New Guinea under the Germans

STEWART FIRTH

MELBOURNE UNIVERSITY PRESS

1982

First published 1983
Typeset by The Dova Type Shop, Melbourne
Printed in Singapore by
Singapore National Printers (Pte) Ltd for
Melbourne University Press, Carlton, Victoria 3053
U.S.A. and Canada: International Scholarly Book Services, Inc.,
P.O. Box 1632, Beaverton, OR 97075
Great Britain, Europe, the Middle East, Africa and the Caribbean:
Eurospan Limited, 3 Henrietta Street, London, WC2E 8LU

National Library of Australia Cataloguing in Publication data

Firth, Stewart, 1944–
   New Guinea Under the Germans.
   Bibliography.
   Includes index.
   ISBN 0 522 84220 8.

   1. Germany—Colonies—New Guinea—
   Administration. 2. New Guinea, German—
   Politics and government. I. Title.

325'.343'09955

To my mother, Phyllis Warren Firth

Contents

Illustrations

Maps

Acknowledgements

Much of this book was written during six months study leave at the Institute of Commonwealth Studies, London, in 1979-80. I am grateful to Macquarie University for releasing me from teaching for this period and to the Institute which gave me a room, congenial company and an ideal location. Macquarie University also provided funds for a research trip to Papua New Guinea in 1979. My research in the Federal Republic of Germany was funded by the Alexander von Humboldt Foundation, an astonishingly generous and helpful patron of my particular academic endeavour, as of others.

For help in the tasks of research I am indebted to the staffs of the Staatsarchiv and Welt-Wirtschafts-Archiv in Hamburg, the Staatsarchiv in Bremen, the Bundesarchiv in Koblenz, the Hausarchiv Sal. Oppenheim & Cie. in Cologne, the Bundesarchiv-Militärarchiv in Freiburg, the Geheimes Staatsarchiv in Berlin-Dahlem, the Australian Archives and Australian War Memorial Library in Canberra, the Mitchell Library in Sydney and the Library of the University of Papua New Guinea in Port Moresby. My thanks for permission to consult the records of the Methodist Church Overseas Mission go to the Reverend John Brown, General Secretary of the Commission for World Mission of the Uniting Church in Australia. Above all I wish to thank Professor Lötzke and the staff of the Zentrales Staatsarchiv in Potsdam, who guided me through the mountain of German colonial records on New Guinea during my three visits.

Donald Denoon and Roderic Lacey read parts of the manuscript and made excellent suggestions. Bill Gammage, James and Helga Griffin, Harry Jackman and John and Ingrid Moses gave information on particular points. My former students at the University of Papua New Guinea, John Waiko especially, gave me a sense of how Papua New Guineans view their history. Peter Hempenstall wrote a valuable critique of early drafts and shared with me, with typical generosity, his own research notes on the subject. Ken Inglis asked the best single question: 'Who are the foreigners in Papua New Guinean history?' For the wider perspective, in which the colonial history of New Guinea is only part of a worldwide phenomenon, I am indebted for ever to Colin Newbury, who oversaw my initial work in this area. And my understanding of encounters between Europeans and Papua New Guineans, a subject which forms the core of this book, comes above all from Hank Nelson, who commented on my drafts at length and prompted me to revise many paragraphs. This book owes much to him. None of these colleagues, however, should be held responsible for my interpretation of German colonial rule in New Guinea.

My wife Beverley tolerated the long gestation of this book with characteristic and unwarranted patience and cheerfulness.

Key to German Geographical Names

Kaiser Wilhelmsland	North-east mainland New Guinea
Neu-Pommern	New Britain
Neu-Mecklenburg	New Ireland
Neu-Lauenburg	Duke of York Islands
Neu-Hannover	New Hanover or Lavongai
Herbertshöhe	Kokopo
Käwieng	Kavieng
Angriffshafen	Vanimo
Berlinhafen or Eitape	Aitape
Kaiserin Augusta Fluss	Sepik River
Dallmannhafen	Wewak
Potsdamhafen	Potsdam Harbour (or Monumbo)
Prinz Albrechthafen	Bogia
Friedrich Wilhelmshafen	Madang
Stephansort	Bogadjim
Konstantinhafen	Melamu Harbour

Key to Pidgin Words

heiltultul	Village medical orderly appointed by the government
kiap	Government official, usually one with magisterial powers
kumul	Bird of paradise
luluai	Village or tribal chief appointed by the government; in Kuanua, the language of the Tolai people, its original meaning was a leader in battle.
saksak	Sago
singsing	Any festival implying dancing (and often feasting)

xiii

Introduction

This book is about the German past of the independent state of Papua New Guinea, the thirty years before World War I when the Germans ruled the north-east of the great island of New Guinea, the island chain to its north known as the Bismarck Archipelago and some of the Solomon Islands. For good reasons it is not a history of all of 'German New Guinea', a territory which has no modern equivalent and which changed its borders on a number of occasions.

As first acquired in 1884, Germany's Melanesian territory or, to give it its official title, 'The Protectorate of the New Guinea Company', consisted of north-east mainland New Guinea and the Bismarck Archipelago. The Protectorate included New Britain, New Ireland, New Hanover and Manus but not Bougainville, Buka and atoll groups in the Solomons such as the Mortlocks and Tasmans. Between 1886 and 1889 this original territory expanded to embrace the Shortland Islands, Bougainville, Buka, Choiseul, Santa Isabel and the northern Solomons atolls as far east as Ontong Java. It now incorporated more of the Solomons than the future territory of Australian New Guinea was to do. Then in 1899 and 1900 a further reshuffle occurred as Germany, Britain, Spain and the United States jostled for the islands of the Western Pacific. First, the German possession, now officially the Imperial Colony of German New Guinea, gained a huge new area of the Pacific north of the equator by Germany's purchase of the Mariana and Caroline Islands from Spain. All these Micronesian islands, with the exception of Guam which went to the United States, were incorporated into German New Guinea as its 'Island Territory'. Second, German New Guinea lost the Solomon Islands of Choiseul, Santa Isabel, the Shortlands and Ontong Java to Britain as a consequence of the deal struck in the 1899 Anglo-German Treaty over Samoa. South of the equator the borders of German New Guinea were now identical with those of the future Australian territory and were the ones inherited by Papua New Guinea at independence in 1975. A final change occurred in 1906, when the German Protectorate of the Marshall Islands, a possession which included Nauru, was also added to German New Guinea. When war came in 1914 German New Guinea was divided along the equator, Japan taking the islands to the north and Australia those to the south.

1

The Germans distinguished between their Island Territory, all north of the equator except for Nauru, and the 'Old Protectorate', that is, the German possessions in Melanesia. Putting the two together was administratively convenient. Police from New Guinea helped the Germans to suppress the rebellious Ponapeans and phosphate royalties from the Island Territory contributed towards the cost of extending control over Melanesians. But Kapingamarangi was the only island north of the equator directly administered from Rabaul and in most ways the two parts of the colony functioned as separate colonial territories, each with its own system of labour migration and subject to different administrative policies. Albert Hahl, Governor of German New Guinea from 1902 to 1914, thought the aim of German policy in the Island Territory was to develop the islanders' ability to buy Western goods, whereas in the Old Protectorate it was to teach people to work on plantations. The bifurcation of the colony under German rule and its subsequent partition between the Japanese and the Australians provide some justification for writing about 'New Guinea under the Germans' rather than attempting a comprehensive account of that evanescent colonial territory called *Deutsch-Neuguinea*.[1]

The Australians who occupied the Old Protectorate of German New Guinea in 1914 found a territory in which Europeans dominated only on the coasts. About 650 Melanesian men wore the khaki peaked caps, sailor shirts and red-bordered shorts of the 'police-soldier', as the Germans called him, and in controlled districts the Australians encountered village chiefs with caps and 'a kind of walking stick with a fancy knob'. These chiefs, according to the Australian military administrator Colonel S. A. Pethebridge, were referred to as 'Loo Loo Eyes' or 'Cooker Eyes'. (He meant the *luluais* and *kukurais*, village headmen appointed by the Germans.) On the copra plantations of the possession there were thousands of New Guinean labourers, 'a great number' of whom 'deserted from their German employers and cleared off into the bush' when they heard about the Australian soldiers, 'thinking that as the German Government no longer had any authority here they could with impunity break their contracts . . .'. The new colonial masters went to considerable trouble explaining to the runaways that, although the Germans were no longer in control of the administration, 'the situation was just the same as before'. It was the old colonial order under new management.[2]

The Australians also found roads. The best one ran for 160 kilometres from Kavieng along the north-east coast of New Ireland, another followed the coast south of Namatanai and a network linked plantations, villages and mission stations with the capital of Rabaul in the Gazelle Peninsula of New Britain. A road with unreliable bridges connected Bogadjim with Madang and Alexishafen and in Bougainville a road ran along the coast from Kieta. Nowhere did the roads lead far inland. The highways of the German territory had been the sea and the rivers, its administrative centres had been placed close to waterways and most of its plantations were within sight of a beach, a lagoon or a bay. It was a maritime colony.

The Germans stuck to the coast for two reasons. First, the inland terrain

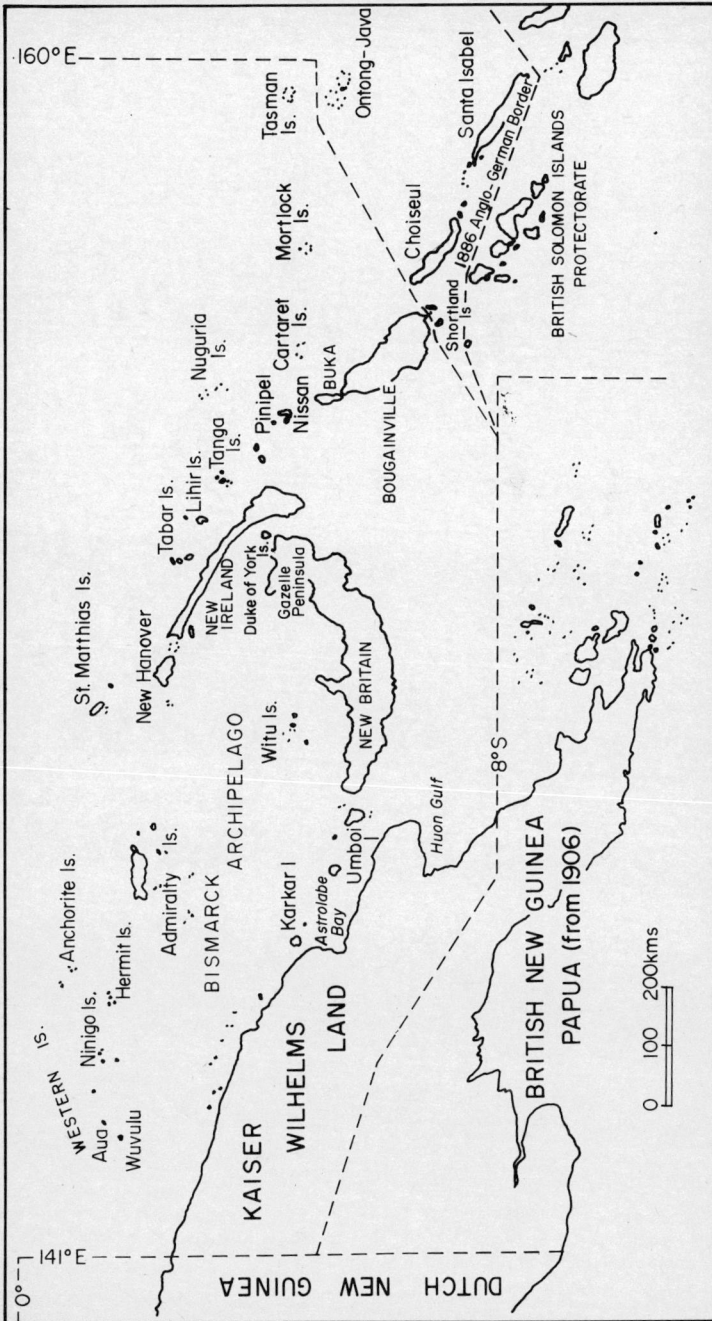

The Old Protectorate of German New Guinea

of the island of New Guinea, Bougainville and the large islands of the Bismarck Archipelago is forbidding in the extreme. The high mountain ranges of New Britain, Manus, Bougainville and southern New Ireland are dissected by precipitous ridges and densely wooded ravines, soaked by rain and obscured by mist. Jungle impedes the traveller everywhere, in places becoming impenetrable, and leeches abound. Along much of the north-east New Guinea range upon range of mountains rise parallel to the coast, sometimes steeply as on the Rai coast and near Finschhafen, sometimes leaving a narrow coastal plain of the kind near Madang, often cut by ravines carrying fast-flowing streams and always densely forested. The typical view from the coast is of endless mountain ridges rising to summits hidden by cloud. Only the river valleys break the mountain barrier. The Sepik and Ramu rivers empty into the Bismarck Sea within twenty-five kilometres of each other in a mosquito-ridden delta of lagoons, floating islands and swamp. The Markham has formed a flat, steep-sided valley which opens into the Huon Gulf but the river is too shallow near the mouth to be navigable. In New Guinea the Germans confronted geographical obstacles far greater than those in Africa, from malarial swamps and flood plains to tropical rainforests, rugged mountains and long stretches of harbourless coastline.

In the second place the Germans were in New Guinea first and foremost to make money, and only secondarily to impose a system of ordered administration on the inhabitants. It was an order of priorities institutionalized in the government of the colony from 1885 to 1899 by a private business firm, the New Guinea Company of Berlin, and perpetuated by the imperial administration of 1899 to 1914, which aimed to create a plantation economy by encouraging private investment. No German governor in New Guinea compares with Sir William MacGregor, Lieutenant-Governor of British New Guinea from 1888 to 1898, for sheer energy in exploring his colonial territory and establishing contact with remote bush communities. MacGregor believed in a rudimentary form of administration for its own sake. The Germans, by contrast, saw administration as a means to an end, which was the rapid economic development of the possession by Europeans, and therefore hardly bothered with foot patrols in mountain country.

The land itself, then, and the Germans' desire to make New Guinea pay determined where they would go as planters, traders, recruiters, officials and to a lesser extent as missionaries. (Lutheran missionaries in the Huon Gulf proved to be the most adventurous of all in penetrating the interior.) The map of German influence became one which was drawn according to the preferences of traders and planters, not according to the presence of population. The Germans did not reach the Highlands, home to hundreds of thousands of people, nor did they more than lightly touch further concentrations of villagers in the hills north of the Sepik River. The overwhelming majority of New Guinea's people, perhaps five in every six, never saw a single German in the thirty years of German rule, even though some of these no doubt came into possession of a material artefact of German origin such as a piece of hoop iron or a nail. To speak of 'New

Guinea under the Germans' is to refer to islands and coastlands: the Gazelle Peninsula of New Britain, its shores free of mangrove swamp, its undulating plateau ideal for copra plantations; north-east and central New Ireland, a coastal strip of fertile soil; east Bougainville near the safe harbour of Kieta; the mainland coast where there are anchorages and level land as at Madang or Alexishafen or where fertile offshore islands dot the roadstead as at Aitape; and numerous island groups and atolls which were far more important to the Germans' economy than they are to Papua New Guinea today: the Duke of Yorks, New Hanover, Tabar, Lihir and Tanga, Nissan, Pinipel, the Carterets, Tasmans and Mortlocks, Nuguria and to the west the Anchorite, Hermit and Ninigo groups.

The questions which this book seeks to answer are familiar in the history of European colonial rule over tropical dependencies. Why did Germany annex the territory? Why did the chartered government of the Neu Guinea Compagnie fail? When the imperial administration took over in 1899, what were its policies on land, labour, shipping, colonial finances and controlling the population? How influential were planters? In what ways did the colonial experience change villagers' lives?

To an extent the answers have a familiar ring. The Germans exploited traditional rivalries in order to achieve political supremacy, obtained land by fraud, theft and purchase, recruited villagers on three-year indentures, imposed labour discipline based on corporal punishment, imposed a head-tax and succeeded in constructing a low-wage plantation economy serving markets in Europe. In the tradition of German colonial capitalism, the German government subsidized the two largest firms active in the territory, the Neu Guinea Compagnie of Berlin and Norddeutscher Lloyd of Bremen, and listened sympathetically to the complaints of all firms that the administration mollycoddled the villagers. The fundamentals of colonization were the same as in a dozen other tropical colonies of the period.

Yet colonial rule in New Guinea assumed a special form, the unique product of interaction between Germans and Melanesians. Where indigenous states did not exist, languages were legion and few people were obvious candidates to become collaborators with the colonial régime, the Germans could extend control over the population only slowly and imperfectly. The impact of the Germans on village life differed widely from place to place, often depending as much on the attitude of villagers as on decisions taken by government officials or missionaries. Much of this book is concerned with events on the colonial frontier, where the Germans and their New Guinean police became an extra factor in local politics, potential allies who could be drawn into backing one community against another. This emphasis is as it should be. German officials had no alternative but to spend much of their time extending control over the villagers of the New Guinea littoral, not purely for the sake of the *pax Germanica* but because control alone brought safety to the plantation homestead, labourers for the plantation lines and teams of villagers to build roads.

The most striking characteristic of German colonial control is its unevenness, dictatorial and destructive in some communities, paternalistic in others and little more than a show of strength in still others. Generally speaking, the Tolai of New Britain came to welcome the Germans as guarantors of a new order of prosperity based on copra trading; the Madangs hated the Germans for being land-robbers; the Manus, Matankor and Usiai peoples of the Admiralty Islands treated the Germans as foreigners who should be killed, ignored or imitated but certainly not obeyed; the Bukas admired the Germans and were eager to serve as police; the northern New Irelanders, at first renowned for their hostility to traders, decided to make peace and obey orders. Generalizations even of this order, however, fail to do justice to the wide variety of responses to the Germans in the villages and hamlets of the territory.

No judgement of German rule in New Guinea is complete without a recognition that many New Guinea villagers were pleased to have the Germans there, whether as allies, providers of iron, healers of the sick, arbitrators of disputes or bearers of a Christian message which promised some protection from sorcery. Equally, no judgement can avoid the fact that the Germans killed more people than the British or Australians in neighbouring colonies in Melanesia, that they tolerated many more labourers' deaths on the plantations, flogged people more frequently and recruited labourers on a scale which threatened to depopulate parts of the country. The Germans were in a hurry to develop New Guinea. They laid down plantations which were to underwrite the export economy of the territory for another half century. But it was development bought at a considerable price in human suffering.

1
Annexation

The police guard of honour presented arms as the Union Jack was run up the flag-pole. The Officer Commanding Native Affairs told his audience: 'Big fellow fight is finished. Germany is finished true. Australia will stop along Kanakas all time. Big fellow King always stop King belong them'. It was Rabaul, 26 December 1919. People from the Baining Mountains in the west of the Gazelle Peninsula of New Britain and from across the sea in New Ireland joined with the Tolai villagers of Blanche Bay in watching a huge bonfire on the top of the 'Mother', the volcanic peak which towers up behind Rabaul, and were told that 'in that fire the last of German rule in these Possessions was destroyed'.[1] Thirty-five years before, in November 1884, the people of Matupit Island had thought they were about to be attacked when 200 German marines came ashore with bayonets to celebrate the declaration of Germany's sovereignty in New Britain.[2] Elsewhere in the New Guinea protectorate which Otto von Bismarck created in 1884 those few coastal villagers who saw the warships and put their marks on incomprehensible treaties of friendship had no better knowledge of the significance of the foreign flag-raising rituals. The vast majority of New Guinea's scattered village population did not know the Germans had come. Yet in the succeeding thirty years the lives of tens of thousands of coastal New Guineans were to be profoundly affected by Bismarck's decision. They would lose land to foreigners, become plantation labourers, replace stone with iron, accept new religious beliefs, suffer from unfamiliar diseases, learn the virtues of European medicine, travel to new places, resist German punitive expeditions, pay head-tax and discover the drastic consequences of disobeying the Germans' orders. However greatly the colonial experience differed from place to place in German New Guinea, change in coastal New Guinea was universal.

The history of colonial annexations suggests that the European powers had a variety of reasons for expanding into the tropical world in the late nineteenth century. To argue, as Lenin did, that territories were acquired simply as investments for surplus capital or sources of raw materials is to oversimplify a complex process. The British, for example, had no domestic motives for taking Fiji or for extending protection over south-east New Guinea a decade later. The impetus came instead from British settlers on the spot, the demands which they made for imperial protection and the political problems which their intrusion into the region created. Britain annexed Fiji to bring order to the frontier of British settlement and it moved into New Guinea to protect the strategic position of the Australian colonies. The earlier British occupation of Australia, New Zealand and Fiji had created its own expansionary momentum, and Britain acted not in response to political pressures at home but because crises had arisen on the frontier of empire.

Germany was different. At the beginning of 1884 the Germans had no colonies at all. By the end of the following year they had colonies in Togo, Cameroun, East Africa, South-West Africa, New Guinea and the Marshall Islands because Bismarck made a decision in principle that Germany was to become a colonial power, a decision dictated primarily by the metropolitan advantages which Bismarck expected would follow. For reasons which have nothing to do with New Guinea Bismarck wanted Germany to have colonies in 1884. Why then did a remote group of Melanesian islands, notorious for fever and rugged terrain, attract his interest? What did he hope to achieve by raising the flag in New Guinea? The answer lies elsewhere in the Pacific, above all in Samoa, where German interests were under challenge from the British and Americans and would be strengthened by Germany's acquisition of New Guinea. What follows, then, seeks to examine not the domestic political circumstances which gave rise to Bismarck's apparent change of course in 1884, decisive though they were, but rather the situation for Germany in the Pacific in the early 1880s, for it was this which ensured that New Guinea would be one of the new German colonies.

Any understanding of the peripheral, as distinct from metropolitan, problems which Bismarck was hoping to solve by acquiring colonial possessions in Melanesia must begin with Samoa, the centre of German commerce in the Pacific Islands for more than a quarter-century before 1884 and the focus of Germany's Pacific ambitions in the 1880s. The Hamburg merchants Johann Cesar Godeffroy und Sohn had opened for business in Samoa in 1857, at the port town of Apia, described by one visiting American as 'composed of a heterogeneous mass of the most immoral and dissolute Foreigners that ever disgraced humanity'.[3] Under the management of August Unshelm Godeffroys quickly grew to become Apia's leading traders, their resident trading agents on the Samoan islands, Uvea, Futuna and the Lau Islands of Fiji trading manufactures for coconut oil, pearlshell and bêche-de-mer.

Godeffroys soon became planters as well, sharing in the short-lived cotton boom caused by the American Civil War. For a few years high cotton prices coincided with an abundance of Samoan labourers, as hungry Samoans were thrown onto the labour market by a long drought, a storm and a pest plague which ravaged their gardens. But when good times came again at the end of 1860s few Samoans wanted to pick cotton, most European planters went out of business and Godeffroys were left as the lone company with sufficient capital to sustain large plantations. Godeffroys' manager was now Theodor Weber, to be remembered by Europeans as a 'Colossus of commercial foresight and enterprise' and by the Samoans as the stealer of their lands.[4] More than any other European Weber exploited the Samoans' differences for European benefit and more than any other German, he created Germany's stake in Samoa, the plantations, trading posts and shipping fleets which were to be the argument for annexation in the 1880s and 1890s.[5]

Weber was an innovator. To provide for future profits, he had coconut palms planted between the rows of cotton on Godeffroy plantations, trees which were to underwrite the prosperity of German Samoa after 1900; to prevent wastage and improve quality, he introduced the conversion of coconuts into copra, the dried flesh of the fruit, rather than relying on coconut oil; and to overcome the main hindrance to plantation enterprise in Samoa, lack of labour, he recruited labourers on indenture from other islands, Raratongans at first and from 1867 Gilbertese.

While the Gilbertese toiled under horse whips and a hot sun in the cotton fields of Samoa, the Godeffroy company's trading agents ventured into the far corners of the Pacific in search of copra, turtle-shell, pearlshell and bêche-de-mer. Ex-sailors and adventurers who spoke the *Plattdeutsch* of Hamburg could be encountered by the 1870s on islands as far apart as Niuafo'ou in Tonga, Abemama in the Gilberts, Yap in the Carolines and even the Anchorite Islands north-west of Manus, where a Hamburg seaman called August Grapengeter traded for a few months before his death in 1873.[6] The visit of a Godeffroy brigantine or schooner once or twice a year was these men's main contact with the outside world, and the means by which island products began the long voyage to European markets. Godeffroys' first permanent trading post in the New Guinea islands was established in 1876 in the Duke of York Islands. Situated between the two large islands of New Britain and New Ireland, and with protected harbours, the island group was an obvious choice for maritime traders, just as it attracted the first settlement by missionaries in the archipelago. The Reverend George Brown of the Methodist Mission arrived at Balanawang Harbour in 1875. The Duke of York islanders were no strangers to Europeans, having traded with passing vessels for decades, and by the late 1870s 'almost all inhabitants of the Duke of Yorks' were said to be able to make themselves understood in English.[7] But the Duke of Yorks was a remote and minor outpost of J. C. Godeffroy und Sohn, who were the giants of the island trade in the 1870s, with traders employed across the Pacific from Tahiti to the Marianas, a shipping fleet which dwarfed its competitors and in Samoa a shipyard, plantations and a cotton-processing factory.

No commercial undertaking as large as Godeffroys could fail to come into conflict with islanders and competing European companies, and just as inevitably, such conflict attracted the political intervention of Germany. Land was the principal source of dispute with the Samoans. In western Upolu Theodor Weber acquired hundreds of hectares as early as 1865, land which was to become Godeffroys' largest plantation, Mulifanua, and in the war of 1867 to 1873 he supplied guns to opposed camps of Samoans in return for further vast tracts of real estate. As consul of the newly unified German empire in 1872 Weber arranged for the commander of the German warship *Nymphe* to fine Samoans caught stealing from German plantations. An argument over the Germans' title to landholdings at Vaimauga, rapidly being turned into a plantation, led to the offshore bombardment of villages by another German naval vessel in 1874. In the growing competition between Britain, Germany and the United States on behalf of their nationals in the Samoan Islands, Weber tirelessly sought German political ascendancy, if need be through a non-German régime. Under the secret agreement between Godeffroys and the American adventurer Albert B. Steinberger, who had begun to exercise a commanding influence in Samoa, Godeffroys would have been guaranteed their landholdings and their right to import labourers as well as having first claim on a copra tax paid by the Samoans when Steinberger took over the government.[8]

The Steinberger strategy collapsed in 1876 because the British deported him. Weber now turned to the trade and friendship treaty, that characteristic instrument of free-trade imperialism, as the best means of preventing the Samoans from granting special privileges to the British and Americans and as the key to securing Godeffroys' predominance elsewhere in the Pacific. The German Chancellor Bismarck supported his consul grudgingly, afraid that an enthusiastic naval commander might drag Germany into jurisdictional arrangements indistinguishable from those of an 'Imperial German Colony', which was the last thing Berlin wanted. Bismarck had no desire to offend Britain or the United States or to do battle with the free-trade majority in the *Reichstag* and he authorized the negotiation of treaties with Samoa and Tonga only on condition that they should not imply German territorial sovereignty. For years to come Bismarck was to oppose any policy of making Germany a colonial power.[9]

At Weber's urging, Germany concluded a succession of treaties with Pacific islanders in the late 1870s, giving its Navy coaling stations and its merchants most-favoured-nation rights in trade. The first was the treaty with Tonga in 1876, a guarantee that J. C. Godeffroy would continue unhindered in virtually monopolizing the lucrative Tongan copra trade. In Samoa Weber's path was less smooth because the councils of chiefs who presided over a weak government of the country believed that Weber was trying to bully them into accepting German annexation. Under threat of German naval retaliation the chiefs were forced to agree to protect German property in July 1877 and under further intimidation in 1878 they emptied their 'meagre treasury' to compensate the Germans for alleged damage.[10] Weber was then delighted to board S.M.S. *Ariadne* on a tour of Godeffroys' Pacific domains, first to Funafuti in Tuvalu, where the Germans concluded a trade and friendship treaty with the chief Jakopo; then via Tabiteua, home of many Gilbertese labourers in Samoa, to Jaluit lagoon in the Marshall Islands, centre of operations for Godeffroys' agent Capelle and his competitors the Hernsheim brothers. Eduard Hernsheim, a Rhinelander by birth and a ship's captain by training, had embarked on the life of an islands trader in the early 1870s, unsuccessfully trying a bêche-de-mer fishery in the Hermit Islands in 1874 and placing traders in the Duke of York group in 1875. His brother **Franz** settled in Jaluit. When the *Ariadne* anchored

in the Duke of Yorks in 1878 it came to offer security to Eduard
Hernsheim's trading post at Makada harbour and to the Godeffroys' agency
at Mioko. For a trifling quantity of trade goods, Topulu and Nerakua of
Makada and ten Mioko men led by Kurerarum put their marks on complicated legal documents in the German language 'selling' the two harbours
to the government of Germany. Back in Samoa in January 1879 Weber
extorted his treaty of friendship from a powerless Samoan government,
which was obliged to recognize German land claims, permit the expansion
of German plantations and the recruiting of labourers from abroad and
tolerate the exercise of exclusive consular jurisdiction by the German consul. The significance of these imposed treaties and farcical purchases of
land was that they showed Bismarck's willingness to resort to active
imperial intervention on behalf of German businessmen overseas. No lover
of colonies, he had nevertheless taken the first steps towards active protection of commerce abroad, that same policy which he was to reiterate four
years later as meaning nothing less than annexation.[11]

The German commercial empire in the Pacific now appeared impreg-
nable. But it was in fact being undermined in Germany, where the
Godeffroy family had for years been investing the proceeds of the South
Seas in coal, iron ore and railway speculations. As the German recession
deepened following the stock market crash of 1873 J. C. Godeffroy & Sohn
was forced to live on credit advanced by London and Hamburg banks.
In an attempt to attract extra capital Godeffroys floated a new company
in March 1878, the Deutsche Handels- und Plantagen-Gesellschaft der
Südsee-Inseln zu Hamburg or DHPG, which took over the firm's business
in the Western Pacific. More than four-fifths of the DHPG's capital of
five million marks was Godeffroy money, however, and Johann Cesar
Godeffroy was soon speaking of the 'disastrous situation' facing his enterprises. When much of the DHPG itself had to be pledged as security on
further loans from Baring Brothers of London, the end was near. After
casting around in vain for yet more loans J. C. Godeffroy & Sohn went
broke in December 1879, 'a deplorable catastrophe' for the 'old and
respected house', as the Prussian minister in Hamburg told Bismarck.[12]

The Godeffroys hastened to make use of their links with people in high
places. Gustav Godeffroy, a director of the Norddeutsche Bank and part-
owner of the pro-government newspaper *Norddeutsche Allgemeine Zeitung*,
appealed for help to his old friend, Gerson von Bleichröder, Bismarck's
personal banker:

> So loyal and influential a man as yourself, one so close to the Chan-
> cellor, will see to it that the laurel wreath which our iron Chancellor
> wound for his brow in the old world will not lose a single, if weighty,
> leaf in the new world.[13]

The 'leaf' which Gustav Godeffroy was afraid that Bismarck might lose
was Samoa, now in danger of passing into British control if British interests
were to buy the DHPG, and he persuaded Bleichröder to arrange a conference with him and the Berlin banker Adolph von Hansemann. From this

conference on 14 December 1879 emerged an ambitious plan to incorporate the Godeffroys' Samoan company in a new Pacific undertaking with twice the capital and to underwrite it with government funds. Within a week Bismarck agreed to put the proposal to the *Reichstag* with his personal backing. The 'Deutsche See-Handels-Gesellschaft', as it was called, came into being in February 1880 to the accompaniment of much beating of patriotic breasts by the pro-government newspapers, which portrayed the subsidization of the company as a national duty. But when the *Reichstag* vote on the Samoa bill was taken many deputies were absent at a Berlin performance of Goethe's *Faust*, and the votes of the Catholic Centre party, combined with those of the left-liberals, were enough to defeat the measure.[14]

Left to itself, the Godeffroys' existing trading and plantation company in the Pacific, the DHPG, might then have fallen into British hands, as Germany's newly appointed career consul in Samoa was urging. Consul O. Zembsch, who replaced Weber in this position in November 1879, thought 'it would be highly desirable if all the plantations and land-holdings of the DHPG passed into non-German hands as soon as possible', a goal which could be achieved by prohibiting further labour recruiting for company plantations; the DHPG's labour system was 'legally and morally impermissible' and the manager of the DHPG in Samoa, August Godeffroy, was a drunkard who should not have responsibility over plantations. The Godeffroy and DHPG company books which Zembsch examined listed the deaths of 677 labourers and their dependants out of 2970 brought to Samoa between 1867 and 1880.[15]

Zembsch's moral scruples cut no ice in Berlin. Under Adolph von Hansemann's direction the DHPG was revived with a twenty-year loan of 1 200 000 marks mainly from the Disconto-Gesellschaft, which was Hansemann's own bank, the Bleichröder bank in Berlin and the Norddeutsche Bank in Hamburg, the last an institution with both Hansemann and Godeffroy connections. Baring Brothers in London, though financially involved in the new DHPG, had lost their stranglehold on it and influence over company policy now lay with Godeffroy men and bankers from Berlin and Hamburg.[16]

The reconstructed board of directors hastened to complain about Zembsch to the government, which told him that his job as German consul in Apia was to 'further German interests through consular and maritime protection', to preserve German treaty rights to land and the importation of labourers and to make official contact with the chiefs of islands likely to be sources of labour. The minute on these instructions to Zembsch was written by the German Foreign Office's most enthusiastic advocate of colonial expansion, Heinrich von Kusserow, who was Adolph von Hansemann's son-in-law. The message to Zembsch was unmistakably clear: what was good for the DHPG, labour trade included, was good for Germany, and there could be no question of sacrificing the company's enterprises.[17]

In the course of reconstructing the Samoa company Hansemann conceived a new colonizing venture which would be centred on Mioko, 'the German Admiralty's harbour on the Duke of York Island'. The scheme was typical of the man in his colonial moods, grandiose and impractical. Born in Aachen in 1826, the son of David Hansemann, Adolph entered his father's bank in 1857 and was its head from 1864 until his death in 1903. While the Disconto-Gesellschaft prospered enough to become one of the leading financial institutions of imperial Germany, Hansemann made colonies something of a rich man's hobby, becoming a member of the *Zentralverein für Handelsgeographie und Förderung deutscher Interessen im Ausland*, an early pressure group for colonial expansion, and of the *Deutscher Kolonialverein*. South-West Africa and New Guinea were later to be his playthings. To Bismarck in 1880 he proposed that the government subsidize a steamship line which would connect Germany with German establishments in the Duke of Yorks, Samoa, Tonga, Fiji and the Marshalls. A Hansemann consortium would then set up trading stations on the northeast coast of New Guinea as a first step towards a German New Guinea. Bismarck, still smarting from the humiliation of his defeat over the Samoa bill, rejected the plan out of hand: though Germans in business abroad might be assured of naval and consular protection they could not expect the government to undertake occupations of foreign territory. Colonies were not on the Chancellor's political agenda.[18]

In the meantime the Germans, once the unchallenged masters of the island trade, began to encounter unprecedented competition from the British in the Pacific. The men on the spot increasingly reminded the German government of its obligation to protect them. The DHPG closed trading posts in the Gilberts and was forced to sell its 'rather valuable buildings' in Rotuma, Fiji, 'at a considerable loss' because the British colonial government tightened port-of-entry regulations so as to channel the trade of outlying islands through Suva and Levuka.[19] Germans who had acquired land in pre-Cession Fiji lost much of it without compensation when the British scrutinized land titles. Above all, just as the DHPG came to rely on Melanesians rather than Gilbertese for its Samoan estates, its labour recruiters were driven out of the New Hebrides by the British and the French and faced fierce competition from Fiji and Queensland labour traders on the beaches of the New Guinea islands. New Guinea began to be noticed in Berlin because it affected the fortunes of Germany in Samoa.

As the mutual fears of the British and the Germans in the Pacific fed upon each other, the reports which reached the Foreign Office in Berlin from German companies and consuls stressed the urgency of the situation and the need to take pre-emptive action to secure German interests before it was too late. The mood was typical of the age of preclusive imperialism, when Europeans strove to acquire colonial territory in order to prevent rival Powers from grabbing it first. Travelling through the New Guinea islands in February 1883 the consular secretary at Apia, Gustav von Oertzen, was amazed by the sight of the thousands of villagers who stood on the beaches of New Britain, New Hanover, the Admiralty Islands and Buka to watch the German naval vessel go by. Germany was playing for bigger stakes in Melanesia than the opening of labour-recruiting areas for Samoa, he told Berlin, for it had the chance of winning the 'untouched and un-exploited half of the South Sea Islands for German trade and German civi-lization' if the German government were to act fast.[20]

The Australasian colonies wanted equally prompt action from the British government. In Queensland the Premier, Sir Thomas McIlwraith, a man described as 'not above doing a stroke of business in land', urged London in February 1883 to authorize him to annex New Guinea because of the danger to the colonies 'if other powers take possession'. He received no authority but when the German vessel *Carola* left Sydney in March he believed German intervention in New Guinea was imminent and despatched the police magistrate on Thursday Island across the Coral Sea to Port Moresby, where the Union Jack was raised and the whole of eastern New Guinea and 'islands and islets adjacent thereto' were proclaimed Brit-ish on 4 April.[21]

To Germans in the islands it looked as if the Australasian colonies were moving Britain along a path of annexation which would squeeze German merchants not only out of trade and land, as had happened in Fiji, but out of labour supplies as well. Weber in Samoa had no doubts about the Queenslanders' motives: they had obviously taken New Guinea in order to monopolize New Guinea labour for Queensland sugar estates, and his own company the DHPG would need a similar guarantee of labour if it were to survive, possibly by German annexation of 'appropriate island groups'. Weber was enthusiastically supported by the new German consul at Apia, Oskar Stuebel, a convinced pro-imperialist for whom company and national interests in Samoa were one and the same thing, and who hastened to advise Berlin that for the sake of the future development of German plantations at least the north coast of New Guinea must be kept free of British occupation. In Germany the head office of the DHPG appealed to the German government to protect its shareholders and especially its mortgagors, the Berlin and Hamburg banks who had advanced the money to keep the company afloat after the defeat of the Samoa bill. The Australasian colonists, said the DHPG, were demanding that Britain annex the Solomons, Marshalls, Gilberts and New Britain, the French had their eyes on the New Hebrides and Germany must stop such annexations or else the German plantations in Samoa would be cut off from their sources of labour.[22]

The British government did not welcome the news that Queensland had annexed eastern New Guinea. The Lord Chancellor was unable to conceive of 'any necessity, or justification, for taking *the whole* of that immense country' and Gladstone was of the same opinion. The Cabinet refused ratifi-cation and Australian fears of foreign intervention in New Guinea were dismissed as 'altogether indefinite and unfounded'.[23]

The British repudiation in July 1883 was of small comfort to the DHPG for by then labour traders from Fiji and Queensland were swarming around the coasts of New Ireland and New Britain, picking up men before the

Germans could get to them. The prospects of sending 600 labourers to Samoa by the end of the year, as the company's agent in New Britain hoped, were diminishing week by week. The 61-ton German schooner *Niuafoou*, for example, reached Nusa Island in northern New Ireland in July 1883 to find that the Queensland ship *Fairy* had beaten it by a fortnight. On one occasion the *Niuafoou* was in the same bay recruiting from west to east as the Fijian schooner *Falcon* recruited from east to west. German recruiters who were used to stepping ashore from whaleboats and saying 'You like go Samoa? Me like plenty Kanakas; you give me plenty boys' found it was no longer enough to offer axes, cloth, tobacco and pipes to compensate the relatives of recruits; to compete with the British, they had to add 'One boy, me give you one musket, plenty powder, ball, cap'. Guns and ammunition became part of the price of New Guinea labourers and as the cost of recruiting grew, the number of recruits fell: whereas the Queenslanders obtained over 1200 New Guinea islanders in 1883 the Germans had to be satisfied with fewer than 300. Increasingly hard pressed for labour, the German plantations in Samoa resorted to keeping men on at work after their contracts had expired, hundreds of them by the end of 1883.[24]

The influx of Queensland labour vessels, the captain of a German naval corvette reported, put the whites in the area 'in a particularly anxious position':

> With the great demand for labourers in Queensland, and the consequent exploitation of these islands, the supply will soon come to a stop, and German interests will be thereby directly injured, since New Britain and New Ireland are the only places whence the Trading and Plantation Company in Samoa can still draw any considerable number of labourers.[25]

A barrage of complaints like this reached Berlin. Eduard Hernsheim, leading trader in New Britain, appealed for German naval protection after Queenslanders, angry that his agent was hindering recruiting, burnt his trading post in the Laughlan group east of Woodlark Island. Theodor Weber of the DHPG pointed to his company's pioneering work in opening a new recruiting field in New Guinea, Gustav von Oertzen of the Apia consulate claimed the Fiji and Queensland labour traders used force and Consul Stuebel insisted that Germany put a warship and an imperial commissioner in New Britain. Bismarck acted even before some of these despatches had arrived in Germany. In September 1883 he protested to Britain about the British labour traffickers and proposed to have a naval vessel permanently cruising in the area during the labour season from May to October; this would supervise recruiting by Germans, 'afford efficient protection to the legitimate commercial interests of the Germans in New Britain and New Ireland, which have latterly attained importance' and 'repel by force violent attacks upon the life and property of Germans'.[26] The protest enunciated no new principle of German policy in the Pacific and was treated as a routine matter in London. Ships of the Imperial Navy, after all, had been acting on behalf of Germans in the islands for more than a decade. But at a time when the Australasian colonies were pressing for annexation, Bismarck's determination to offer further protection to Germans in the islands could change in significance. A commitment to protect by naval power might, under further threats to German companies, be extended in the direction of imperial sovereignty.

Consul Stuebel urged Bismarck to establish *de facto* German protection of Samoa and the New Guinea islands without delay, by declaring that Germany would not permit any foreign power to take possession of those island groups. Such a declaration was in his view needed to ensure the survival of the DHPG, the embodiment of independent German interests in the Pacific. In the long term whites were destined to take the place of islanders 'since the native races in contact with a white population gradually die out', and Stuebel wanted those whites to be Germans.[27]

The Australasian colonists were also talking the language of race nationalism. At the Sydney Intercolonial Convention of late 1883, which brought together leaders of all the self-governing colonies in Australia and New Zealand, delegates were unanimous on the issue of New Guinea: Britain ought to annex it immediately and any further foreign acquisition of territory in the Pacific south of the Equator would be 'highly detrimental to the safety and well-being of the British possessions in Australasia'. The Victorian delegation, the Premier of Victoria said afterwards, had gone to Sydney 'not in the lust of territory in any shape or form, but as a matter of defence in years to come' so that future generations of Australians 'would not have an enemy dwelling on their borders'. But at the Colonial Office Lord Derby was astounded by the naïveté of this Australasian Monroe Doctrine and confided to Gladstone that it was 'mere raving' which could scarcely have been 'seriously intended: though it is hard to fix the limits of colonial self-esteem ... '. Gladstone agreed and early in 1884 Britain assured Germany that it did not intend to act on the resolutions of the Sydney convention.[28]

Whatever Gladstone might say, Bismarck was becoming increasingly perturbed by what he regarded as the limitless ambitions of the British to extend sovereignty in Africa and the Pacific. While London continued to return blunt negatives to German inquiries about the Fiji land claims and the Sydney convention called for the western Pacific to become a British lake, reports reached Bismarck that Britain planned to annex Togo in west Africa and had signed a treaty with her ally Portugal approving Portuguese territorial rights at the mouth of the Congo. Worst of all from the German point of view, the British government delayed for months answering a German request for information about Britain's intentions in South-West Africa, which the Cape Colony government wanted Britain to annex. Pushed by sub-imperialist settlers, the frontiers of the British Empire seemed about to be redrawn again to enclose yet more territory on terms which would disadvantage German merchants. Bismarck's patience was reaching its end by early 1884, and he directed his ambassador in London to be frank in complaining about the treatment of Germans in Fiji. He was now seeking a way for Germany to acquire colonies without also incurring imperial expense and—what for Bismarck represented a strong objection to colonial expansion—without giving the *Reichstag* a further hold over government expenditure. Colonies of the traditional kind were a solution he would not accept. But colonies administered and paid for by companies under royal charter, as suggested in a Foreign Office memorandum of 8 April, offered an obvious escape from the impasse. The idea came from Hansemann's son-in-law Kusserow in the Legal-Commercial Division and was probably decisive in changing Bismarck's mind about colonial acquisitions.[29]

Hansemann's hour had arrived. Once Bismarck changed his mind about raising the German flag Hansemann, with reliable inside knowledge of the Chancellor's intentions, revived his plans of 1880 and proceeded to organize the investment of speculative capital in a New Guinea consortium which would apply for a charter to govern New Guinea territory. Inviting the Cologne banker Albert von Oppenheim to join the consortium on 30 May 1884, Hansemann mentioned that Bismarck's banker Bleichröder had already decided to participate in the 'colonial endeavours' as 'a quite different wind is now blowing from the Wilhelmstrasse'. The Hansemann scheme, as outlined to Bismarck on 27 June, was to colonize north-east mainland New Guinea and its offshore island chain, leaving south-east New Guinea alone, and it received Bismarck's secret approval on 20 August.[30]

A clandestine German expedition, fitted out in Sydney to look like a routine voyage by the DHPG, sailed to the north-east coast of New Guinea via New Britain. The northern New Guinea coast was explored, so-called treaties concluded with village people and land supposedly acquired from its owners. Official confirmation of this charade of negotiations between Germans and New Guineans followed in November 1884, when German marines raised the flag in the Gazelle Peninsula, the Duke of York group and on the mainland coast at Madang and Finschhafen. The news which was to cause a minor crisis in Anglo-German relations, since Bismarck had been careful to keep the British in the dark about his annexation, did not reach the British government until 17 December. A telegram received by the British Admiralty stated that the German flag had been hoisted 'on the north coast of New Guinea from 141 meridian as far as Huon Gulf, including Admiralty, Hermit, Anchorite, New Britain, New Ireland groups'. In the subsequent division of territory between the two European powers, agreed in April 1885, the German border was extended as far south as the Waria River.[31]

Bismarck was besieged with requests for further annexations. The DHPG wanted Germany to take Samoa, Tonga, Fakaofo in the Tokelau Islands, Uvea, Futuna, Niue and parts of the Gilberts and Ellice, the Marshalls, Carolines, Solomons and New Hebrides. Hernsheim's company asked Germany to take possession of the Ellice, Gilberts, Marshalls, Carolines and Nauru, while in Apia Consul Stuebel actually went ahead and unilaterally annexed Samoa for the *Reich*, confident of support and congratulations from Berlin. Bismarck was prepared to make Samoa German but he could not endorse Stuebel's initiative because of agreements already made with Britain and the United States and he was to remain tied by American opposition for years to come. No Pacific island, as Bismarck well knew, was worth a quarrel with a major power. He withdrew German forces from their brief occupation of the Carolines in 1885 when Spain protested and he gracefully submitted to Papal mediation in the matter. After that, his acquisitions were confined to undisputed territory.[32]

The Marshall Islands became a German colony on 15 October 1885. The DHPG and Robertson & Hernsheim, which were reckoned to have two-thirds of the copra trade of the group in 1884, had both appealed for its annexation and agreed to merge in a single company to represent them in the Marshalls and the rest of Micronesia. By the Anglo-German Declaration of 4 and 10 April 1886, the powers delineated those areas of the western Pacific where each surrendered its claims to possible annexation. Samoa and Tonga, the two most valuable island groups at issue, were excluded from the agreement—but Buka, Bougainville, the Shortland Islands, Choiseul, Santa Isabel, Ontong Java and Nauru all lay on the German side of the line of demarcation and Germany incorporated them into her Pacific possessions. The northern Solomons became part of the Protectorate of the Neu Guinea Compagnie, as the new colony was called, and Nauru joined the Protectorate of the Marshall Islands. By 1889, as the imperial flag went up on Santa Isabel and Ontong Java, Germany's first period of expansion into the Pacific islands was over, and another was not to come until the dissolution of the Spanish colonial empire in 1898 and the Samoan civil war of 1899.

Bismarck undoubtedly thought New Guinea to be of little value in itself. Writing privately to the German ambassador in London in 1885 he stressed the pro-colonial force of German public opinion: 'The smallest corner of New Guinea or West Africa, even if completely worthless in an objective sense, is at present more important for our policy than the whole of Egypt and its future'.[33] Bismarck shared none of Hansemann's illusions about New Guinea's economic potential and the main reason he annexed it was that the act of annexation served his political purposes in Germany. Hans-Ulrich Wehler has argued that Bismarck's grab for colonies was dictated by the needs of domestic politics, the most dramatic in a series of attempts to arrest the decline of German capitalism during the long depression which began in 1873. The decision to authorize chartered companies to administer tropical territory in the name of the *Reich* was not a sharp break with previous policy but a further development of endeavours to provide state assistance to industry, as Bismarck had tried to do in the Samoa bill of 1880. In an era before Keynesian economic theory, colonial expansion, with its promise of new markets for German goods and opportunities for German investment, was the instrument of an embryonic interventionist state wishing to moderate the effects of a cyclical downturn in the German economy. More immediately, the patriotic appeal of raising the flag and resisting the arrogant English overseas led to the crushing defeat of the anti-colonial left-liberals in the *Reichstag* election of October 1884 and generally discredited Anglophile liberalism. 'Pragmatic expansionism', says Wehler, was accompanied by 'social imperialism', a conscious government policy of focusing public opinion on national achievement so as to weaken the forces of democratization, liberalism and socialism in Germany, with the objective of entrenching the power of the aristocratic Prussian élite.[34]

Granted that domestic politics were uppermost in Bismarck's mind when he determined upon the general principle of acquiring colonies, the acquisition of New Guinea in particular requires further explanation. Why New Guinea? The German commercial stake in New Guinea and the Bismarck Archipelago was small. No German traders lived on the mainland coast and the few dozen copra and pearlshell traders of a variety of nationalities whose settlements dotted the Gazelle Peninsula of New Britain, the Duke of Yorks, northern New Ireland and the Western Islands were not the main object of the protection which Bismarck extended to the archipelago named after him in 1884. The two big firms, the DHPG and Robertson & Hernsheim, were estimated by an enthusiastic consul to be exporting 1000 tons of copra each by 1884 and in the Anglo-German propaganda war which followed German annexation the German Foreign Office made much of their alleged commercial importance. But they were used as a justification for what Germany would have done anyway.[35]

Samoa was the island territory which mattered to the German government in the early 1880s, the subject of endless negotiation with Britain and the United States, the centre of German commerce and plantation agriculture in the Pacific islands, the prize which German consuls and businessmen on the spot pressed Bismarck to take as a German possession; and it was only because of Samoa that New Guinea entered into Bismarck's calculations. Once the DHPG in Samoa became dependent on the labour of men recruited in the New Guinea islands the fate of the two widely separated island regions was intertwined. Germany's stake in New Guinea was real enough by 1884, but it was in the village men who went on board the DHPG's schooner the *Niuafoou* for transshipment to Mioko and Samoa rather than in piles of coconuts exchanged for sticks of Niggerhead tobacco. New Guinea, because of its labour, happened to be one of the underpinnings of the German claim to Samoa at a time when the German government expected Samoa to be involved in the general demarcation of protectorates by Britain and Germany. Consul Stuebel rarely missed an opportunity to remind Bismarck that the New Guinea islands and the German plantations in Samoa went together, the one guaranteeing the success of the other; and Bismarck accepted the argument. As John Bates Thurston, the British Commissioner chosen to report on Samoa, commented in 1886, Germany 'has lately brought under its influence certain large and populous islands for the sake, as it would appear, of, among other things, conserving the Samoan plantations, which otherwise might fall into neglect or ruin'.[36]

Bismarck annexed a colonial empire in Africa and in the Pacific above all because he wanted symbols of national success, strength and unity which could be trumpeted before the people; and he included part of New Guinea in that empire because the Melanesian labourers on the plantations of a

Hamburg firm in Samoa had become a national interest. Unless they continued to pick cotton, clear land and plant seed coconuts, Germany might lose its chance to raise the flag over Samoa. As the colony of a chartered company, moreover, the Melanesian possession would cost the German government nothing beyond the expense of naval patrols. These were the considerations which swayed the German Chancellor in the European summer of 1884.

By its annexations in the western Pacific Germany guaranteed Melanesian labour to the DHPG in Samoa, protected German traders in the Marshall Islands and placed a vast tract of tropical forest in New Guinea, the Bismarck Archipelago and the Solomons under the control of Adolph von Hansemann's Neu Guinea Compagnie, formed in 1885 in order to profit from the government's policy of handing over the new colonies to chartered companies.

Five years before, the German era in the Pacific Islands seemed to have come to an end. J. C. Godeffroy & Sohn had declared bankruptcy. The DHPG into which the Godeffroy family had put its money, was also on the point of collapse, and the *Reichstag* had refused to subsidize any new Pacific undertaking. Now the future of German investment was assured, at least in the Marshall Islands and New Guinea, where privileged companies would enjoy the direct protection of the *Reich*. And in Samoa, which Germany could not yet annex because of the competing claims of Britain and the United States, the plantations of the DHPG had a secure supply of labour from New Guinea. The DHPG's critical labour shortage was over by 1886. Its plantations in Samoa recorded an annual average of 458 new arrivals in 1885, 1886 and 1887 compared with 224 in 1884, and the advantage was written into law when the German government determined that the DHPG should be the only company, German or otherwise, permitted to export labourers from the new German territories in Melanesia.[37] For the next thirty years the recruiting schooners of the DHPG continued to visit the bays and inlets of the New Guinea islands, bringing villagers back to the Duke of York Islands for transshipment to Samoa, and providing a reminder of one of the original motives for German annexation.

Hansemann, the financier who never went to the Pacific, was principally responsible for this revival of German fortunes. It was he who arranged the loan which kept the DHPG solvent in 1881, who first thought of the idea of a 'German New Guinea' and who had the money and contacts when the time came to found the Neu Guinea Compagnie.

2
Kaiser Wilhelmsland
1885–1899

On 5 November 1885 groups of Yabim-speaking people living on the coast of the Huon Peninsula witnessed the coming of strangers different from any they had previously encountered. The strangers were not canoemen of Tami on a trading voyage or coastal people coming north for refuge from attacks by mountain warriors, but unknown and unexpected foreigners. The people took the opportunity to trade, offering tools as items for exchange, but the strangers wanted pigs and fruit rather than tools, and instead of making a brief visit, they began to clear the bush and build a house on an island in the harbour they called Finschhafen. An old man greeted one of the strangers as an old friend and embraced him.

The stranger's name was Dallmann, one of five Germans and thirty-seven Indonesians who had left Cooktown, Queensland, a week before, sailing across the Coral Sea and past the eastern islands of the Protectorate of British New Guinea in the steamers *Samoa* and *Papua* bound for a new colony with a new name: Kaiser Wilhelmsland, as north-east mainland New Guinea was now called, part of the larger 'Protectorate of the New Guinea Company' which included the offshore islands lying to the north. At the end of 1885 Kaiser Wilhelm I approved further rechristenings: New Britain became 'Neu Pommern', New Ireland 'Neu Mecklenburg' and the Duke of York Islands 'Neu Lauenburg'. The Germans were putting an official stamp on their Melanesian possessions, which were extended between 1886 and 1889 to embrace Buka, Bougainville, the Shortland group, Choiseul and Santa Isabel.

The people of Finschhafen began to doubt the wisdom of welcoming the Germans and Indonesians after barely two months. In January 1886 warriors massed in canoes, threatening to attack the foreign settlement and withdrew only because of the arrival of a German steamer. The Germans, who were as new to imperialism as the Yabim, presented the villagers with pieces of the black-white-red flag of the Imperial Fatherland, 'to signify that from now on the common flag is to be a mark of the alliance of friendship and of "mutual" support'. 'We were pleased', a Company official reported, 'to see that the natives greatly respected these flags and immediately put them up in tall coconut palms. In the next few days several of them appeared and presented themselves for work, and soon many were

21

willing to sell us the cultivable land near the station.' But by 1887 the New Guinean settlements closest to the German station were almost deserted and the Germans had 'bought' Suam village from its inhabitants, paying one axe and two pieces of iron for each house.[1] By the talismanic significance which they attached to the pieces of black-white-red cloth, by their possession of iron, by their demand for the food, labour and land of the villagers, and by their evident intention to stay, the Germans soon showed themselves to be strangers of a unique kind.

Other coastal people met the Germans in 1885 and 1886. The people of Dugumor and Tobenam watched a small party of Germans and Indonesians build huts and plant tobacco at Hatzfeldthafen. They attacked the Indonesians in July 1887, killing one and seriously wounding four others, and fled before the Germans burnt their houses and canoes.[2] The villagers of Astrolabe Bay already knew about Europeans before the Germans came to Constantinhafen near Garagasi in May 1886. From Bilbil island south to Bongu and as far east as Gumbu people remembered 'Maklai', Nikolai Nikolaevich Miklouho-Maclay, the Russian scientist who had visited them in 1871-72, 1876-77 and 1883, and lived among them as a friendly observer, careful not to intrude upon traditional custom. In a vain gesture of protest, Maclay appealed to Bismarck not to annex the 'Maclay coast' of New Guinea in 1884, only to have his name used by the German flag-raising party as a way of overcoming New Guineans' mistrust. 'Aba Maklai', Otto Finsch of the German expedition had shouted on reaching Constantinhafen in October 1884, proclaiming his friendship with the Russian in the language of the Bongu people. They welcomed him. Now again in May 1886 the entire populations of Bongu, Gorendu and Gumbu helped to clear the bush and build the German settlement and were said to be friendly with the colonists.[3]

Wherever the Germans travelled on the coast of Kaiser Wilhelmsland they saw evidence of highly developed art and decoration in everyday life. Using stone and shell axes and knives fashioned from bamboo, the New Guineans produced intricate carvings on everything from houses and canoes to bowls and wooden spoons used in the preparation of sago. Along the coast of Astrolabe Bay men and women decorated themselves with bamboo combs, cassowary feathers, tortoise-shell ear rings, and elaborate necklaces and bracelets of teeth and shell, and near Finschhafen the women lived in houses adorned with scenes of fantastic sexual feats. The Bilbil people of Astrolabe Bay were famed potters, carrying their earthenware on trading voyages in decorated outrigger canoes, paddling with richly carved oars when the winds did not fill the mat sails. The wooden spears, clubs, swords, slings, shields and bows and arrows used by the coastal New Guineans were not mere instruments of warfare like the Germans' Mauser rifles, but objects of artistic endeavour as well.[4] For all the diversity of their languages and customs, and despite mutual enmities, the coastal communities of New Guinea organized their economic micro-systems in similar ways, as the universal practice of decoration showed. They shared an economic culture markedly different from that of the Germans. They worked not to achieve profit, accumulate re-investible capital, rationalise production or improve living standards, as the Germans did, but for other purposes: to live well on sago, breadfruit, taro, yams, bananas, sweet potatoes, fish and pigs; to acquire wealth for exchange; to perform the rituals which honoured the dead and guaranteed favourable intervention by the gods in human affairs; and to announce the place of people and things in this world by decoration and depiction.

Such a gap between the indigenous and foreign conceptions of the purpose of work was not new in the Pacific. It had characterized the encounter between Islander and European since Captain Cook first observed the Hawaiians more than a century before. But in Kaiser Wilhelmsland it was particularly striking because traders did not precede the Neu Guinea Compagnie (NGC). The villagers had no experience of Europeans who wanted vast tracts of land and armies of disciplined plantation labourers. They had virtually no experience of Europeans at all. And the contrast in assumptions between colonizer and colonized was to determine the success of the NGC to a far greater extent than Adolph von Hansemann realized as he sat in Berlin promulgating regulations for his colony.

'Adolph Hansemann governed New Guinea in the morning hours before he came into the bank', a fellow banker recalled. Hansemann threw himself enthusiastically and ignorantly into his colonial hobby. He talked of selling the open coastland of north-east New Guinea for sheep grazing, an absurd proposition in the hot wet climate of the region. He expected his colony to be a magnet for German immigrants, drawing them away from traditional destinations in North America and Australia to the new Germany of the South Seas, and in September 1885 the NGC announced that conditions would be suitable for settlers within a year.[5]

The terms of the German government's charter to the Company appeared highly attractive to Hansemann and his fellow investors when it was granted in 1885. The NGC gained the exclusive right to take possession of all 'unowned land' and to buy or lease land from New Guineans and except in foreign relations and the administration of justice, it could exercise the sovereign authority vested in the Kaiser; it was guaranteed the protection and support of the Imperial Navy.[6]

New Guinea for Hansemann was real estate and he was the developer. As the founding statutes of the NGC proclaimed, its aim was to 'prepare the way for settlement' and to undertake trade and agriculture on its own account only to the extent needed to sustain the enterprise and encourage other investors.[7] Hansemann expected his outlays on shipping, exploration and land to be richly rewarded when the immigrants flooded Kaiser Wilhelmsland to buy his town, suburban and rural lots. They would pay him many times as much for land as his agents paid the New Guineans, and his company would impose lucrative taxes on the settlers.

First reports were encouraging. The colonists in Finschhafen thought the soil and plant life of that part of the coast comparable with that of Java, and the climate much more pleasant for Europeans than in the Indonesian Archipelago. After being honoured by Queensland colonists with a banquet in Cooktown, Vice-Admiral Georg, Freiherr von Schleinitz, the first *Landeshauptmann,* or administrator, of the new colony, reached Finschhafen with his wife and children in June 1886. Within weeks one of his daughters fell seriously ill with malarial fever but Schleinitz was optimistic about the prospects for German colonization. The New Guineans impressed him: they appeared to be peaceable and aware of the advantages brought by European settlement. Iron and cloth earned by New Guineans in Finschhafen was already being traded to distant villagers who had no direct contact with the Germans, and Schleinitz was confident that the New Guineans would recognize work as the source of their new wealth. The Finschhafen station, a collection of wooden huts, stores and houses manned by the administrator, a station manager, a forester, storeman, gardener, doctor, cook, tradesman, sailors and Malay and Chinese labourers, struck a visiting naval commander as well-organized and purposeful, a good beginning for Germany's colonizing venture. On a voyage several hundred kilometres up the Sepik River in August 1886 the Germans were delighted with its navigability and apparent potential for timber-getting. They encountered people who valued tobacco and smoked cigarettes rolled in leaves, carried axes of stone and shell, knew nothing of iron, lived in large decorated houses and travelled the river in long canoes, as many as twenty-five men standing in a line to row a single canoe. Schleinitz indefatigably explored the coasts of mainland New Guinea and New Britain and discovered workable phosphate in the Purdy Islands.[8]

Hansemann believed in issuing orders to his employees to cover every eventuality in New Guinea. Nothing was to be left to chance. Before a single bag of copra was traded the Berlin office fixed the price of copra and attached precise values to the hoop iron, axes, pearls, cloth and tobacco which the colonists used in dealings with the New Guineans. Even empty packing cases had to be accounted for. The scientific party engaged by the Company in 1886 was directed to proceed from the coast as far inland as the border with British New Guinea and to return by a different route; then to repeat the exercise so as gradually to 'open up the whole territory'. Its task was to present a comprehensive report on the climate, rocks, soils, plants and animals of New Guinea and to determine the political and social organization of the New Guineans.[9]

Orders were one thing, but the ability of Company officers to follow them was quite another. Men with no experience of the Pacific suddenly found themselves living on the edge of the New Guinea jungle, subject to fever, cramped in tiny huts, forced to live on a diet of salted meat and bread and inundated with paper work from Berlin. The scientific expedition's only achievement was to ascend the Sepik. Otherwise the scientists could do no more than make a few brief forays inland. They had counted upon recruiting New Guineans but could persuade no one to become carriers. Far from rejoicing in their tribulations on behalf of the Fatherland the NGC's employees grew despondent and resented the military discipline imposed by Schleinitz. The early enthusiasm soon dissipated.[10]

Violent clashes between Germans and New Guineans were inevitable. The first came in 1886 at the mouth of a river flowing into the Huon Gulf when New Guinean fighting men threw spears at a party of Germans in a boat; the Germans retaliated with gunfire and burnt 'the hostile village'. In a second attack in July 1887, this time at Hatzfeldthafen, warriors speared one Malay to death and wounded five others. While the tiny group of colonists awaited reinforcements and maintained a strict watch in case of further attack, they learnt from the people of the mountain village of Tambero that the culprits came from two coastal villages and another mountain village. As so often in the history of German rule, the colonial masters had to rely on intelligence from New Guineans in matters of war. What the villager told the European might be true, a slanted account designed to attract European support or an outright fabrication. German punitive parties reduced the two coastal villages to ashes, and the Tambero people 'expressed their satisfaction over the punishment of the villagers, from whose arrogance they, as the much weaker ones had also had to suffer . . .'.[11] Laden with gifts from the Germans, the Tambero people must have rejoiced at having such powerful allies.

The incident revealed the Germans' weakness. Without the naval protection promised to the Company under its imperial charter none of the three widely separated settlements at Hatzfeldthafen, Constantinhafen and Finschhafen would be a match for a concerted New Guinean attack. Yet when Schleinitz asked the commander of the S.M.S. *Carola* to arrest men from a village five kilometres up in the mountains behind Hatzfeldthafen, the commander flatly refused. 'It is quite impossible to take natives prisoner or to make them stand and fight', the commander explained to the Admiralty. New Guineans invariably fled before a landing party, which was left with nothing to do beyond burning 'a number of almost worthless huts'. As for requests for help from the NGC, the Navy was entitled to accept or reject them without giving reasons and was by no means intended to serve as the Company's 'executive and police force'. Police were a Company responsibility. The commander of the *Carola* was expressing a view widely shared by his colleagues in the Australian Station of the German Navy and supported in Berlin. The dispute between NGC and Navy remained unresolved until 1890 when the Foreign Office imposed strict limits on the use of the Navy 'for the protection of settlers or for the punishment of natives'. Naval vessels were permitted to shell villages from offshore and land detachments of sailors for the most straightforward actions but were otherwise under no obligation to assist the Company. In the meantime the Company bought fifty Chassepot carbines from the Prussian Ministry of War, recruited an army Lieutenant and raised a tiny police force, the core of which appears to have been twelve Buka men with experience of rifles. The full complement of thirty-six men was apparently not obtained, and the 'police-soldiers' of the late 1880s did little to provide the security envisaged by Hansemann.[12]

In expectation of white settlers the NGC acquired vast tracts of land, especially along the coast of Astrolabe Bay. Here a Company officer, Jan

Alexishafen

Siar I.
Panutibun I.
Biliau I.
Kranket I.
MADANG (Friedrich Wilhelmshafen)

5°15'S

Gogol

Yabob I.

0   5   10kms

Bilbil I.

River

R.

Gorima
Malaga

Nuru

ASTROLABE

BAY

Erima   Erima Harbour

Bogadjim
Stephansort   RAI   COAST
Constantinhafen   Gumbu
Gorendu
Bongu

Myou

146°00'E

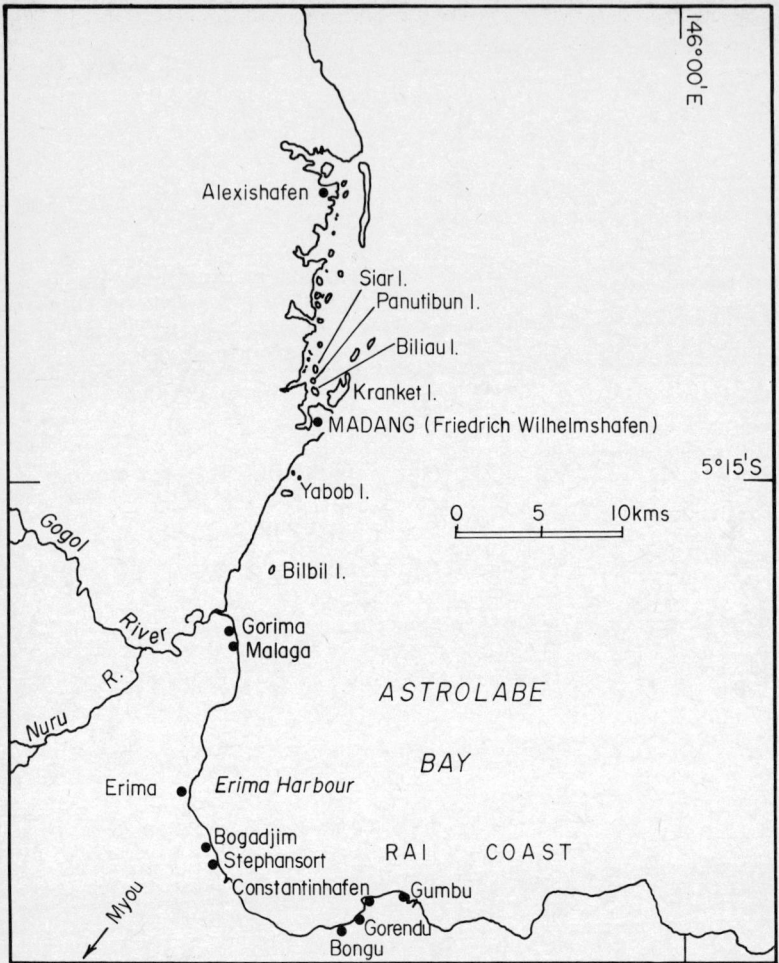

Astrolabe Bay

Kubary, bought 36 000 hectares, much of it for little more than strings
of pearls given to Yabob and Bilbil men who were not the owners of the
land anyway. The alienation of this land was to fester like a sore in the
relations between the Germans and the people of the Madang and Rai
coasts. The NGC's legal entitlement to land derived from the imperial
charter permitting it to take possession of 'ownerless land' and to 'conclude
contracts with the natives about land and rights to the soil'. The right was
an exclusive one, and the protections for New Guinean land owners spelt
out in the Company's land legislation of 1887 amounted to little of consequence. Conscientious Company officials refused to buy land if New Guineans did not wish to sell, but in general the only effective restriction on

German acquisition of land was the Company's military weakness. Many New Guineans appear not to have known that the Germans intended to occupy their land permanently. The basis of the New Guinea Company's enterprise, land, was mostly acquired by fraud and deceit, at best as the result of mutual misunderstanding.[13]

The Protectorate of the Neu Guinea Compagnie was declared open for settlement in September 1888. Prospective settlers were offered land to buy or lease, informed that roads and bridges were under construction and assured that New Guinea's soil was fertile. The response to this invitation mocked Hansemann's dream of ruling a new Germany in Melanesia. The offices of Burns, Philp in Cooktown and Brisbane, agents for the NGC, were not besieged by German-Australians eager to emigrate. On the contrary, a mere handful of settlers went to New Guinea and they were seeking work with the Company, not plots of land. To make the colony pay the Company had no option but to invest in large-scale plantation agriculture. The plantations, at first cultivated merely to show settlers the colony's fertility, now became the Company's only hope of a return on capital. In the first three years of colonization the protectorate did nothing but absorb the Company's funds. Over three million marks were sunk in the enterprise by April 1888, and a further million was spent in the following year. Governor von Schleinitz quarrelled with head office about policy and his contract was terminated in mid-1888. The only solution, Hansemann decided, was to seek the help of the German government, and on the analogy of the German Protectorate of the Marshall Islands, where the Jaluit Gesellschaft paid imperial officials to run the administration, Bismarck agreed to a change of course in New Guinea. From November 1889, for a trial period of three years, the *Reich* administered New Guinea at the expense of the NGC.[14]

Hansemann's mistakes were fundamental. He over-regulated a colony whose only potential attraction to settlers might have been free land and absence of government. The Company's conditions of land purchase were far more onerous than those in the Australian colonies, requiring payment of cash sums in advance and leaving all land near water under Company control.[15]

Having ensured that New Guinea would not be a settler colony, Hansemann embarked upon the creation of a plantation colony. He ignored the lessons which might have been learnt from planters elsewhere in the Pacific, preferring to take the Netherlands East Indies as his model of development. The success of plantations in New Guinea, as the estates of the Samoan-American Emma Forsayth in the Gazelle Peninsula of New Britain showed, depended on good soils, a correct choice of crops, cheap labour and vigorous trade with the New Guineans. 'Queen Emma', as she was called, followed the practice of planters in Samoa by interplanting cotton with coconut palms, in order to have a saleable crop during the decade before palms came into full bearing. In 1889 her plantations produced over twenty-two tonnes of cotton, more than a hundred times as much as came from the NGC's plantations on the mainland. Her fifteen traders in the

Gazelle Peninsula and elsewhere in the Bismarck Archipelago gathered the copra which brought money for further plantation expansion, and labourers from no further away than Buka worked in the cottonfields. With little initial capital, her business nevertheless flourished, financing an investment in copra plantations with cotton and trade copra.[16]

The natural advantages which enabled settlers to link trade with plantations in New Britain were lacking on the mainland coast. The porous, volcanic soils typical of the Gazelle Peninsula were rare, and coconut palms were by no means prolific, growing in small stands near villages and too few to be the basis for a copra trade between villagers and Germans. Plantation agriculture in Kaiser Wihelmsland, as Hansemann was to discover, had to be financed entirely from outside sources.

The decision to concentrate on the mainland rather than the islands was itself an error for a company bent on making money from plantations. But the error was then compounded. Hansemann's most serious miscalculation was to expect the peoples of coastal Kaiser Wilhelmsland to provide labour for his plantations. The Pacific labour trade had not reached north-east mainland New Guinea and villagers knew nothing of indentured labour until the arrival of the Neu Guinea Compagnie. What they then saw proved unattractive. They wanted hoop iron, axes, beads and cloth and in the first year of German settlement worked enthusiastically to earn them but such goods rapidly lost value, especially as villagers found the Company men to be keen buyers of spears, shields and other local artefacts. By 1888 hardly a New Guinean in the vicinity of Finschhafen would work for hoop iron. When the villager agreed to work for the Germans, a Company official complained, he did so out of curiosity rather than a desire to improve his condition. And those clans who worked as groups imposed their own terms on how jobs were to be done. The people of Gorendu and Bongu, for example, built a fence around part of the NGC's Constantinhafen plantation in order to protect it from wild pigs, but every few days they alternated fence-building with work in their gardens and could not be made to appear for work at any particular time.[17]

Eager to discern the slightest sign of a change of heart by coastal peoples, the Company recorded the 'pleasing fact' that in February 1889 eighteen young men from the villages near Finschhafen signed labour contracts for work elsewhere in the colony and the Company Governor thought it was evidence of a new attitude towards 'regular work' on the part of the 'native population'.[18] Such optimism was unfounded. Few mainland New Guineans put their marks on German labour contracts until after the turn of the century and in the meantime the NGC had to rely on migrant labour from the Bismarck Archipelago and the Solomons, the Dutch East Indies, Singapore and the Chinese treaty ports.

'Samoa', 'Fiji' and 'Mackay' were familiar destinations to men in the coastal villages of New Ireland before the coming of the Germans and the promises made by an NGC recruiter on a voyage to south-west New Ireland in October 1887 were equally familiar: 'plenty taro! plenty yam! plenty coconut he stop!' But the New Irelanders knew nothing of the new

place which the recruiter kept mentioning, 'New Guinea', and many shared
the feelings of the man who declared: 'me stop here; by and by me go back
Fiji'. The 200 or so New Guinea islanders who dared to go on board the
Ottilie on that occasion, and who huddled under blankets on deck at night
as it steamed towards Finschhafen, were among the first of some thousands
of villagers from the Bismarck Archipelago and the Solomons who crossed
to the mainland during the 1890s. By March 1894 about 2800 islanders
had worked on contract in Kaiser Wilhelmsland, of whom about 1600 were
New Irelanders. Local mainland recruits in the same period numbered
about 600.[19]

The NGC's labour legislation of 1888 was detailed and specific. It put
control of recruiting in the hands of the Company, created 'labour depots'
through which all recruits were to pass before and after indenture, specified
the space and rations which each man was to have on board ship and required
contracts to be made before two witnesses fluent in German or English.
Disciplinary measures could take the form of reducing rations for up to
a week, withdrawing customary extras such as tobacco, requiring unpaid
work of up to three hours a day on as many as three days a week, confinement
for up to three days a week, and flogging. Flogging was to be administered
only if the worker were healthy and the maximum he could be given was
ten strokes of the lash a week. In cases of particularly recalcitrant workers
all these forms of discipline could be imposed at once. The principal
responsibility for ensuring that the labour regulations were observed fell
upon the *Stationsvorsteher*, or officer-in-charge, at a Company settlement.
It was he who was supposed to judge whether the contracts and lists of
workers were in order and whether the recruits fully understood what they
were doing in signing a contract. His permission was needed before a ship
left port and before workers could be landed. He was to inspect labour
depots, issue certificates and supervise floggings. Impressive as the legislation was on paper, much of it was ignored in practice under NGC rule
as officers came and went, stations were abandoned, plantation managers
took the law into their own hands, labourers deserted and official records
were neglected. The most important effects of the 1888 legislation were
to perpetuate in German New Guinea the three-year indenture common
in Samoa, Fiji and Queensland, and to institutionalize corporal punishment
as a form of disciplining labourers.[20]

Hansemann was convinced that however effective his recruiters might
become on the beaches and in the villages of the colony, the people of
New Guinea would be 'neither numerous nor capable enough' to man plantations on the scale he envisaged. Labourers accustomed to the climate
and to the cultivation of tobacco, cotton, coffee and cacao were needed
in large numbers, and he appealed to the German government for help
in getting skilled coolies from the Dutch and Chinese. The Dutch
demanded concessions. They objected to the fact that coolies from the
Netherlands East Indies, because they were coloured, were classed as
'natives' under German law and could therefore be flogged for disobeying
employers, a type of punishment which the Dutch no longer used for that

purpose in their own colony. They wanted more than the vague assurance of the German ambassador in the Hague that the treatment of labourers was 'particularly humane and mild' in the Protectorate of the Neu Guinea Compagnie, and the Company therefore exempted such coolies from corporal punishment. About 125 Javanese reached Kaiser Wilhelmsland during 1890 and a further eighty Chinese and five Malays were recruited in Singapore. The fate of the Singapore recruits should have been a warning to the Company. Some failed to embark in Singapore, others died of cholera on the voyage, a majority smoked opium and none had ever worked on a tobacco plantation even though they were all signed on as tobacco labourers.[21]

To specialize in different types of plantation agriculture Hansemann established subsidiary companies, for cacao and coffee the Kaiser Wilhelmsland-Plantagen-Gesellschaft formed in Hamburg in November 1890 and for tobacco the Astrolabe Company which followed a year later. The Kaiser Wilhelmsland-Plantagen-Gesellschaft, capitalized at 500 000 marks under the chairmanship of the Hamburg ship-owner Adolph Woermann, was managed on the spot by a cacao planter with experience in Trinidad. Land near the village of Gorima in Astrolabe Bay was made available by the NGC, cacao seed brought from Ceylon, expensive cacao-processing machinery landed from the NGC steamer *Ysabel* and New Irelanders provided as labourers. Nothing was to be spared in confirming Hansemann's judgement that the soil and climate of north-east mainland New Guinea were ideal for tropical plantations.

By paying government officials to run the colonial administration, the NGC hoped to be able to 'devote itself with undivided attention ... to the exploitation of the land and its resources' while retaining full control of the colony.[22] The Company expected the Imperial Commissioner appointed by the government to be a cipher. But Fritz Rose, the Prussian civil servant who took the job, was far from that. Determined to assert the independence of the imperial administration, he was a fearless critic of the NGC and refused to be swayed by its complaints about him.

As soon as he arrived in Finschhafen in late 1889 Rose reviewed the Company's labour legislation and suggested changes. Officials had frequently been unable to establish the identity of labourers and the regulations were amended so as to make every recruit identifiable. House-girls, usually living with Company men as concubines, were declared to be 'labourers' so as to bring them under the protection of the law. Shocked by the arrival in Finschhafen of venereally infected labourers and by the callous treatment of two Tolais on board a Company ship, Rose issued a further ordinance providing for medical supervision of recruits. When the NGC's directors in Berlin contested Rose's facts and demanded alterations in the ordinance, Rose delayed more than six months before complying and in doing so complained bitterly of the Company's unwillingness to let the local administration have a free hand.[23]

Rose further offended the NGC by forcing the dismissal of the officer-in-charge of Finschhafen station, Julius Winter, a tough colonial adventurer of Hungarian origin who had reached Kaiser Wilhelmsland in 1887 by sailing in a small vessel from Australia. The Company had given him a job and because of his skill as a recruiter of mainland labourers he had become one of its valued employees. Rose, punctilious, aloof and an upholder of the law who believed that labour recruiting was 'in truth nothing other than the sale of human beings', was appalled that this 'rough, uneducated man' Winter should have the responsibilities and disciplinary authority of an officer-in-charge. The two soon quarrelled and Rose found himself ostracized by the Company men in Finschhafen. Winter kept a house-girl, and when he flogged a Tolai called Hannes for trying to seduce her, he was charged with breaching regulations. In his defence he appealed to the need for the whites to maintain their authority over the blacks, and said he would have flogged every one of his labourers, 'perhaps even more severely', for that reason alone; he had acted with a view to the moral effect on his house-girl; he had used the regulation flogging rope, about three feet long, and if he had gone to the trouble of notifying the court officially of the punishment, as the law required, time would have been lost and no impression made on the black workers. Winter was found guilty and Rose persuaded the pliable general manager of the Company in Finschhafen to dismiss him. The NGC's directors in Berlin had already asked the Colonial Department to restrain Rose's 'bureaucratic tendency' and Rose was ordered to avoid taking measures 'which seem likely to restrict the Company and its enterprises'. The primary task of the imperial administration, he was told, was to further the interests of the Company. The news that Winter had been sacked provoked another blast by the Company against Rose.[24]

The NGC later claimed that the hardest blow to its finances came between February 1891 and September 1892, the second half of Rose's administration of the colony. Only a small amount of phosphate from the Company mine on Mole Island in the Purdy group reached Hamburg before the mine was closed after a storm wrecked all the installations. The Company steamer *Ottilie* was wrecked in the same islands in March 1891 and the hulk *Norma*, with large stocks of uninsured goods on board, sank. In the early months of 1891 one after another of the colonists at the tiny capital of Finschhafen died from malaria, including the Company's general manager. Following each burial the *house belong trink* was crowded with the remaining colonists, who would drown their fears through the night and sometimes stay at the bottle until the next victim succumbed. The thirteenth victim was the Company doctor, who died on 12 March, and when a steamer arrived the next day it was stormed by settlers demanding to be evacuated. More than a third of the white population was already dead. A temporary settlement was made at Stephansort, on the coast about fifteen kilometres south of the Gogol River, where the colonists camped in plantation sheds and a further move to the new capital of Friedrich Wilhelmshafen (Madang), was not complete until September 1892.[25]

Relations with the villagers who came into contact with the Germans in Kaiser Wilhelmsland deteriorated as the plantations expanded. At Gario near Bogadjim and at Erima local men clubbed one Company labourer to death and shot another in early 1891 after fruit was stolen from village gardens. Rose found himself lacking the means to exercise any government control over Germany's native subjects in Kaiser Wilhelmsland. Neither the *Reich* nor the NGC was prepared to provide a sea-going vessel for the sole use of the imperial administration and the German Foreign Office established strict limits on the use of the Navy in protecting the colonists, leaving them virtually dependent on twenty-four police and any plantation labourers who could be spared to swell the ranks for particular expeditions.[26]

The impotence of the administration, and the difficulties inherent in any attempt to impose foreign rule in New Guinea, were revealed in Rose's response to the multiplying conflicts of 1891. First he had to deal with the murder of two missionaries of the Rhenish Mission Society, F. W. Scheidt and Friedrich Bösch. On a visit to Malala Harbour in 1891 the missionaries bought, or at least believed that they bought, a small peninsula together with its bananas and coconuts, as the site for a new mission station. Leaving Bösch with five labourers to begin work on clearing, Scheidt went to the NGC settlement at Hatzfeldthafen to get corrugated iron and provisions, returning with another European and eleven labourers. The mission boat had to be rowed the last part of the way because the wind was calm and as it approached the peninsula warriors armed with spears waded into the water and attacked the foreigners, who made desperate attempts to save themselves by jumping overboard. All were killed except two labourers who fled back to Hatzfeldthafen to raise the alarm.

Rose organized a large expedition, fourteen Europeans, the police troop and about 130 plantation labourers, who sailed to the scene of the murders. But before the boats were close enough to the beach for the Germans to open fire the villagers disappeared into the bush and the expedition was forced to press inland, tracking the fugitives in unfamiliar country in the hope of encountering them. The advantages were all on the side of the villagers. Few were found and Rose decided to surprise the big village of Simbini in a dawn raid on 30 June. After marching for two hours through the darkness the German column reached the village as day broke. 'We were extremely disappointed', wrote Rose, 'when we found it completely deserted'. Warned well in advance of the Germans' arrival the villagers had even had time to strip their palms of ripe coconuts. Rose ordered the village to be set alight and went inland: 'We were about to return when the boy leading the party caught sight of natives and in a short time shot two of them, who turned out to be women'. The expedition killed a few more villagers, cut down hundreds of coconut palms and smashed canoes.[27]

Retaliation was not the same thing as control, as Rose soon discovered. Six weeks later, on 14 August 1891, a plantation overseer from Hatzfeldthafen, Ludwig Müller, disappeared with five labourers and a party sent to find him was attacked near the village of Tobenam. Rose returned to the area with two detachments, found no one in Tobenam and was unable to catch anyone alive because his police were so keen to shoot. Coming across two huts in the bush, Rose ordered a man to be brought before him:

I had him brought out of the hut—a big man in his best years, at whom the leading boys had immediately opened fire. My hope of getting a native alive in my hands, in order to obtain more detailed information about the causes of the recent unrest, was thwarted. The man, with severe wounds to his left knee and left groin, was already taking his last breaths.[28]

A careful search of Tobenam revealed the decomposing bodies of Müller and three of his New Guinean companions. Rose had good grounds for suspecting the Tobenam people of having committed the murders but he cast his net wider as well, attempting to punish neighbouring villages simply because they were allies of Tobenam. The police continued to kill villagers in the Hatzfeldthafen area until, on Rose's advice, the NGC abandoned the station in November 1891.[29]

The second major conflict between Germans and villagers in 1891 began when two Malay overseers and six labourers were killed at the Gorima plantation of the Kaiser Wilhelmsland-Plantagen-Gesellschaft early in July. Rose took immediate action. With armed police, thirty-five spear-carrying labourers and a few European volunteers he proceeded by boat and on foot to the new plantation, where he was met by a grisly scene: eight corpses with numerous spear and arrow wounds. The labourers' trade boxes lay scattered about, torn open and their contents stolen. Leaving a party to bury the dead, Rose set off with a party of New Guineans in search of nearby villages and destroyed the first one he reached. On the following day he pressed north to the Gogol River. Here his police crossed the river ahead of him. 'After half an hour', Rose reported,

> about ten shots were fired, whereupon I went over the river with the rest of the party. The police soldiers had ferreted out fugitives, a man with two women and a child were found lying in a place under bread fruit trees and bananas, they were all killed.

Cloth from the plantation store was found in the women's string-bags, 'eloquent proof' to Rose that the villagers put to death by his men were not innocent.[30]

The causes of the attack on Gorima plantation appeared clear to Rose. The contract of sale for the plantation land was made only with one group of people, the Malaga, and not with the inhabitants of numerous other villages in the neighbourhood. The villagers feared that the Europeans would move further inland. Tools and other trade goods on the plantation were much desired by people nearby. And in addition the attack was an indirect consequence of the brutal treatment meted out to plantation labourers by the *master belong glass*, the bespectacled plantation manager Ludwig Kindt, who was said to have held men to the ground with his foot while he thrashed them. Earlier in 1891 the entire labour force had escaped from Kindt in a stolen boat and sailed to Finschhafen, and the New Guinea islanders and Javanese subsequently employed at Gorima were constantly deserting to avoid the beatings of their employer, leaving the plantation in order to live off the surrounding countryside and steal from village gardens. Twenty Javanese disappeared entirely.[31]

Yet Rose wanted to know more about the villagers' hostility to the Germans, and so he turned to the Bilbil people, who possessed extensive contacts throughout the Astrolabe Bay because of their trade in pots and clay. The Bilbil were delighted to entertain him and at a feast to which he was invited they recounted the story of the Germans' fight near Gorima again and again. A few weeks later the Bilbil came to the Germans of their own accord to warn them that the defeated people planned to attack Gorima once more, and offering help from their own warriors and others. The ambitions of the Bilbil and their desire to manipulate the Germans for their own advantage were so obvious, however, that Rose declined their offer of assistance and took only his police on his punitive expedition. The police found plates, trade tobacco, a large axe and other goods stolen from the Gorima plantation in Myou village and responded by burning houses and shooting dogs and hens.[32]

The Germans' encounters with the people of Astrolabe Bay and Hatzfeldthafen in 1891 had all the marks which were to characterize future collisions between Europeans and villagers on the frontier of control in New Guinea, whether under German or Australian rule. Rose did not know who had killed the missionaries or attacked the Gorima plantation. He destroyed villages which were close to the scene of the crime or might possibly have been implicated. He was unable, perhaps unwilling, to bring a single villager to court. On patrol his police went ahead of him, a law unto themselves, shooting at anybody they saw. For intelligence about the enemy he depended on villagers whose own motives were to use the Europeans as allies against other peoples. Far from the villagers being introduced to Western notions of jurisprudence, it was the colonizing power which was adopting Melanesian customs of warfare and retribution, sending raiding parties to kill small numbers of the enemy and burn property. Because of the hostilities in Kaiser Wilhelmsland and continuing troubles in New Ireland Rose asked in September 1891 for more police, fifty instead of twenty-four, for the appointment of a police master to be based in northern New Ireland and for a regular shipping service to Nusa and the north-east coast of New Ireland. The NGC rejected every request, disclaiming responsibility for the disorder in the colony and reminding the Colonial Department of the imperial protection promised by the Charter of 1885: protection was provided to Germans in East Africa and South-West Africa at imperial expense and should be extended to the Protectorate of the Neu Guinea Compagnie.[33]

The Colonial Department of the Foreign Office refused to admit the need for more imperial control in New Guinea and described Rose's 'expeditions for the punishment of the natives' as 'generally successful'. Existing forces, consisting of the police, plantation labourers and German volunteers, were said to be quite adequate for the protection of the settlers. Rose knew better. During his time as imperial commissioner he found it 'unthinkable' that the administration should leave the villagers to themselves, intervening only sporadically, and when he left the colony in 1892 he offered the German government his prescription for better relations between the colonizers and the people of Astrolabe Bay. A survey of the New Guinean settlements in the area was essential, he thought, so that the Germans would know just who the villagers were and what land they occupied. Afterwards German officials could consider appointing village agents who would be consulted about the acquisition of land for German stations, the definition of reserves, the settlement of disputes, and so on.[34] The idea was ignored at the time, but it exactly prefigured the system of government-appointed *luluais* introduced in New Britain and the Short-lands in the late 1890s.

With Finschhafen closed and the Kaiser Wilhelmsland-Plantagen-Gesellschaft dissolved, Hansemann put his faith in a new subsidiary firm to grow tobacco. This was to be plantation agriculture on a grand scale, centred on Astrolabe Bay and run by the new 'Astrolabe Compagnie' which came into being in October 1891. More than half the capital of 2 400 000 marks was subscribed by the NGC and by Hansemann personally, the rest by investors based mainly in Berlin, Hamburg and Bremen. Making the most of temporary unemployment in the tobacco industry in Sumatra, the new company engaged managers, overseers and coolies. About 1700 Malays and Chinese sailed in five expeditions to Kaiser Wilhelmsland between August 1891 and February 1892, and began to clear the bush, hoe and plant for the Germans, who expected the first tobacco crop in 1892. But work soon ceased.

Severe outbreaks of malaria and dysentery were followed in December 1891 by an epidemic of influenza which brought work to a standstill for weeks on end. A planter recalled hearing 'croaking and groaning' from within the 'pig sties' which served as labourers' quarters when he arrived in Madang in late 1891. At Stephansort the labourers' hut and the hospital were the one building and under it sick labourers lay with the pigs, too weak to climb the stairs. Often corpses lay for hours beside the living before being carried off with a makeshift pole. New Guinea islanders suffered particularly, many fleeing into the bush to escape, and Rose described 'the number of black boys carried off' in the epidemic as 'shockingly high'.[35] Of the 313 Chinese on one plantation in October 1891 only 110 were capable of working eight weeks later and by Christmas eighty-three were dead. By the end of March 1892 only 420 Chinese were left in Kaiser Wilhelmsland, yet at least 988 had arrived in the previous eight months, and instead of the 2250 labourers which the Astrolabe Compagnie had reckoned on having in April 1892, it had 1450.[36] How many people died in these years will never be known, but it was clearly plantation mortality on a scale never experienced in Queensland, Fiji or Samoa.

When the administration of the colony reverted to the Neu Guinea Compagnie in September 1892, the new *Landeshauptmann* was Georg Schmiele, a short, fat man with a round face and grey-flecked moustache whose principal virtues in the eyes of the Company were his experience as a magistrate in the Bismarck Archipelago and his optimism about the future of the colony. Like Hansemann in Berlin, Schmiele had little faith in the New Guineans as developers of their own country. He looked instead to the models of colonial development provided by Java, Sumatra and Ceylon, and was convinced that Kaiser Wilhelmsland, lacking a 'useful native population', needed a mass influx of another race of people 'standing higher' than the villagers of New Guinea.[37]

New Guinea to the British was part of the Pacific, a colony where they could apply the lessons of ruling Fiji. New Guinea to the Germans was part of the East Indies. The NGC was impressed by the example of the tobacco industry in Sumatra, where tobacco exports to Amsterdam rose fivefold in the decade to 1886, and saw experience in the Dutch East Indies as qualifying a man for work as a plantation manager in New Guinea. Three of the four managers hired by the Astrolabe Compagnie had been in Sumatra and the fourth was sent there on a study tour. Schmiele himself went to the Dutch colony before taking up his post and Curt von Hagen, the former Prussian artillery officer who ran the Astrolabe Compagnie before becoming *Landeshauptmann* in 1896, was an ex-Sumatra man. Such men tended to judge success or failure in New Guinea by South-East Asian standards. Compared with Sumatra in the 1870s, Kaiser Wilhelmsland did not appear especially unhealthy and in any case, said the Astrolabe Compagnie doctor, 'every tropical colony has to be manured with human bodies before it can bear fruit'.[38] To supplant the original inhabitants of New Guinea with thousands of immigrants seemed a natural objective to men familiar with the large-scale migration of labour in the Malay Peninsula and Indonesian Archipelago.

It was easier to rhapsodize about New Guinea's possibilities than to make them come true. Hansemann smoked New Guinea cigars exclusively, but tobacco came from Kaiser Wilhelmsland in such small quantities that few other smokers could have done so. The flow of coolie labour from South-East Asia was effectively controlled by the British and the Dutch, who created numerous obstacles to recruiting by the Germans. In December 1892 the government of the Straits Settlements amended the Crimping Ordinance of 1877 so as to make recruiting of coolies for employment outside the British Empire dependent upon the prior approval of the governor. The amendment's principal object was to 'restrict the emigration of labourers from this Colony for labour in foreign places', and when it appeared that the Straits Settlements government would interpret this as a prohibition in the case of German New Guinea, the NGC appealed to the German Government to intercede for it at the highest level.[39]

The Company managed to recruit over 450 coolies from Singapore during the first seven months of 1893 but every recruitment had to be separately negotiated with the British authorities, who would not give permission to the Germans on a permanent basis. The British were worried about the anti-Chinese attitudes of the Australian colonials, who, they thought, would object strongly to constant immigration of Chinese into New Guinea because of the danger of Chinese finding their way to Australia. From the German point of view the British attitude was further evidence of that 'change towards ill-feeling' in colonial questions which had occurred in British foreign policy, especially as the British continued to let the Dutch take thousands of coolies from Singapore to Java and Sumatra.[40]

Fortunately for the NGC the outbreak of the Siam crisis in late July 1893 brought Britain closer than ever to the Triple Alliance and Rosebery at the Foreign Office decided to override Colonial Office objections to emigration of Chinese labourers from Singapore. A compromise was reached with Germany in October 1893 and the German ambassador in London, Count Hatzfeldt, was told that Britain could now meet some of the requirements of the 'New Guinea Company, in which the German Government take so marked an interest'.[41] The Germans were promised up to 800 coolies a year for three years in return for an undertaking that those coolies who did not wish to remain in the Protectorate of the Neu Guinea Compagnie would be returned to Singapore, and that the rest would be prohibited from going to ports in British New Guinea or Australia.

The Dutch were meanwhile creating difficulties of their own, following an exposé of the crowded graveyards of Kaiser Wilhelmsland in a Surabaya newspaper.[42] They delayed giving approval for the recruitment of 180 coolies from the Dutch East Indies and finally rejected a request for a further 200 in early 1894 because of suspicions about the fate of those recruited in 1890, few of whom had returned. They agreed, however, to a suggestion of the German Consul in Batavia that a Dutch official be sent to investigate, and following his visit to Kaiser Wilhelmsland in July 1894, the governor-general of the Dutch East Indies gave permission for the 200 to go, on condition that his government be informed every two months of any coolies' deaths, and that provision be made to prevent coolies gambling away their earnings on the voyage home.[43]

Disease, partly introduced and partly indigenous, added to the Germans' losses in Kaiser Wilhelmsland. Most people on the plantations, whites and non-whites alike, had an attack of malaria at least once a month. NGC employees with chronic malaria who were sent back to Europe became known on the ships of Norddeutscher Lloyd and in Singapore as 'New Guinea corpses'. To combat disease, the Germans erected primitive 'hospitals', built labourers' quarters high off the ground, laid dry gravel paths, used fine-money paid by the workers for the care of the sick, had *kadehs* or stores set up under Chinese and Malay management to provide coolies with fresh food, and introduced a system of employing newly arrived Chinese for only eight hours a day with four hours off in the noon heat. The results were disappointing. The imported workers, whether New Guinean or Asian, were more susceptible to the diseases of the mainland than locally recruited workers, and in any case they brought serious diseases with them. Many Malay coolies, for example, carried the indelible blue stamp of the Dutch East Indies Army at the base of their spines, indicating that they had once had beri-beri and were therefore unsuitable for future employment as soldiers. In the twelve months to 1894 one in four of all Malays employed by the Germans contracted beri-beri, a vitamin deficiency disease which could kill a worker or keep him in hospital for two years. The smallpox and influenza epidemics of 1893 and 1894 affected the imported New Guinean workers, who lacked immunity even to malaria. Of 306 recruits from New Hanover and New Ireland who arrived in Kaiser Wilhelmsland in July and August 1894, for example, nearly half were in hospital with malaria by the end of October. The Chinese were also unhealthy. One lot of them was described by the Astrolabe Compagnie doctor as 'a completely wretched, run-down, anaemic rabble, enervated by opium, scum who had in fact been picked up in the streets of Singapore and could find employment no other way'.[44] He claimed that the 25 per cent mortality rate could be attributed at least partly to the effects of drug addiction. In their haste to colonize the Germans themselves were being exploited by labour recruiters in Surabaya and Singapore, who supplied sickly unemployables instead of strong, skilled labourers. Only a small proportion of the coolies was used to working with tobacco and many had never been field-labourers at all. The healthy young coolie whom the doctor in Singapore passed as 'fit for field labour' would often be replaced on the way to the ship by an aged weakling, and since the British in Singapore would not allow seriously ill people ashore, the Germans were obliged to restore them to health in Kaiser Wilhelmsland.

From 1893 each year brought a smaller rather than a larger crop of tobacco. The human cost mounted. So much opium was imported for the coolies that in the three years to April 1894 the import duty on it provided nearly half all tariff revenues for the colony. Smallpox brought from Java or Singapore raged among the coastal peoples of Kaiser Wilhelmsland, reaching the Witu Islands off west New Britain. When he visited the Ali, Seleo and Angel Islands off Aitape in 1896, the commander of the survey vessel *Möwe* estimated that the smallpox had killed, on average, half the islanders. In the New Guinea islands, Kaiser Wilhelmsland was gaining the reputation of being the place where there was 'no kaikai, no sunday, plenty fight, plenty die'. Men sought vengeance for the loss of kinsmen on plantations far from home. NGC recruiters in the area of the Lihir Islands near New Ireland were subjected to what appeared to be a planned attack in March 1894, when nine new recruits fell upon them with their bare hands while kinsmen gave support with axes. The German helmsman and at least two New Guinean crew were killed. In July 1894 Company recruiters were again attacked in New Ireland, and in April 1895 the acting Company Governor reported little desire among the New Irelanders to sign on. He attributed it to a good season in New Ireland and the recent return of large numbers of labourers with trade-goods but fear of Kaiser Wilhelmsland may also have played a part. On the plantations of the Astrolabe Compagnie the New Irelanders were thought by the Germans to be weak in constitution and refractory in their attitude to work. New arrivals from New Ireland and New Hanover accounted for 80 per cent of the numerous deaths among the company's islander workforce in the terrible months of October, November and December 1894.[45]

Kaiser Wilhelmsland had by now proved to be an utter fiasco in colonization. Yet even as the reports of disaster reached his desk, Hansemann pretended all was well. The official Company gazette predicted improvements in all directions during 1895 and pointed to the renewal of labour contracts by Javanese and Chinese as evidence that they themselves no longer thought the climate unhealthy. In fact, as Hansemann himself admitted later, medical records revealed that 537 plantation labourers died in Company hospitals in Kaiser Wilhelmsland in the year to March 1896 out of an average total workforce of 1946. In its last two years the Astrolabe Compagnie, capitalized at 2 400 000 marks, lost 1 312 837 marks because of poor tobacco prices in Europe, droughts, and inability to procure a 'robust labour force'. Optimistic in public, Hansemann was privately trying to extricate his companies from their over-extended investments as early as January 1895, when he appealed to the government for help. He now wanted to withdraw permanently from the colonial administration, have the imperial charter revoked and allow the German government to assume administrative authority, and while negotiations on a full transfer of power took place, the Bismarck Archipelago was put under the control of imperial officials paid by the NGC.[46]

Retrenchment and rationalization of the plantations soon followed. The Neu Guinea Compagnie absorbed the Astrolabe Compagnie, debilitated coolies were sent home before the end of their contracts and the jungle was allowed to creep back over erstwhile tobacco fields. The British, though not the Dutch, refused to allow the NGC to recruit any more coolies, leaving it once more largely dependent on the labour of New Guineans. But New Guineans did not fill the gaps left by departing Asians and at the end of 1897 the NGC's directors were still resolving that the recruiting of black workers be energetically undertaken.

Yabim from the coast of the Huon Gulf had been more willing than any other mainland men to sign on for work with the Germans, yet even they were refusing Company recruiters by the end of the 1890s. The Company blamed the Yabim's changed attitude on missionaries of the Neuendettelsau Lutheran Mission, evangelizing in the area since the arrival of Johann Flierl in 1886. A recruiter returning to the Huon Gulf in 1898 found one Yabim village, previously a frequent supplier of labourers, deserted. He rang the bell used by the missionaries to call the people together, but this time no one appeared. At another village he claimed to have been told that the missionaries virtually ordered villagers to stay and build a mission station instead of going on board the recruiting vessel. According to the Company, the mission used not only warnings but also presents of tobacco and trade-goods to stop New Guineans signing on.[47]

The Neuendettelsau missionaries were opposed to the recruiters for several reasons. For their own safety alone they were unwilling to be a party to Company recruiting in case they be held responsible by a recruit's tribesmen for his death. In the second place, missionaries were themselves recruiters and the plantations were therefore their competitors. Under the boarding-school system adopted by the Neuendettelsau mission, pupils were attracted to school by the offer of trade-goods in the same way in which labourers were attracted to the plantations. After perhaps a year's work doing odd jobs on the mission station and learning hymns, prayers and bible stories, the pupil was paid off with the usual axes, knives, cloth and beads. At Simbang mission school in 1898, for example,

> There were six boys from the villages around Finschhafen who had proved themselves diligent learners. Their relatives also came to discharge day, in particular to receive the wages Missionary Pfalzer had laid out ready in the school.[48]

It seems as if some Yabim, at least, were emboldened to sign on as plantation labourers by their experience of earning trade-goods at school, despite the warnings of missionaries. At the end of the 1890s ex-pupils of the Neuendettelsau Mission schools were common among the mainland labourers in Astrolabe Bay. Thirdly, the missionaries objected to the deception practised by Company recruiters and to Company methods of payment. The veteran missionary Georg Bamler, who had worked in Kaiser Wilhelmsland since 1887, wrote in 1898 of people being told they would be away only ten months and then having to work for forty months, and of kidnapping by the Company recruiter, Ludwig Kärnbach. 'But', he added, 'one has no authentic witnesses, blacks do not count before the law ...'. Bamler could understand the Company's unwillingness to spoil the market by giving away too many axes and knives, but he described as 'worthless' the shirts, suits, hats, perfumes and umbrellas supplied to Company labourers as wages. By 1898 forty to fifty Yabim had died at Stephansort plantation in Astrolabe Bay, perhaps a twentieth of the Yabim population. Who would want to blame the New Guinean, Bamler asked, when he wondered whether his children had been born for himself or for the whites? As in the archipelago the recruiting difficulties of the NGC in its last years of rule are probably attributable far less to mission influence than to New Guineans' fear of dying on the plantations. The Company thought fear of ill-treatment on the plantations also deterred New Guineans from signing on. When a doctor in Kaiser Wilhelmsland complained in 1898 that Europeans were assaulting labourers, the directors in Berlin reminded the New Guinea manager that rumours of cruelty greatly impeded recruitment.[49]

The negotiations for a general settlement which the NGC began with the imperial government in 1895 were prolonged for another three years. An agreement for the transfer of sovereignty came before the *Reichstag* in the summer of 1896, but it was rejected as scandalously favourable to the Company. It would have given the Company an economic monopoly of Kaiser Wilhelmsland and southern New Britain for a period of seventy-five years (to 1971) or up to 4 600 000 marks for surrendering that monopoly. Defending its record to shareholders against charges made in the *Reichstag* that it had carried out 'pure mass murder' of coolies the NGC explained that although it was 'unfortunately correct' that a 'large number' of coolies brought from Singapore in late 1891 had died, this was not the Company's fault. And to the critics in the *Reichstag* who objected to giving the Company exclusive rights to recruiting in Kaiser Wilhelmsland for

twenty years, it replied that it had invested a large amount of trouble and
money in accustoming the New Guineans to work.[50]

The matter now went to the Colonial Council, an advisory body of colonial investors and businessmen, created in 1891 to placate the right wing
of the German colonial movement. Hansemann himself was a member,
together with Reinhold Kraetke, former acting governor of the Protectorate
of the Neu Guinea Compagnie, Richard Hindorf, a former Company
official and from 1897 Simon Alfred, Freiherr von Oppenheim, a Company
shareholder. The Council recommended that the NGC should surrender
all privileges in return for compensation of 4 000 000 marks and a land
grant of 100 000 hectares. In further negotiations between NGC and government the Colonial Department offered 50 000 hectares of land instead
of 100 000 and would not publicly guarantee preferential labour recruiting
rights for the Company in Kaiser Wilhelmsland. But government officials
assured the NGC in private that it could count on imperial co-operation,
a promise later honoured when Berlin overruled Governor Hahl in order
to give the Company recruiting privileges on the mainland. The agreement
signed in March 1899 required the government to pay the NGC ten annual
instalments of 400 000 marks, each instalment to be spent on what were
liberally defined as 'economic enterprises in the interest of the colony';
the Company had to take possession of its 50 000 hectares of land in Kaiser
Wilhelmsland within three years; and, while losing its land monopoly for
the colony as a whole, the Company was given exclusive mining rights
in the area of the Upper Ramu River.

The Neu Guinea Compagnie was one of the great disasters of late nineteenth century colonialism. To create the externals of colonization—
shipping connections, settlements, exploratory expeditions, town plans and
regulations—was not the same thing as founding a flourishing colony, as
the rusting machinery and abandoned plantations of Kaiser Wilhelmsland
showed. Land in itself was not an asset unless settlers could be persuaded
to come and, with no assurance of a secure livelihood in New Guinea, they
sensibly stayed at home. Hansemann fell back on the alternative of tobacco
cultivation, described by the veteran islands trader Eduard Hernsheim in
1888 as 'praiseworthy and patriotic no doubt, but an impossible undertaking from a commercial point of view'.[51] And so it proved to be.

Hansemann was constantly misled by thinking of New Guinea as an
extension of the East Indies and by assuming that the larger mainland would
be a more profitable area of investment than the smaller archipelago to
the north. From those two false assumptions flowed virtually every difficulty which the NGC encountered.

The example of Sumatra encouraged Hansemann to invest ex-
travagantly, especially in shipping, which was a severe drain on Company
finances in the early years. The NGC enthusiastically established its own
fleet in 1885, purchasing two steamers new from a Danzig shipyard and
maintaining a shipping connection between Kaiser Wilhelmsland and
Cooktown. But because this arrangement was expensive and made the
Company dependent on the British merchant marine for supplies from Ger-

many, the Company transferred its entrepot to Surabaya in Java in 1889 and used the Dutch line Stoomvaart Maatschappij Nederland for shipments to and from Europe. In March 1891 the NGC steamer *Ottilie* was wrecked in the Purdy Islands and Hansemann decided to rely on chartered vessels for the colony's links with the outside world, employing his own smaller craft for inter-island transport. Almost a third of all Company expenditure up to 1893 was on shipping and the direct returns from freight were negligible. The solution to the Company's shipping problems, as later to its potential insolvency, came in the form of government aid. In 1893 the Bremen firm Norddeutscher Lloyd was granted an imperial subsidy to establish a regular service between New Guinea and Singapore, connecting with its subsidized run from Bremen to Shanghai.[52]

The decision to concentrate on the mainland rather than the New Guinea islands had multiple consequences, none of them favourable to the NGC. In the first place, the more prevalent malaria of the mainland coast killed Melanesians, Chinese, Malays and Germans in numbers so great as to constantly disrupt the Company's operations. A count made of labourers recruited in the New Guinea islands from 1887 to 1903 showed that of 2802 listed as having worked in Astrolabe Bay and western Kaiser Wilhelmsland, 1129 died during their period of contract.[53] Of the Company governors, only Kraetke and Skopnik completed their short terms of service. Schleinitz's wife died in the colony and he resigned early; Schmiele died while on leave; Rüdiger left before the end of his appointment because of failing health. The two general managers of the Company sent out during the interregnum of imperial administration, Arnold and Wissman, both died within months of arriving in New Guinea. Hagen's brief tenure of the office of *Landeshauptmann* ended in 1897 when he was shot dead by a policeman from Buka called Ranga. After being forced out of Finschhafen by malaria in March 1891, the German colonists did not re-establish a permanent centre of administration until September 1892, at Madang.

In the second place the mainland offered fewer opportunities than the islands for the Germans to trade with the villagers and employ them as labourers. Inclined to dismiss the New Guineans as of no account, Hansemann never understood that his success depended upon their co-operation. The foreigners in the Bismarck Archipelago, old hands of the Pacific, knew better and built their prosperity on trading with the villagers for copra. The schooners which plied between the Gazelle Peninsula of New Britain and northern New Ireland, New Hanover, the Admiralties, the Shortland group and atolls from Ninigo in the west to Ontong Java in the east carried thousands of tonnes of trade copra in 1899, dwarfing the output of the mainland; and the plantations which the foreigners laid down on the Gazelle Peninsula during the 1890s were financed with the proceeds of copra trading. Except for Ludwig Kärnbach at Aitape, the NGC had no traders to forge significant economic links with the villagers and break down suspicions about labour recruitment. Most of the Company's labourers and virtually all its capital were expensively imported from abroad.

The political strategies of the NGC offered no way out of this economic impasse. In the scores of small, distinct communities along the coast of New Guinea the authority of 'big men' waxed and waned in accordance with their success in organizing feasts, making alliances and waging war. In the absence of leaders with control over thousands of people, indirect rule through collaborating élites was impossible, and the Company resorted to sporadic and ineffectual punitive expeditions, burning huts and shooting women, children, pigs, dogs, hens and occasionally a warrior. It was not a form of government but a succession of raids. Hansemann went on claiming that the Charter of 1885 promised his Company imperial protection at imperial expense; the Navy disagreed, refused to offer more than strictly limited help and helped to leave the coastal peoples of Kaiser Wilhelmsland as independent in 1899 as they had been in 1885.

Without the 'pioneering work' of the NGC, said a Company pamphlet of 1899, 'Kaiser Wilhelmsland would have as small a number of plantations as British New Guinea'.[54] Maybe so. But the price of this plantation development had been human suffering and death on a scale unknown on the British side of the island. Hansemann's reward for being ignorant, inept and ruthless, was a government subsidy on the profligate scale typical of the period when the conservative Gerson von Buchka was Colonial Director. Buchka's concessions to colonial companies in Africa were notorious and he conceded vast tracts of New Guinea to the Company with the same casual ease. Delivered at birth by charter, and nourished through an extended childhood by government subsidy and concession, the Neu Guinea Compagnie continued to exert a powerful influence over colonial policy even after the coming of the imperial administration in 1899.

3
The Islands under Company Rule 1885–1899

North-east of the high mountains of east New Britain stretches a fertile, densely populated peninsula which played a central part in the colonial history of Papua New Guinea. The Gazelle Peninsula, so named after the German warship which visited New Britain on a scientific expedition in 1875, includes the provincial town of Rabaul. From Rabaul a network of roads carries cars, open trucks and people on foot to copra and cocoa plantations, tradestores selling tinned fish and rice, numerous villages of wooden houses with corrugated iron or thatch roofs, schools surrounded by neat lawns and airy, white-painted United Church and Catholic churches. Monuments record the coming of the missionaries in the 1870s and 1880s. Man has not ripped the heart out of this place on earth by mining, clearing or urban sprawl and the Gazelle Peninsula looks much as it was when Europeans intruded a century ago. Vegetation and topography dominate: many villages are hidden by plantations or forest, and Rabaul itself is dwarfed by the three volcanic mountains under which it shelters. Around the western and southern shores of Blanche Bay the land rises steeply to a plateau, covered with grass in the 1870s and now extensively planted with coconut palms and cacao trees. In a country of swamps, ridges and mountain chains, the Gazelle Peninsula is a rare patch of broad coastal plain with deep, rich soils.

The foreign settlers who came to the New Guinea islands before German annexation knew what to look for if they were to make a livelihood: convenient anchorages, plenty of coconut palms and not too much malaria. In the Gazelle Peninsula they found all these and in addition a local population who were keen traders, the Tolai. Forests of coconut palms grew on the shores and hills of Blanche Bay, providing a natural surplus of coconuts for trade, and in the earliest commercial encounters between foreigners and Tolai a tonne of copra, worth 400 marks in Europe, could be had for six marks worth of stick tobacco, empty bottles and beads. Within a few years the Tolai had doubled or trebled their asking price and as the European market for copra weakened the golden opportunities for foreigners disappeared; by 1884 villagers were demanding cartridges for Snider rifles instead of gunpowder and lead-shot, brass Jew's harps instead of iron ones, higher quality axes, and breech-loading rather than muzzle-loading fire-

arms. They had even begun producing artefacts specifically for the eager
European buyers on board visiting naval vessels. But profits could still
be made by foreign traders.[1]

The market places of the coastal Gazelle Peninsula, situated in neutral
territory between villages and spaced between two and five kilometres
apart, quickly accommodated foreign trade. Women, protected by their
menfolk, traditionally brought lime, betel-nut, fish and fresh produce to
exchange with the women of neighbouring villages. The European traders
added a new element to these exchanges by employing Tolai as agents to
go to market with tobacco, knives, axes and iron to buy thousands of coconuts for making into copra.

The Tolai people numbered perhaps 30 000 in the 1880s. Like most
other New Guinean peoples, they were not a single unit of political organization but a series of segmented descent groups living in separated hamlets
and villages. Descent was matrilineal and the land jointly owned by
matrilineages. While centralized Tolai authority was unknown, within
villages the *lualua*, or 'first men', of clans, held control over clan land and
could command kinsfolk to cultivate it. The *lualua* owed their power to
seniority. But status, in the form of a kind of generally recognized title,
also came to men for achievement as warriors or entrepreneurs. People
called the successful fight leader a *luluai* and the man who had accumulated
a rich store of shell-money and other valuables a *uviana*. For the great
man who succeeded in many spheres and was often a *luluai* and a *uviana*
at the same time, they reserved the title *a gala*. The *a gala* was entrusted
with the clan's shell-money and it was he who bought wives for the young
men who were then required to work off their debt to him. In the 1880s
no Tolai dared to go beyond the confines of his clan lands without his
sling and stones, nor did he go to market without the protection of muskets,
spears, axes and clubs. The planter Richard Parkinson called it 'a permanent
state of war'.[2]

At least until the turn of the century relations between the Tolai and
the colonizers were deeply influenced by Tolai custom in making war and
peace, settling disputes and engaging in trade. Inter-Tolai warfare was a
frequent occurrence at the time of annexation, perhaps because of the
increased military power of coastal villages with access to European
weapons. Villages protected themselves with guards, fences and concealed
ditches dug in forest paths. Influential men in districts threatened with
attack appealed for allies by sending shell-money to neighbouring warriors,
who indicated their willingness to join an alliance by accepting a gift. Bands
of warriors were summoned by the beating of the war-drum or *garamut*,
hundreds at a time going into battle. But the battle itself was not always
fought to the death; instead, in a kind of chivalrous warfare unknown to
Europe, warriors often shouted insults at each other, threw stones and withdrew with few injuries. Peace was settled by paying compensation in shell-
money.[3]

To acquire great amounts of shell-money was the ambition of every Tolai man. Variously called *dewarra* or *tambu*, the small nassa shells threaded on rattan cane and measured in fathoms were the key to the Tolai's success in life. With them, wrote Parkinson, the Tolai

> buys his ornaments and his wives, with dewarra he buys himself out of every predicament and complication, with dewarra he placates his embittered enemy even when he has killed his immediate relative . . . Money is power in New Britain as elsewhere. He who possesses most dewarra enjoys the highest esteem and exercises the greatest influence. The women must work from morning till night throughout their lives in order to obtain dewarra for the man; the men covet their neighbour's treasure and devise schemes to steal it.[4]

In what is now the Kokopo area of the Gazelle Peninsula men paid one fathom of shell-money for about eighty kilograms of yams in the mid-1880s, ten fathoms for a large pig, twenty fathoms for an older woman and up to 100 fathoms for a nubile young girl as a wife. A canoe built in the Duke of York group, on Watom Island, or on the western side of the peninsula at Kabaira, the places which specialized in canoe-building for sale to villages elsewhere, could cost as much as 150 fathoms and would be greatly prized by its owners. The destruction of canoes by German punitive expeditions in the colonial period represented considerable loss to Tolai communities.

The Tolai were a horticultural and fishing people. In gardens close to the scattered groups of houses which constituted the village, the women grew coconuts, yams, taro and sweet potato. Fishing was men's work, mostly performed by trapping fish in cane baskets lowered from canoes, and coastal communities with a surplus of fish would trade them to inlanders who did not need all their taro. The men built houses, felled trees, dug out stumps and fenced gardens to keep out wild pigs.

Foreign settlement was centred in the Gazelle Peninsula and the Duke of York Islands from precolonial times onwards, but it extended into numerous other island localities which enjoyed the same combination of accessibility from the sea and ample supplies of coconuts. Intermittently driven away by fever or islanders, foreign traders lived on New Hanover, the Admiralty Islands, the Shortland Islands and on most of the isolated atoll groups: the Western Islands, the Nuguria group, Nissan, the Mortlock Islands, the Tasman Islands and Ontong Java. But only the north of New Ireland could be compared with east New Britain in commercial importance. Here at Nusa Island Eduard Hernsheim established a trading post in 1880 and quickly developed a network of agents who made the most of the New Irelanders' initial unfamiliarity with European manufactures.

The foreigners found anchorages in the maze of islands between New Ireland and New Hanover; and on the north-east coast south from North Cape, where the sea beats upon rocks and coral reefs, they discovered flat, fertile land covered with coconut palms. The northern New Irelanders grew taro, yams, breadfruit and bananas, raised pigs and fished, living in dispersed hamlets of two or three dozen people of the same matrilineal clan. The men caught sharks with a unique instrument of wood and cord, attracting their prey to canoes by making clapping sounds and then pulling the lassoo tight. *Tapsoka*, made in New Hanover from red and white shell, served as money and conferred power and prestige on the owner. At the centre of the ritual life of the people was the *malanggan*, a word describing both ceremonies which honoured the dead and the carvings which accompanied them. Using dried shark-skin to sharpen their knives, dead leaves for polishing and mixtures of lime and tree-sap for colours, the select group of *malanggan* carvers produced the designs which belonged to their particular community, each design with its own mythical or historical ancestry. Fantastic images of men, men-beasts, phalluses, birds (often hornbills), snakes, fish and pigs emerged from the secret enclosures where the carvers made their masks and figures. But it was the weaponry of the Tigak, Kara and Nalik speaking peoples of northern New Ireland which the traders came to know best in the twenty years to 1900, the slingstones, long-handled steel axes, decorated spears with bamboo shafts and hard palm-wood tips and firearms used to kill foreigner after foreigner whose presence was resented.[5]

Within the one colony, the Protectorate of the Neu Guinea Compagnie, two quite different forms of colonization developed. Kaiser Wilhelmsland and its horrors were the direct creation of colonial planners in Berlin. Company officials, the majority from Prussia, came to Kaiser Wilhelmsland on short-term contracts, observed the stiff formalities of rank to which they were accustomed and were glad to leave the colony alive. The origins of colonization in the Bismarck Archipelago, by contrast, lay in the Pacific islands rather than Europe and in the attractions of fertile coastal localities for the heterogeneous collection of ex-convicts, missionaries, labour recruiters, ship's deserters and adventurers who moved from island to island in the nineteenth-century Pacific.

Germans were a minority among expatriates in the Bismarck Archipelago and the German Solomons in the 1880s and 1890s. As late as 1897 British colonials, Fijians, Chinese, Scandinavians, Belgians, Dutchmen, Frenchmen, Spaniards, Samoans and others outnumbered Germans by more than three to one. Many settlers had lived in other parts of the Pacific before coming to New Guinea. Eduard Hernsheim sailed south from the Carolines to the Duke of Yorks in 1875 and later recruited traders from Ponape; Richard Parkinson worked for Godeffroys in Samoa before marrying Phebe Coe and moving to New Britain in 1882; Phebe Coe's more famous sister, Emma Forsayth or 'Queen Emma', spent time in Tahiti, the Marshalls and Samoa before she took up residence in the Gazelle Peninsula; Friedrich Schulle, trader, came to northern New Ireland in 1884 from Fiji; Joseph Haas, trader, was from New Caledonia. The examples could be multiplied. The few hundred foreigners living in the Bismarck Archipelago in the 1880s and 1890s included French and Belgian survivors of the disastrous Marquis de Rays expedition, a swindle which had dumped prospective colonists in a non-existent colony in southern New Ireland in 1880. The Methodist Mission was staffed by Australians and Fijians, the head of the Sacred Heart Mission from 1889 was the Frenchman Louis Couppé and the shipwright of the settlement was Ah Tam, a Chinese. This polyglot community ignored the Neu Guinea Compagnie and took the island peoples seriously as opponents and allies. They could not afford to do otherwise because the basis of their livelihood, trade, depended on the co-operation of the villagers. In the Gazelle Peninsula and elsewhere in the islands New Guineans and foreigners met, co-operated, disagreed, traded and fought in ways little affected by the NGC, the German government or the Imperial Navy. Rather were relations between islander and intruder determined by which side had more power at any particular time; or, more accurately, by which side saw advantage in using its power against the other, according to the ambitions of clans and big men to augment their political influence, the desire of traders to survive in a hostile environment, rises and falls in the price of copra and shell and, as well, the behaviour of lonely, often alcoholic, traders on remote outposts of the colonial frontier. To complicate the situation, islanders often joined the foreigners as allies against local enemies.

The proclamation of German sovereignty in 1884 did not bring German colonial rule to the Bismarck Archipelago. It represented instead a claim to exercise control in the future, and for the moment nothing changed at all in relations between settlers and villagers. The trading agent for the big firm, dependent on a modest monthly wage and small commission on the copra he collected, living on salted meat and rice and effectively in the power of his New Guinean neighbours, continued to be the foreigner most likely to be attacked or driven away. Villagers on the west coast of the Gazelle Peninsula stole all the property of the DHPG's trading post at Kabaira in January 1885; a trader at Kabakada lost more goods to thieves in May; Hernsheim's station at Kabakada was burnt to the ground in June; and a few months later a fire at Tamalili in the eastern Gazelle destroyed forty tons of copra belonging to the DHPG. In northern New Ireland Kabien men attacked a trader called Svente Carlson with axes, tomahawks and rifle-butts as he stood in his boat at Kabatheron Island in May 1885, an incident which Carlson blamed on a competing trader's incitements to murder him; the Kapsu people cut down several hundred coconut palms on land belonging to the Hernsheim company and at Lessoa they murdered a European and a Solomon Islander in September 1885; Djaul Islanders speared another European to death a few weeks later; and at the end of the year an agent for the trader and planter Thomas Farrell met his death.

The imperial commissioner in the Bismarck Archipelago, Oertzen, reported that the island warriors had become 'so provocative and dangerous that the utmost danger appears to threaten all settlers, both their persons and their property', and after five further raids by northern New Irelanders on trading posts he asked the imperial cruiser *Albatross* for assistance. The arson and theft at Kabaira on the western side of the Gazelle Peninsula were traced to a wealthy big man of the district and a renowned enemy of the whites, To Vering. A party of about thirty German marines was sent to impose a fine on him but he refused to accompany them and instead arranged for several hundred warriors armed with guns to appear on the hills surrounding the landing corps. The Germans were forced to withdraw. They returned the following day with reinforcements, only to be 'suddenly attacked by an almost invisible enemy' and compelled to undertake a second humiliating withdrawal. The intervention of the *Albatross* in the Gazelle Peninsula, Oertzen admitted, had diminished rather than increased the Tolai's 'fear of our weapons'. 'They do not recognise us as the unconditional victors', he wrote, 'otherwise they would not have shot at the troops on the last day but would rather have asked for peace and, as a sign of submission, would have brought the diwarra ... which we demanded'. In northern New Ireland the marines of the *Albatross* landed a number of times to inflict punishment: at Kabien village; at Mangai, where they were opposed by spear-carrying warriors who shouted a war-cry and who yielded 'only after a great number of them had fallen victim to the Mauser rifle'; at a place the Germans called Balgai (Bagail, near Kavieng), scene of the arrest of five prisoners and the killing of one who tried to escape; at Maiom, whose inhabitants met them with spears and gunshot; and elsewhere. Yet as subsequent conflict along the trading coast of New Ireland was to show, the safety which these reprisals brought to the foreigners was short-lived.[6]

Oertzen decided to put an end to the trouble in the Gazelle Peninsula with a massive demonstration of German military might. The attitude of the people in the area between Kabaira, Rakunai and Kabakada was hindering the 'spread of civilisation', by which Oertzen meant the spread of traders, and he thought the villagers deserved a fine of 2000 fathoms of shell-money, together with the confiscation of all their arms and ammunition. The difficulty, as a Methodist missionary at Kabakada foresaw, was that the people would retire as the sailors advanced:

> there will be no chance of striking a blow that will tell the natives that opposition is useless & submission is the wiser course. Secure in their fever-stricken glens and gullies they will not need to fight in order to compel the retreat of the whts. but will quietly wait for them to go away thinking it all a good joke. [sic]

Planning to encircle and capture To Vering on the morning of 19 June 1886, 500 men landed from the frigates *Bismarck* and *Gneisenau* and the corvette *Olga* and marched in the heat up and down steep ridges in search of the enemy. But no enemy was to be found. The villagers, having seen the German men-of-war anchor hours before, hid deep in the bush and rendered the expedition pointless. To Vering remained at large, the fine of shell-money was unpaid and the warriors still had firearms.[7]

The naval interventions of 1886 revealed numerous obstacles in the path of a colonial administration in island Melanesia. Islanders fled on the approach of a warship, amply forewarned by 'bush telegraph', their drum signallers, and in their home country they could ambush German landing parties at will. The German marines were poor warriors in unfamiliar and mountainous jungle terrain and required local guides, who were hard to procure. The marines pounded villages with 15-centimetre shells, bivouacked ashore and burnt gardens and hamlets. On 11 November 1886 they hanged a man called Wobau from Kapsu in northern New Ireland for reporting the movements of a German landing detachment.[8] He was convicted of espionage under martial law, an offence which symbolized the new loyalties the colonial administration was attempting to enforce on an uncomprehending population. None of these measures brought New Guineans under the control of the foreigners who now claimed to be their masters.

Traders had no particular interest in establishing the authority of the Neu Guinea Compagnie. They wanted to make a living. Once they saw the Navy in action in New Britain and New Ireland, they quickly called for it to stop disrupting peaceful commerce: better to trade on the islanders' terms, after all, than not to trade at all. Eduard Hernsheim, whose experience of the Bismarck Archipelago was longer than that of any other foreigner, thought the relationship between whites and islanders had been generally amicable since the 1870s and that conflicts were usually the product of misunderstanding. The Navy, he thought, would always fall short in the task of creating colonial order, because naval captains could never afford the time to pursue fleeing villagers on land. The only answer was a police force of at least 100 trained men. Oertzen asked the NGC for just fifteen police in 1885, only to be told that the Company could not provide them and that he should depend on the Navy, and when Oertzen left New Britain in 1887 settlers remained as exposed as ever to New Guinean attack. His parting prediction was that the Company would bear a 'heavy responsibility' if it delayed any longer in fulfilling 'the first duty of a state', to keep person and property safe.[9]

For another decade in the coastal Gazelle Peninsula and for longer elsewhere in the islands the relations between New Guineans and foreigners were hardly influenced by government. Adolph von Hansemann said order was for the Navy to impose, the Navy and the Colonial Department retorted that it was a Company responsibility; and nothing effective was done. Without a steamer, without sufficient naval assistance and without enough police the colonial administration was inconsequential, its meagre power being exercised intermittently and in response to New Guinean initiatives. The Company doubled the size of its police force for the whole colony from twenty-four to forty-eight during the 1890s but the police, who spent a great deal of time building roads and houses for the Company, were militarily puny.

Northern New Ireland

More than half of all labourers recruited in the Bismarck Archipelago in the 1890s came from New Ireland and New Hanover, and of this group the majority were from northern New Ireland. Work on contract in east New Britain, Samoa and mainland New Guinea became a tradition for the young men of northern New Ireland long before government was imposed, and their experience of recruiters and plantation overseers pro-

Adolph von Hansemann

Dr Albert Hahl in 1896

Bishop Ludwig Couppé

Reverend Johann Flierl senior

Men of Sissano, north-
west coast of Kaiser
Wilhelmsland, in the
1890s: the two warriors
in the centre wear a
broad bark belt as
protection from arrows
and spears

A young married couple,
Siar, Astrolabe Bay, in
the early 1890s

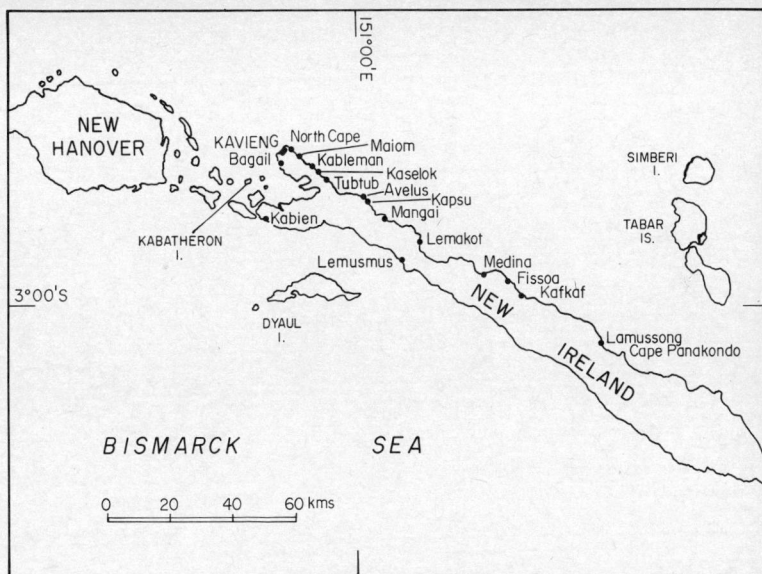

Northern New Ireland

vided first-hand knowledge of the wealth, power and vulnerability of the white man.

During 1886 and 1887 villages along the coasts of New Ireland as well as the Duke of Yorks and New Britain celebrated the return of time-expired labourers from plantations. 'The return of many men from Queensland, Fiji and Samoa has not been an unmixed blessing', wrote a missionary: 'Contagious and Epidemical diseases have been introduced by them and have carried off large numbers both on New Britain and New Ireland . . . The dysentery has been a frightful scourge'.[10] A further 150 New Irelanders drowned in the wreck of the *Young Dick*, which foundered on the Great Barrier Reef near Cooktown, and Eduard Hernsheim became alarmed by the resentful 'mood of the natives'. For the sake of the copra trade, in danger of being disrupted by the recruiters, Hernsheim had already succeeded in having the northern tip of New Ireland officially closed to recruiters from March 1886, a restriction which survived the complaints of the Neu Guinea Compagnie until September 1887.[11]

The New Guinea labour trade to Queensland and Fiji had virtually ceased before German annexation. Under regulations issued by the Queensland government in March and June 1884, Queensland recruiters were forbidden to supply arms and ammunition to Pacific islanders and to recruit labourers in New Guinea, New Britain, New Ireland and adjacent islands and from July 1884 the prohibition on supplying arms was extended by the Western Pacific High Commission in Fiji to all British subjects. But the labour trade to Samoa, which German annexation of the Bismarck

Archipelago was intended to protect, continued in full swing. In a formula suggested to the German government by the DHPG itself, that company became the sole beneficiary of a special exception in the laws governing the migration of labour from the Protectorate of the Neu Guinea Compagnie. By a proclamation of August 1885 the 'natives' of the Protectorate could not be taken outside its borders as labourers 'except for German plantations' and 'from those parts of the Bismarck Archipelago where this previously occurred'. The DHPG's right to the labour of New Guinea islanders survived until World War I. An official estimate, roughly reliable, put the number of labourers taken from German New Guinea to Samoa between 1885 and 1913 at 5746.[12]

Many men were away from the hamlets of northern New Ireland during the 1890s. If they were recruited for Samoa, they travelled in small schooners to the Mioko agency of the DHPG in the Duke of Yorks to wait, sometimes for weeks or months, for the ship from Apia. In Kokopo they put their marks on contracts and (after 1895) were examined by a doctor for signs of tuberculosis or venereal disease. After a voyage across the Pacific lasting from three to five weeks, they spent three years loading coconuts into ox-carts, weeding, cutting copra and packing. For disobedience, insubordination, desertion, fighting, stealing, mistreating animals, damaging equipment and assaulting overseers they were fined, flogged, compelled to work extra terms of service or confined to the penal labour division at Vaitele plantation, which was set up after the mass desertions accompanying the Samoan civil war of 1888-89. Here labourers were locked up while not working, those suspected of trying to escape being shackled in foot-irons. Well over a hundred labourers a year were escaping from the Samoan plantations in the early 1890s, perhaps one in every eight, and 78 deserters from one plantation were crossed off the company books as uncaptured in 1893.[13] Old deserters made converts. As a plantation manager explained in 1893, 'Ragaub, 7391, a good, willing boy and efficient worker' had decamped after the deserter Ratonga, labourer No. 7408, sneaked back one night to the labourers' quarters and told them that 'life is much better with the Samoans than on the plantations—they did not need to work and could do as they pleased'.[14] An unknown number of New Irelanders decided to spend the rest of their lives in Samoa. Those who completed their contracts received twenty-five Samoan dollars a year (about £5 in the sterling of the time) and spent the money on expensive goods in the company store before making the long trip home.

Samoa, with an average annual mortality rate on the DHPG plantations of about 10 per cent in the 1890s, was undoubtedly preferable to Kaiser Wilhelmsland as a destination for recruits, as the attacks on Neu Guinea Compagnie recruiters in New Ireland in 1894 were to show. And the Gazelle Peninsula, where most New Irelanders went, had the attraction of being closer to home, healthier, and a place where village women brought fresh food to the plantations for sale to the labourers.

The historical record is too slight for firm conclusions to be reached about the effect of the labour trade on the relations between northern New

Irelanders and the foreign traders who lived amongst them. All that seems clear from the endemic disorder of northern New Ireland in the 1890s is that foreigners were not held in awe by the people but rather treated as ordinary men who were potential allies or enemies, to be welcomed, given compassion, respected, ignored, exploited for their wealth and skill, or killed as circumstances demanded.

Some traders appear to have infringed local custom and paid the penalty with their lives. Frank Bradley, for example, after working for five months at Tubtub, talked of buying a local girl called Marankas as a wife. Whether he paid for her or not is unclear, but she spent only a day with him before he was slain with an axe by men of the district in July 1889, a murder which S.M.S. *Alexandrine* avenged a few months later by destroying the 'beautiful and large village' of Avelus (Ngavelus). In the house of the influential man, Anati, the Germans found a copy of the works of Schiller, looted the previous year from the possessions of Robert Hoppe, a Hernsheim agent killed at Kapsu.[15] The naval expedition was followed by one of the colony's first true police patrols between November 1889 and February 1890, when six trained police under a German officer visited Kavieng and Tubtub and exercised what the Germans thought was a 'considerable influence' for peace. But within weeks a French ship's deserter from New Caledonia, Joseph Haas, newly sent to Tubtub, died from the blows of a tomahawk wielded by an Avelus man. The instigator of the killing was said to be Luange, one of the two big men of the Avelus people and renowned for his enmity towards Europeans, and his motive allegedly was to get the Frenchman's Snider rifle and ammunition. At Kaselok warriors twice attacked trading boats in April 1890, killing a Solomon Islander called Lungi and stealing trade-goods.[16]

The New Irelanders' view of the situation was reported by a European:

> This is what the natives tell me: 'Yes, all the man he like kill 'em white man. Man he like musket and ball and plenty something belong white man, he very good'
> When I tell them that by and by a man of war will come to punish them, they laugh at me and say: 'Man-war he all same one bloody fool, he no save kill 'em kanaka. He make fire house, never mind. He no save go bush. Kanaka he no fraid belong man-war. Man-war he come, kanaka he go bush alright.
> Before, kanaka he kill 'em some white man, then man-war he come, white man belong him he come shore and he give 'em tobacco. He no kill 'em kanaka all same you speak.[17]

The traders were hard-living, often dissolute. Friedrich Schulle was given to rages in which he strung up his labourers and thrashed them with a bamboo cane until the blood flowed. He regularly drank himself into fury and insensibility and indulged in sexual excesses with local women without bothering to pay the customary compensation. His employee, the Norwegian Alexander Gunderson, stationed 100 kilometres down the coast from the north cape at Bosso, was said to shoot at the Bosso people and was probably drunk when they killed him in April 1891. Gunderson set out on a voyage from Bosso to Kapsu together with two Buka labourers and a number of Bosso men; according to the Buka, he was thrown overboard by the villagers, who returned to plunder his station of its rifles and ammunition. The next man foolish enough to venture to Bosso as a trading agent, a Filipino called Cordelo, was murdered with a tomahawk later in 1891 and became the seventh or eighth trader to be killed on the east coast of New Ireland since 1886. Not all died at the hands of northern New Irelanders: Studzinka and Hoppe, agents for Hernsheim, were slain by their Solomon Island labourers. But the northern New Irelanders had firmly established a reputation for getting rid of foreigners whom they disliked and the occasional visit of a naval cruiser, such as that of S.M.S. *Bussard* in 1892, did not lessen the risks of being a resident trader.[18]

The list of traders and recruiters killed in northern New Ireland and its offshore islands grew steadily longer: Carl Rojahn and his Japanese employee, Junzo Arinaga, put to death by Kabien warriors in 1894; a 'Negro sailor', a German labour recruiter and a Buka labourer axed by Lihir Islanders while trying to sign men on for the Neu Guinea Compagnie in 1894; four Tolai attacked and killed by the Kabien people in 1895; the Japanese Sugino and his labourer To Vianne killed at Kableman in 1895; the Dutchman Anat and his Samoan assistant Clark murdered by Simberi Islanders in 1897; ten Buka and a Tolai working for a white trader in Kapsu killed at Panakondo in 1899.[19]

Men such as William Leonhardt, who was said by a man from Kafkaf to have gone to the coast where the women were fishing and taken one by force whenever he felt in need of sex, were much more likely to be dealt with by village justice than by the colonial administration. And village communities were free to wage war without government interference. The Kabien people, for example, were continuing to undertake expeditions of war against the Djaul Islanders and the Lemusmus people of northern New Ireland in the late 1890s, having decided not to sign on as labourers or have anything to do with the Germans. Some traders may have exacerbated inter-village warfare. Leonhardt, for example, joined Johann Lundin to trade for Hernsheim at a village in north-east New Ireland in October 1896. The village was at war with the Medina people, who, led by former police, attacked and wounded the two traders and their Buka labourers in March 1897, forcing them to abandon the trading post.[20] By his very location the trader conferred advantages on his host community and aroused the jealousy of others who had to pay more for trade goods bought from village intermediaries. He became part of the village politics whether he liked it or not.

As imperial commissioner from 1889 to 1892, Fritz Rose had proposed tough measures. In order to safeguard the investments of Eduard Hernsheim, Friedrich Schulle, Emma Forsayth and the DHPG, he wanted an expeditionary force of a dozen Europeans, sixty armed police and labourers and ninety men from Kavieng armed with spears and axes to spend time pacifying northern New Ireland. But the venture was too expensive for Hansemann. The NGC had not chosen the reckless white traders of New Ireland, he said, and it would not spend money looking after them. No naval vessel, apart from the survey ship *Möwe*, visited the colony between December 1893 and January 1896 and north-east New Ireland continued to be neglected by the authorities.[21]

The Outlying Islands

Small island and atoll groups attracted settlers in the Bismarck Archipelago and the Solomons from the time Eduard Hernsheim first tried fishing for trepang in the Hermit Islands north-west of Manus in 1874. Such islands were often rich with coconut palms, trepang and turtleshell and easily accessible from the sea, unlike many stretches of coast on the big islands. By 1892 Hernsheim maintained trading posts on the Hermits and Anchorites, Queen Emma had one each on Rambutyo in the Admiralties, the Witu Islands off west New Britain, Nissan, the Nuguria and Mortlock groups, and Australian firms worked the Shortland Islands of the Bougainville Strait.[22]

Outlying islands were especially difficult for the NGC to police. Few traders based in Sydney or the Solomons bothered to make the journey to Kokopo in New Britain, the German port of clearance, before visiting German island groups in the Solomons such as Ontong Java or the Tasmans. A man from Ontong Java called Bari, who had been to Sydney three times and spoke good Pidgin, claimed that 'English captains' regularly came to the atoll to buy copra. He said 'Captain Tom' bought twenty tons of copra from the Ontong Java King Uila in about 1892, giving in return two boxes of dynamite, twelve bottles of gin, a sack of rice, a tin of biscuits and a Snider rifle with fifty cartridges. 'French Peter', a trader based in Roviana on New Georgia, was taking islanders from Ontong Java to work for him, breaking the German law forbidding the emigration of labour except to German plantations.[23]

Ontong Java, a huge atoll of more than twenty larger islands enclosing an extensive lagoon, had been visited by copra traders and labour recruiters since the coming of the brig *James Burnie* in 1874. Its population, which was to decline rapidly after the turn of the century, may have numbered over 2000 in the 1890s under the rule of King Uila. Speaking an Austronesian language with many clearly Polynesian elements, the people of Ontong Java accorded an authority to their kings and priests which was rare in Melanesia. Under Uila, no one returned from fishing without sending the best of the catch to the king, no one collected coconuts without giving him the biggest and no beautiful young girl refused to share his bed. Some Ontong Java islanders obeyed another chief, Vailua, in the early 1890s but it was to Uila, ruler of most of the group, that the Germans presented the official deed of annexation.[24]

One of the Australians who was caught and fined for illegal incursions into German territory, Captain Thomas Kirkpatrick of Sydney, said that at the time of trading and recruiting on Ontong Java about 1891 he 'was not aware that the German Government had assumed control over or annexed this Group of Islands'.[25] Kirkpatrick could be forgiven for not knowing. Santa Isabel and Ontong Java, annexed in October 1889, were late additions to the Protectorate of the Neu Guinea Compagnie and no German official lived in any of the German Solomons under Company rule. They were German in little more than name. In the far west of the colony the international border was equally ignored. A trader for the Carolines firm of O'Keefe, based in Yap, came south to the Hermit group in 1890 and for two years traded in spirits and copra without paying customs duties, illegally supplied arms to the islanders and contravened numerous German regulations.

Imperial Commissioner Rose was determined that Queen Emma rather than the Australians should have the trade of the Polynesian outliers. After Australian skippers told the Tasman islanders that the German régime was bad and oppressive, Emma's trader on the atoll had to flee for his life and at Ontong Java King Uila, no doubt encouraged by receiving a European boat from an Australian, ordered his subjects to make copra for the men from the south. Business had become 'almost impossible' for Queen Emma by the time Rose went to the atolls in 1892 on board S.M.S. *Bussard*. The demeanour of the Ontong Java people impressed him as much as their tall stature, heavily tatooed bodies and nasal shell ornaments. The priests sat on mats apart from the rest of the people, cooling themselves with triangular fans and unmoved by the arrival of the German party. King Uila, solemn and dignified in hat and coat, welcomed Rose, assured him of his loyalty and undertook to sell copra only to Emma's agents. At the Tasman Islands, where women sang, danced and clapped in Rose's honour, the people also agreed to stop trading with the Australians and remained friendly until they realized that Rose had come to take away some of their countrymen, one a man suspected of attempted murder and two others, influential islanders, who were to be shown the settlement at Kokopo in order to impress them with the power of the colonial administration. Even the most generous offers of mats failed to secure the release of the captives, and with cries of anguish the islanders chased the Germans' dinghies through the shallows, tried to climb aboard and were pushed back by the police.

Bari, the Ontong Java interpreter, went on the man-of-war to New Britain together with the Tasmans. 'Naturally intelligent' Rose called him and likely to be 'of considerable use' in explaining the workings of the government to the Tasman Islands chiefs, Puli and Fotau. Bari was the typical mediator in the colonial situation, telling each side what the other was doing. King Uila wanted information about the foreigners in Kokopo and sent Bari there to get it, and the Germans were glad to have someone capable of conveying their demands and wishes to the chiefs and to the prisoner accused of trying to kill Emma's trader. The prisoner was sentenced to three years' gaol and 'from conversations' which he had with Bari, the German imperial commissioner was satisfied that Puli and Fotau understood the true purpose of the colonial administration: not to impose force arbitrarily but to bring justice and protect those islanders 'who behaved themselves well'.[26] Whatever the Polynesians actually thought, Bari alone was the Germans' source of information about them.

Informer against the Australians, advocate of the government to the chiefs of Ontong Java and the Tasmans, Bari had been an employee of Queen Emma for seven years and played a central role in establishing her control over the Polynesian outliers. He was still in Kokopo in 1892 when the Germans decided upon a punitive expedition in defence of Emma's interests on Nuguria, another Polynesian atoll in the German Solomons, and the Germans insisted that he accompany them as interpreter. Queen Emma's brother, John Coe, disappeared while trading at Nuguria in 1890 and was at first presumed lost at sea but two Nugurians later claimed that John had been murdered and his boat hidden in mangroves. Emma sought vengeance, supplied an official party with plantation labourers as troops and had them transported from the Gazelle Peninsula in her schooner *Three Cheers*. The expedition included Puli and Fotau, who seized the opportunity of inflicting injury on the Nugurians on their way home to the Tasmans. It followed a predictable course, burning houses and making arrests of suspects to be tried for murder. When the Nugurian chief Soaa barricaded himself in his people's great sacred house, Captain Stalio, Emma's lover, stood up momentarily from behind his cover to appeal to him to surrender and was shot dead.[27] By the standards of the Germans in New Guinea the death and destruction wrought by the expedition to the Nuguria group were insignificant—at first. Soaa and one of his kinsmen perished in the sacred house as it burnt to the ground; two other Nugurians were sentenced to prison and an Ontong Java man called Reggi was hanged at Kokopo for his part in the murders. The terrible legacy of the expedition was still to come, and was described without regret by a German naval commander who visited the islands in January 1893:

> The only trader living there came immediately on board and reported that conditions on the islands were now completely satisfactory and he did not fear any hostilities from the natives. At present only about 80 people live on the islands. The troops which undertook the punishment last September introduced influenza and 90 persons have been killed by this disease.[28]

In a few months the population had been halved.

By the end of the 1890s Queen Emma had a plantation on Nuguria employing fifty labourers. All the atolls were important as sources of copra for the Germans, and all the atoll peoples suffered a decline in population under German rule.

The Gazelle Peninsula of New Britain

Before annexation Queen Emma had laid claim to hundreds of thousands of hectares of land in the Bismarck Archipelago, and for years to come was in dispute with the government over the legality of her titles. But as far as the New Guineans were concerned, all that mattered was whether

Europeans occupied land and used it for plantations, and it was not until 1890 that the Tolai of the eastern Gazelle began to become alarmed about the spread of Emma's plantations. The land crisis for the Tolai, still not solved today, began in the 1890s and their attempts to solve it in that decade took the form of violence against the foreign occupiers. When the strategy failed, they were forced to accept the mediation of the government in land disputes and to make the most of the European presence. Some decisions they never accepted. At first, however, the Tolai response to encroachment on their land was to seek to expel all intruders.

When Queen Emma ordered a road to be built from Ralum to the NGC station at Kokopo in March 1890, local men accosted the road gang. A man asked Emma's son Coe Forsayth where the road was to go and said: 'Whatfore you make road all same?' Forsayth answered: 'Road belong everybody: whitemen, bouka, kanaka, papine', but the villager disagreed, claiming that the land belonged to his people. A few moments later the villagers attacked, killing a Filipino overseer called Moses with an axe. As far as the Germans could determine, the murderers saw the road as threatening fishing sites and desecrating a sacred place; they were especially angry with the Filipino because 'he slapped his buttocks in their face in return for the *tabu* they offered in order to prevent the road making'.[29]

In an initial punitive expedition against Bitarebarebe on 30 March 1890 eighty plantation labourers from Ralum, including New Irelanders with spears and Buka with bows and arrows, joined police in destroying hundreds of houses. The Germans demanded that the murderers surrender, but no murderers were forthcoming. Instead, a large force of warriors from Bitarebarebe and Tingenavudu, armed with rifles, spears and long-handled axes, attacked the plantation's advance posts on the beach on 1 April and were driven back by gunfire from the plantation labourers. 'Gunagunei and Bitarebareba' wrote Richard Parkinson at Kokopo that night,

> have allied themselves with Tingenavuddu and Malagunan, districts further inland, and claim they will not give in but will attack Ralum in broad daylight. I regard this as a kind of military stratagem and expect them to use the bright nights for an attack . . . Around Ralum the cotton bushes have been pulled out and piled up to form entanglements with guards positioned behind. In Malapir there is a strong detachment with orders to concentrate at Ralum in the event of a mass attack.[30]

The foreigners were living from hour to hour in the expectation of a renewed onslaught but when a second expedition advanced inland on 3 April, it succeeded only in chasing people through thick grass and killing a woman and two men. The warriors and their families fled to the plateau of the south-west, leaving large amounts of shell-money, clothing, beads, weapons and ammunition scattered in the grass.

As Tolai big men sued for peace by presenting the Germans with traditional gifts of shell-money, the Imperial Judge Georg Schmiele thought executing 'perhaps two of the guilty ones would ensure complete security'. Yet in fact the affair revealed the extraordinary weakness of the German

administration. Far from arresting and shooting numerous alleged ringleaders, as they would do when faced with similar incidents after the turn
of the century, the Germans in 1890 lacked the military strength to do
more than collect shell-money fines and offer rewards for the capture of
the murderers. Schmiele was at pains to mollify and negotiate rather than
punish. At a meeting with people of the Kokopo district he asked whether
they had any complaints against the whites, agreed to discuss compensation
in future before removing houses or trees, promised to uphold fishing rights
and distributed tobacco. It was almost as if the Tolai had imposed conditions in agreeing to peace, and the subsequent execution of To Ruruk
of Bitarebarebe, hanged before a crowd of settlers and villagers on 2 September 1891, failed to convince the Tolai that the Germans were an unbeat-
able enemy.[31]

As in most punitive expeditions in the Bismarck Archipelago in the
1890s, a few police fought alongside much larger numbers of plantation
labourers on loan from their employers. The first expedition against
Bitarebarebe in April 1890, for example, consisted of '24 Solomon Islanders
(axe-carriers), 30 New Mecklenburgers (spear carriers), 6 police-soldiers,
5 whites and half-castes'.[32] Such hastily assembled parties of mainly
untrained men might be led by an official but they were essentially organized by planters, motley little armies of ill-disciplined vigilantes. In the
heat of the fight they frequently killed women as well as men and could
not be stopped from burning everything in sight: houses, canoes, carvings,
fish-baskets, rafts and other possessions of the 'enemy'. The usual tactic,
later to become standard practice in colonial Papua and New Guinea, was
to attempt to surprise villagers by marching on them in the darkness before
dawn, but if it were to fail the punitive party would spend many hot hours
in pursuit. Naval bombardments and hangings apart, the methods of warfare adopted by the foreigners were those employed by New Guineans
for centuries. To the Tolai the foreigners must have seemed like another
clan, wealthier and more aggressive than many, but demanding and accepting shell-money in the usual way, fighting with spears and axes as well
as guns and making alliances with neighbouring communities.

The foreign clan was in armed conflict with the Tolai once more in
1890, this time in expeditions against the Rakunai people living in the hills
behind what was then Vulcan Island in Blanche Bay. The Rakunai had
killed a trader, a New Hebridean known as Jimmy, for enjoying the sexual
services of a Rakunai girl without paying compensation to her father. For
the Germans, imbued with notions of a hierarchy of races, the murder of
an islander was a minor offence and the German authorities agreed that,
since the dead man was 'after all only a coloured', the Navy should not
intervene. But the Rakunai were also boasting that spears were being sharp-
ened to kill the Imperial Judge, Schmiele, and were said to be making raids
on their neighbours. As news of the Rakunai challenge spread to other
Tolai communities Schmiele became convinced that the authority of the
government was being undermined. He decided to act. Under Schmiele's
leadership two punitive expeditions were undertaken in September and

October 1890. In the first he was assisted by nineteen warriors from Barawon on the shores of Blanche Bay, offered to him by the big man To Kinkin, and his force engaged the enemy in desperate combat only to discover afterwards that the 'enemy' were the wrong people. The Rakunai people were triumphant, sending word to Schmiele that they would eat him and the Barawon men. On the second occasion, a party of whites, police and labourers carrying a total of thirty-seven guns killed at least seven Rakunai warriors. Yelling a battle-cry and swinging rifles and spears, the Rakunai men burst upon the foreigners from a distance of 200 metres without cover and ran straight into German fire. They were driven back immediately and did not dare return for their dead and wounded until the Germans were on a distant ridge towards the coast.[33]

Opposed by any one community at any particular time, the foreigners could usually be confident that another community not far away welcomed the government as a potential ally against enemies. But to be offered assistance by a village in making war on another village was not evidence of official control. Warriors were offered on the villagers' own terms and for their own purposes, not conscripted. As the Germans discovered, the exploitation of traditional rivalries could never form the basis of permanent colonial rule because villagers co-operated with the government when it suited them rather than from fear, respect or loyalty. Only direct and constant foreign intervention in village affairs by means of appointed headmen could establish the authority of the colonial administration in New Guinea.

The truth of this was borne home to the foreigners in 1893, when villagers of the eastern Gazelle Peninsula united to expel the colonists in the so-called war of the bullet-proof ointment. The immediate object of the Tolai campaign was the NGC plantation at Kokopo which had expanded rapidly since Richard Parkinson recruited hundreds of Tolai, New Irelanders and Buka for the Company in 1889. Not only were clans losing land, but the imported labourers were guilty of raping village women and destroying gardens. The inland villages between Ralum and Kinigunan feared further depredations and turned to a prophet from Viviren further inland, a man called Taulavai who claimed to have invented a mixture which, if rubbed on the body, created invulnerability to bullets. Taulavai sold his precious ointment for 1000 fathoms of shell-money.

From the start of hostilities at Kokopo in July 1893, when four warriors were killed attacking the NGC plantation, the war continued for months. Constant guerilla raids on the plantation were answered with the usual punitive expeditions, some of which were assisted by Tolai friendly to the foreigners, but the inland people refused to make peace. Three hundred men of Tingenavudu, Malakuna, Bitarebarebe, Balnaburur and Ulagunan advanced in two columns on the Kokopo plantation on the morning of 17 September, uprooting cotton plants until they were driven back by the foreigners. By then the warring Tolai had buried at least forty kinsmen killed in battle, yet they remained defiant.[34] Governor Schmiele went from Madang to New Britain to persuade the hostile groups to submit to German rule and seal the peace with traditional payments of shell-money. On the

day fixed for the peace settlement, 26 October 1893, the leaders of the
movement against the foreigners failed to appear and Schmiele spent fruitless and humiliating hours waiting for them. 'The natives', wrote someone
from Ralum plantation,

> have lost too many in the fights with the Herbertshöh people. they
> will not be quiet again until either some of their dead are paid for
> in blood or Tamboo. these are native ideas and it is quite impossible
> to make them understand otherwise. only by giving them a thorough
> thrashing and drive them away from our lands then we may have peace.
> Herbertshöh is under guard—morn and night—against the Kanaka's,
> they prowl around the Station at all hours, trying to shoot white and
> black . . . [sic][35]

The Germans attempted such a 'thorough thrashing' in December 1893
when sixty sailors from the naval cruiser *Sperber* were put ashore to work
with police in surrounding the offending villages, an operation which even
the NGC admitted was 'not accompanied by success'. The detachment of
sailors, noticing movement in front of them, made the mistake of opening
fire on the police troop led by the NGC manager Paul Kolbe.[36]

Having failed on land, the Germans trained the *Sperber*'s guns in the
direction of the inland villages and shelled them from offshore. Whether
this demonstration of naval power led to the subsequent capitulation of
the hostile Tolai is unknown. The Germans thought it did, pointing to
the fact that the people sued for peace within three days of the bombardments, but one Tolai oral tradition says that everything changed when the
police and plantation labourers got hold of the 'bullet-proof ointment'.
Whatever the reason, the Tolai were suffering from the effects of the war
by the end of 1893. They had lost kinsmen and were unable to get the
trade-goods and tobacco to which they had become accustomed.[37]

The war of the bullet-proof ointment shook German confidence in a
system of governing which depended on reprisal: waiting for the New
Guineans to act first, then responding with punitive measures. 'Conditions
in Blanche Bay', wrote Governor Schmiele, 'absolutely demand a more
or less direct government of the tribes' because the foreign settlements
from Ralum to Kinigunan had taken so much land that the Tolai would
have to come to terms with the foreigners. As things stood, the New Guineans were left to themselves as long as they were peaceful and 'hit on the
head' when, 'perhaps for a just cause', they took up arms. The only solution
for the government was to appoint 'men of trust' and to give them 'a certain
authority, so that they are able to maintain order in their districts'.[38]

The idea of appointing government chiefs was not a new one in the German colony. Rose suggested it for Madang in 1892 and Schmiele, as
Imperial Judge in the Bismarck Archipelago, actually appointed a man
called Terriki to be 'king' of the Nuguria Islands in 1892. Terriki possessed
no authority over the Nugurians and by the time an official next visited
the atoll, they had sacked the Germans' 'king' and replaced him with a
man of their own choosing, Pulewa.[39] The experiment ended there. When
the war of 1893 rekindled the Germans' interest in official chiefs the NGC

indicated support for the scheme without ensuring that anything further was done. Village affairs did not interest Hansemann, whose preoccupation in the mid-1890s was to free the Company of its administrative responsibilities.

The NGC's dual role as a business undertaking and a government proved especially burdensome in the Bismarck Archipelago, where it imposed taxes on competing firms and incurred the wrath of the Sacred Heart Mission over a disputed land claim. The long wrangle with Bishop Louis Couppé, who was supported by the Catholic press and the Centre party in Germany, convinced Hansemann that he could only lose more money by trying to ride 'in both saddles', and in January 1895 he appealed to the German government to take over administration of the Bismarck Archipelago and the German Solomons. The *Reich* assumed authority in the colony's eastern district, that is, the islands, in April 1895.[40]

Albert Hahl, a short, solidly built lawyer of twenty-seven, arrived in east New Britain as an imperial official in the Protectorate of the Neu Guinea Compagnie in January 1896. As imperial judge or administrator in New Britain 1896 to 1898, vice-governor in the German Caroline Islands 1899 to 1901, acting governor of German New Guinea 1901 to 1902 and governor 1902 to 1914, Hahl was to have a decisive influence on German colonial administration in Melanesia and Micronesia. Born in the Bavarian village of Gern in 1868, he was the son of a Protestant brewer. He studied law at Würzburg, worked for the Bavarian Ministry of the Interior at Bayreuth and for the Colonial Department in Berlin and prepared for service in German East Africa but was posted instead to the Protectorate of the Neu Guinea Compagnie.[41]

Hahl was energetic. As soon as he had recovered from an eight-day bout of malaria, he explored the Gazelle Peninsula on horseback to discover its potential for planters and traders. He was immediately impressed by the vigour of Tolai trade. The inland villagers supplied Queen Emma's plantation with all its yams and taro, staple foods for the labourers; on the beach near Kokopo people went from house to house every third day offering garden produce for sale; at Takabur, inland from Kokopo, he saw about 400 women with laden baskets in the market-place and was told of other large markets further south; and the market near Malaguna attracted crowds of north coast people, who came across the hills to trade with the Matupit islanders and other villagers of Blanche Bay. Hahl wanted to encourage such market trading and within weeks of his arrival was planning a network of roads to open up the Gazelle Peninsula, including a road around the bay linked with the north coast by a pass. He took heart from Bishop Couppé's success in recruiting villagers to widen the existing path from the coast to the mission station at Takabur.[42]

The directors of the NGC had always believed that foreign economic development would come from concentrating on plantations. Hahl quickly decided this view was wrong: trade came before plantations and should be encouraged in the Gazelle Peninsula and elsewhere in the islands: trade in copra, galip nuts, trepang, turtleshell, and foodstuffs for plantation labourers. But only a few short stretches of road existed, sea communications with Sydney were deficient and local wars, especially in New Ireland, frequently destroyed trading relationships. The NGC had so failed to protect foreign life and property that the islands' firms carried out their own private punitive expeditions or added their forces to the police to make official action possible. Company legislation concerning such matters as quarantine, labour depots and labour discipline was ignored by settlers. In the Gazelle Peninsula land was a source of endless contention between settlers and Tolai and likely to cause another war like that of 1893. Hahl soon realized that Company 'rule' was a fiction, for no real government existed and the preconditions for rapid foreign development in the New Guinea islands had never been created. His answer to these problems was specific and practical: first, build roads and provide the administration with a sea-going vessel; second, settle the issue of land ownership in New Britain by setting aside 'native reserves' protected from foreign encroachment; third, appoint chiefs and empower them to adjudicate minor village disputes in the name of the government.

In the Gazelle Peninsula, Hahl noticed, 'the young people are accustomed to working for the heads of their families in return for food and small payments, often in order to work off bride price'.[43] He adapted the traditional system to have roads built by the Tolai, paying them in food, shell-money and iron tools to construct bridle-paths and roads which by 1898 stretched from Kokopo halfway around the bay towards the site of modern Rabaul, inland towards Vunakokor, from Matupit to Rabaul farm, from Malaguna to Ratavul and along the north coast as well. To the amazement of other officials Hahl's orders were obeyed. At his command Tolai villagers cut roads, kept them in good order and planted coconut palms.

Mutual self-interest explains the relationship between Hahl and the Tolai. He wanted influence. They wanted land. He learnt the Kuanua language, studied Tolai custom, listened at length to villagers' grievances and arbitrated in village disputes. Above all he took action to prevent further dispossession of village landowners. Without specific justification in law, but for good political reasons, Hahl created land reserves for groups of villagers who said they had not understood the meaning of the original sale of their land, and he persuaded large landholders that they would be serving their own interests by surrendering some of their claims. By 1901 the government had established twelve New Guinean land reserves, all in the Gazelle Peninsula, and was to set up more there and elsewhere in the colony. They were the fruits of a policy designed to avert further major hostilities by making strategic concessions. The Vunabalbal people, for example, were permitted to stay on land which was legally Queen Emma's on condition that they planted coconuts, a requirement which they were happy to fulfil at a time of rising copra prices.[44] Planting and production for the European market became an alternative to war for a number of Tolai communities, who apparently decided trade with the foreigners was preferable to trying once again to drive them away.

Hahl believed in shooting people who inflicted harm on Europeans or interfered with the work of labour recruiters, missionaries or traders. In his first six months in east New Britain he repeatedly took to arms against the islanders but by his own account 'unwillingly' and because he lacked the resources to do anything else:

> The success of weapons always seems highly questionable to me, consisting as it does in killing a number of people who could not run fast enough and in burning down settlements. But often, because of scarcity of resources, a quick raid is in fact the only option left to achieve redress. With the help of S.M.S. Bussard the people in Mankai, east coast of New Mecklenburg, were called to account; I required the Varzin [Vunakokor] natives to conclude peace and took armed revenge for the breach of that peace; I took punitive action south of Kuras, west coast of New Mecklenburg, because of the murder and eating of escaped labourers and the theft of goods. Recently in Kabanga on the eastern side of the Gazelle Peninsula I was able to impose peace on the disputing parties by negotiation, supported by the presence of the police troop. Here the administration's concern lay in the security of the trade which has already been vigorously developed.[45]

The logical extension of negotiating in particular disputes, as the Germans had realized since the early 1890s, was to institutionalize negotiations by appointing chiefs, and Hahl began to do this from August 1896 onwards, first of all in the Gazelle Peninsula and in 1897 in the German Shortland Islands. Again Hahl tried to blend European and local custom. The chiefs were given the Kuanua name *lualua* at first and later *luluai* and were presented not only with a cap but with a stick as well, like the sticks which traditional Tolai *lualua* carried to signify their authority. The government *lualua* were told to be unquestioningly obedient to officials, to protect the whites, to settle disputes among their own people and to depend on the government for defence and security.[46]

Hahl was no martinet. In the case of a Tolai convicted of the murder of a white man, he showed unusual sympathy for a German colonial administrator of the time. Totaia, a man from Vunamarita in the Gazelle Peninsula, was handed over to the Germans in May 1896 by a man from Kabakada in return for ten fathoms of shell-money. He had been wanted for questioning about the death in 1895 of a trader whom he confessed to having hit with the handle of a boat's rudder. An experienced labourer who had worked in Samoa and Kaiser Wilhelmsland, Totaia claimed he was driven to the murder by the trader's constant ill-treatment. In judging the case, Hahl conceded that Totaia had been provoked, then sentenced him to death anyway on the grounds that 'the severest punishment' was 'the only possible atonement for the murder of a white person'. Yet Hahl soon granted a reprieve: 'Five months in a gaol in Herbertshöhe is in my view a punishment as severe as death itself. I can no longer bring myself to advocate the fulfilment of the sentence after the man has suffered horribly . . .'. Totaia's death sentence was commuted to a year's hard labour, which he did at the New Guinea Company plantation at Kokopo before returning home in October 1897.[47]

One naval commander described Hahl as feared by the New Guineans for his strictness and respected for his impartiality and fairness. The description is a familiar one from the age of colonial expansion, a statement of the empire-builder's virtues: indefatigable in extending the *pax Germanica* and firm but just in his dealings with the 'natives'. Hahl would undoubtedly have liked it. He was keen to make the New Guineans a subject people, available for service as labourers and collectors of coconuts. Besides appointing *luluais*, he trained a voluntary reserve of police and took personal command of punitive expeditions. For as long as the NGC had to pay for control in New Guinea, however, 'security conditions', to use the words of a naval report, would not be 'in accordance with the prestige of the flag under which the territory has the honour to stand'.[48]

Foreign enterprise in the Bismarck Archipelago and the German Solomons remained unprotected until the end of Company rule. No administration official visited the north-east coast of New Ireland for at least two years after October 1896, for example, even though it was an important source of copra and labourers. In desperation a trader wrote to Hahl: 'I beg of You Sir to take some steps and give thise people a warning above all the guns for as long as they have it in there possessions there will never be any peace, & I also never feel safe as I use to be' [sic]. There was little Hahl could do. He had explained why to the provisional Company governor a few weeks before, when he feared an outbreak of inter-tribal fighting in Bougainville and the Shortlands: the Company must first police the sea and coasts with a ship. The Company had no such intention and as late as March 1899 was reiterating the view that it was entitled to imperial protection at imperial expense under the charter of 1885, 'not merely against foreign enemies, but also against the natives'.[49]

Unprotected, the settlers in the islands achieved much more than the NGC on the mainland. For every tonne of copra exported from Kaiser Wilhelmsland in the year to April 1899 more than twenty tonnes were shipped out of the Bismarck Archipelago on the Burns Philp steamer to Sydney or the Norddeutscher Lloyd steamer to Singapore and Europe. After fourteen years of 'rule' the islanders remained independent. The coastal Tolai of the eastern Gazelle had decided to co-operate with the foreigners, but they exploited whatever advantages they possessed and by the end of the 1890s foreign traders were complaining bitterly of having to use shell-money. The Tolai would accept nothing else, forcing the foreigners to compete among themselves in buying the currency. The northern New Irelanders continued to kill foreigners and engage in warfare with each other. On the outlying islands and atolls the reception enjoyed by traders depended entirely on the islanders' decisions and not at all on the government.

The subjugation of coastal New Guinea to the Germans was to begin in earnest when the imperial government assumed power over German New Guinea in 1899.

4

Opening the Country
to the White Man
1899-1907

With the exception of the Dutch, the European powers in Melanesia before 1914 all wanted their possessions to become plantation colonies. After a long decline since the mid-1880s the European price of copra began to rise in 1898 and doubled its 1899 level by 1913. Businessmen dreamt of fortunes to be made in supplying raw material for soap and margarine, colonial administrators welcomed plantation investment and Melanesians lost land and worked for planters on an unprecedented scale. In the British Solomons, Lever Brothers Limited became the first large British company to invest purely in Pacific copra plantations when it began operations in 1905; in Papua white settlers rushed for land after Australia assumed control in 1906; and in German New Guinea planters increased the area of cultivated plantation land in the 'Old Protectorate' from about 4500 to over 34 000 hectares between 1902 and 1914.

Control, land, labour, shipping and colonial finances were the keys to success in building plantation colonies in Melanesia. How was government control to be extended over numerous, independent, scattered hamlets? Under what conditions was land to pass into European hands? By which methods were labourers to be encouraged or required to work on roads and plantations? How was copra to be shipped cheaply to metropolitan markets? Who was to pay for colonial administration—the colony or the metropolis? These were the questions which preoccupied administrators. In the case of German New Guinea the administrators were influenced by a recent example of what not to do: the Neu Guinea Compagnie had lacked control over the villagers, planted the wrong crops, wasted money on shipping and lost countless labourers through sickness and death. 'In the country around Astrolabe Bay', wrote Albert Hahl with some exaggeration in 1901, 'about ten thousand labourers lie buried'.[1] The incoming imperial officials were determined to avoid those errors. Only if he was alive, accustomed to central government and willing to trade and become an indentured labourer did the New Guinean serve the Europeans' purpose for him in a trading and planting economy. This was the lesson which the Germans drew from Company rule, from both the disasters of Kaiser Wilhelmsland and the insecure colonization of the archipelago, and its first corollary was that all else would fail unless the colonial government in Kokopo created colonial order in the villages of New Guinea.

In no other colony in the world were so many of the colonized peoples strangers to each other in language and identity. The German extension of control was therefore certain to be irresistible, for no group of people was strong enough to withstand the Germans, but also slow, for none was large enough to make a single conquest especially significant for the whole of the Old Protectorate. A 'successfully completed punitive expedition does not have a far-reaching effect', one annual report complained, 'practically every individual tribe has to be made to feel the power of the Administration before it can be induced to desist from robbery, murder and cannibalism'.[2]

Rudolf von Bennigsen, the new governor who reached New Guinea in July 1899, initially fell into the trap of thinking that the mere sight of himself and his entourage would engender respect for the government. His more famous father supported Germany's colonial expansion in the 1880s as leader of the National Liberals in the *Reichstag* and he himself entered the colonial service in 1893, working in the German East African government and in the Colonial Department of the Foreign Office. Visiting the Admiralty Islands Governor Bennigsen went ashore at Mok near Baluan Island and was greeted 'in the most friendly and peaceful way' in the villages of the Manus people. Clad in laplaps laced up with strings of shell-money and chewing betel nut, the men offered to trade pigs and artefacts. Bennigsen responded by telling them not to fight with their neighbours and at a small island nearby he warned the 'wonderfully built men, obsidian spears swinging in their hands' that the government would punish those who broke the peace. Bennigsen had no doubt that the voyage of a German warship through the Admiralties, the appearance of the police and the friendly intercourse between Germans and islanders would deter the Manus from future crimes and promote European trade in the area. Yet a few weeks later the big man Nauvain and his two sons from Mok murdered two labourers and the Hernsheim trader Maetzke. Bennigsen was surprised. He put a price on the heads of the murderers, dispatched six police to guard the Hernsheim trading post and appealed to Berlin for a fast, armed steamer to be made available to the governor.[3]

Preaching peace was not enough. Police were needed, trained in the use of weapons and stationed at strategic points throughout the Old Protectorate. At the prompting of Albert Hahl, by now vice-governor of the Island Territory, Berlin provided funds for a new station in northern New Ireland at a site close to the major trading posts, Kavieng. Under Franz Boluminski, a former employee of the Astrolabe Company, the Kavieng station rapidly extended government influence after its foundation in 1900. The legend of Boluminski heard in Papua New Guinea today sees him as a worker of wonders, transforming a battlefield into a haven of peace by sheer strength of personality, but in fact the ground for his success had been well prepared before he came. At Fissoa, for example, several warring peoples had broken spears and exchanged *tapsoka* in about 1898, making use of the trader Wagenbrett as mediator; and so many others had taken the opportunity of visits by Hahl to make peace that in 1899 the acting governor predicted an easy pacification for northern New Ireland without recourse to bloodshed.[4] Boluminski set the government seal on a movement of peacemaking already being undertaken by northern New Irelanders. With his eight police he visited the villages assuring the people that they would be protected if they handed in firearms, stopped fighting and brought their disputes to him for arbitration. While his wife won confidence by treating the sick, Boluminski paid the people of Bagail near Kavieng in tobacco and *tapsoka* to collect the stones and coral for the foundations of his residency, and he convinced a number of villages to build a coastal road, which by August 1902 stretched more than 100 kilometres south-east of the government station. Most people worked willingly for cash, tobacco and pipes; a few were forced to participate by having to pay fines, including the villagers of Avelus, whose homes had been destroyed in 1889 by a German man-of-war. Boluminski gave portraits of Kaiser Wilhelm II to village leaders and explained that this 'most powerful Luluai' required Germans to pay taxes and serve as soldiers, whereas he asked of New Guineans, who had no money, that they work on roads. His *luluais*, like those elsewhere in the Old Protectorate, wore a black cap with a red band and carried a long, black stick with a white metal top to symbolize government authority. For a district officer who believed that the future of the Bismarck Archipelago lay in 'rationalised plantations', the consequences of colonial order in northern New Ireland were gratifying. He established a government plantation at Kavieng, which was weeded by neighbouring villagers in return for the right to grow crops between the coconut palms, and by 1904 nine private planters had land under cultivation and were employing about 500 labourers.[5]

Governor Bennigsen was a simple man who enjoyed touring his colony and observing the life of the New Guinea villager. World-weary bureaucrats in Berlin reading his report of a visit to Fissoa in northern New Ireland in 1900, for example, had to wade through a description of the beauty of the village, the fast-flowing mountain stream which ran through it, the 'golden light of the setting sun' filtered through breadfruit and palm trees and the 'pretty, happy children' who imitated him when he collected insects. His aim for German New Guinea was to make it safe and profitable for settlers, and he rhapsodized about Hernsheim's trading post on the island of Nusa, with its well-built jetty and stores, as an 'attractive picture of European civilisation in the South Seas wilderness, here still almost virgin in character'.[6] To promote this spread of European culture Bennigsen took measures rather less romantic than his depiction of New Guinea: he appointed *luluais* in the Gazelle Peninsula and the Duke of Yorks, sixty-seven by mid-1900, to supervise road-building and settle minor village disputes; and he sent the police and the Navy to shoot people who were interfering with traders and missionaries: in January 1900 to the Kabien people of northern New Ireland, six of whom were shot, and to Baluan and Pityilu in the Admiralties, whose inhabitants fled to the main island; in March 1900 to Hansa Bay and Aitape, where at the request of a Catholic missionary the government forces burnt down pagan sacred houses in the villages of Pro and Vokau; in April 1900 to Kabanga and Londip on the eastern side of the Gazelle Peninsula; in August 1900 to the Baluan people of the Admiralties once again; in February 1901 to the Witu Islands off west New Britain.[7]

Bennigsen also took action to give Europeans in east New Britain the advantage in trade. The Tolai had become the Germans' bankers, insisting on being paid for copra in the *tambu* or shell-money which they alone supplied. When Europeans wanted to buy copra they had to turn to the Tolai for the necessary shells and were charged at 'absurdly high' exchange rates. Playing one trader off against another, many Tolai had also persuaded their foreign customers to accept whole coconuts instead of ready-cut copra. For a colonized people who were supposed to be learning valuable habits of industry in the service of their masters the Tolai were inconveniently independent, and in order to curb their business acumen Bennigsen outlawed the use of shell-money in commercial transactions between Tolai and foreigners and prohibited traders from purchasing whole coconuts.[8]

To be governor of a German colony was not to be in charge of colonial policy but to be one among a number of decision-makers, especially in vital matters of land and labour policy. In theory a German colonial governor was an autocrat, responsible to the Kaiser alone; in practice he had to deal with the Colonial Department of the Foreign Office, the body of officials who acted for the Kaiser in colonial affairs. They might approve or reject his suggestions on the basis of general colonial policy, and in the case of German New Guinea they regarded the Neu Guinea Compagnie as a national interest which must not be offended. Bennigsen had little success, for example, in his efforts to restrict the Company's land claims. The NGC not having complied with the conditions under which it was supposed to acquire its land concession of 50 000 hectares, he proposed to limit its future acquisitions. The Colonial Department denied his authority in the matter.[9]

An official called Boether visited Hansa Bay, Wewak and Aitape in July 1900 and decided that most of the NGC's land there had been acquired by fraud. In most cases, including those where the Company had bought whole islands, the people with whom the contract was made did not own the whole area which it specified. 'In so far as they understood the Europeans' intention at all', many villagers believed that they were negotiating about permission for a Malay or Chinese to settle on the land as a copra trader or that the few trade goods given by the Company men during a brief encounter were to pay for artefacts such as spears or shields. Nowhere did the people realize that they were parting with their land. The representatives of the NGC, said Boether, had acted with 'direct unscrupulousness', claiming land about which they had not even consulted the villagers, forging native signatures and on some occasions 'buying' land by recording the sale on a map without bothering to come ashore. Boether's zeal was not appreciated in Berlin either by the NGC's directors or the Colonial Department. The Department held that 'contracts as they are made with natives of the kind living in Kaiser Wilhelmsland can never bear a rigorous juristic examination' and that officers of the imperial administration should be guided by considerations of fairness towards the Company, which might otherwise fail to acquire the land reserved for it under the transfer agreement of 1899. Boether refused to register numerous land claims of the NGC in Kaiser Wilhelmsland but the Company successfully complained about the 'hostile attitude of the Registration Office in Friedrich Wilhelmshafen' and in 1902 the Colonial Department instructed the government of German New Guinea to allow the Company new land concessions.[10]

From the NGC offices in the Unter den Linden in Berlin, the ageing Hansemann barked out orders as if the colony were still his. The Company claimed 6000 hectares of densely populated land on the eastern side of the Gazelle Peninsula between Cape Gazelle and the Warongoi River but lost it after Heinrich Schnee, imperial judge, found in favour of a group of Tolai who took the Company to court in 1900. Hansemann was furious, and personally intervened to prevent the appointment of Schnee as acting governor of the colony in 1902. As Fritz Rose of the Colonial Department explained, Schnee was denied his post simply because of the 'resolute opposition' of Hansemann:

> Given the great importance of the New Guinea Company in the Protectorate, it did not appear correct to cause a bigger conflict over a personal issue, even though the arguments which Herr von Hansemann produced to account for his attitude can in no way be agreed to.[11]

Hansemann was equally influential over labour policy. Governor Bennigsen at first revoked the old Company law on labour discipline without replacing it, advising employers to exercise a 'moderate right to punish on the analogy of regulations at home', but Hansemann protested that removing authority to discipline plantation labourers was tantamount to prohibiting plantations. A new ordinance filled the gap in June 1900 and was to remain in force until the end of German rule. Under its provisions a labourer could be punished for 'continued neglect of duty and laziness', 'insubordination or leaving places of work or service without reason' and 'other major violations' by being fined up to twenty marks, locked up, birched with a 'light switch or sapling' or 'flogged with a simple wooden stick'. The level of corporal punishment, up to twenty-five strokes a fortnight, was higher than that suggested by the Colonial Council in 1897 and equalled what it recommended for criminals. Such were the penal sanctions of labour law in German New Guinea. They could be enforced by the authorized employer on his plantation.[12]

In drafting the 1901 labour ordinance, which governed recruiting and employment until 1910, the Colonial Department lent heavily on the advice of the NGC. The only kind of labour recruiting subject to control was 'by sea', that is, when the place of work was more than three nautical miles from the recruit's home and the journey either to work or to the recruiting authorities was made by sea. Labourers' contracts could be extended repeatedly and the government had to give reasons for refusing an application to recruit. The DHPG of Samoa was debarred from seeking labour in the NGC's home territory, Kaiser Wilhelmsland. In law the working conditions of the labourer remained much the same as in Company times: in return for food, lodging and medical care, transport to and from his place of work, and a wage paid either in cash or kind, the labourer was to work a ten-hour day, from sunrise to sunset with two hours off at midday, six days a week, for the standard three-year contract period, though contracts of up to five years were permitted. The whole object of the legislation was to allow the employer a free hand in his treatment of the labour force, and, as well as leaving local employment unregulated, it made no provision for government inspection of plantations. Ration levels, as a medical report later showed, were scandalously low.[13]

The NGC might be respected in Berlin as the authority on the needs of the colony, but it continued to mismanage its enterprises. Still following a grand concept of colonization in which Asian labourers would toil on tobacco plantations and in goldmines, the Company established a resident recruiter in Hong Kong in 1900 and imported 200 Chinese from Swatow the following year, only to see a repetition of the failures of the 1890s. The Chinese were sickly, useless for heavy work in the early months of acclimatization and they picked a crop of tobacco leaves so puny that the Company at last abandoned the dream of creating a new Sumatra. Copra replaced tobacco as the leading crop in Kaiser Wilhelmsland after 1901 and the Asian labour force was allowed to dwindle.

The NGC's mining ventures prospered no better. The Ramu Expedition found traces of alluvial gold, spurred on by the promise contained in the transfer agreement that the Company would have exclusive rights to any precious metals found in the upper Ramu River region, but by 1901 exploratory patrols were suffering severely from lack of labour. The Chinese from Swatow proved poor carriers and locally recruited villagers deserted the lines, leaving the Germans dependent on New Guinea islanders from the archipelago and draining the plantations on the coast of their labour. The search for gold in the Ramu ended in failure in 1902.[14]

A second venture was capitalized at 500 000 marks by a syndicate in which the NGC took a half share and the other half was subscribed by a collection of banking interests typical of German colonial investment. The Berlin banks were represented by Hansemann's own Disconto-Gesellschaft, with an 18 per cent share, and with a less confident 4 per cent each by the Berliner Handelsgesellschaft, S. Bleichröder, Deutsche Bank, Mendelsohn & Co., Robert Warschauer & Co., and Count Henckel von Donnersmarck. Godeffroy's Norddeutsche Bank in Hamburg and Sal. Oppenheim Jr. & Co.'s Cologne Bank also contributed 4 per cent each. The 'Huon Gulf Syndicate', as it was called, obtained the exclusive right to mine in the river basins of the Huon Gulf for twenty years, on condition that it establish one or more colonial companies within five years from the grant of the concession in June 1901. Exactly the same problems of sick and deserting labourers as in the Ramu undertaking now dogged the

Huon Gulf expeditions, which after two years were likewise given up.[15] Rudolf von Bennigsen left the colony because of ill-health in mid-1901. In his two years as governor there had emerged a pattern of political forces which his successor as governor, Albert Hahl, was to resist, modify but never abolish. On the central issues of colonial policy the governor's discretion was limited. He could order punitive expeditions, request the assistance of the Navy, appoint *luluais* and decide where villagers would build roads, but he had to refer regulations on commerce, land and labour to Berlin. The Colonial Department's attitude to New Guinea was summed up by a Berlin official who said that the average colonial administrator was a necessary evil rather than an agent for good: 'the fewer officials, the fewer mistakes are made'.[16] Berlin intended the governor to follow in the footsteps of the white settlers, helping them to help themselves in colonizing New Guinea. In the official mind of the Colonial Department the aim was rapid economic development by private plantation companies and the role of government was to act as their servant.

The political pressures on the colonial bureaucracy were parliamentary as well as commercial. Officials had to consider not only the opinions of Adolph von Hansemann, but also those of the Budget Commission of the *Reichstag*. Originally Bismarck had intended to keep *Reichstag* interference in colonial affairs to a minimum by giving colonies to chartered companies, thus avoiding direct imperial expenditure and Parliamentary scrutiny of budgets. But when the chartered companies in Africa collapsed the German government was forced to finance colonial administration, and in 1892 the *Reichstag* succeeded in bringing colonial expenditure under its control, as it was constitutionally entitled to do. All government expenditure in the German colonies, whether it originated in imperial subsidy or local taxation, became subject to the approval of the *Reichstag*. Each year Colonial Department officials pared their estimates to the bone in order to ensure easy passage for colonial budgets through the *Reichstag*, and in the case of German New Guinea they were particularly keen not to spend money on anything more than the bare essentials of administration. One official privately described the funds for New Guinea in 1899 as 'miserable'.[17] The reason for this was that the government was already committed under the terms of the transfer agreement to pay the NGC compensation of four million marks, divided into ten annual instalments of 400 000 marks each.

Under the accounting procedures which the Colonial Department followed, the annual compensation payments to the NGC counted as part of the imperial subsidy to the colony. Every year until 1909 German New Guinea's budget included an amount of 400 000 marks not available to the governor at all, and the colonial administration had to compete against the NGC for imperial funds. In 1899, 1901 and 1902 the *Reich* gave more to the Company than to the government of the Old Protectorate and though the *Reichstag* was to approve more generous budgets up to 1906, Governor Hahl remained starved of funds for all but the most essential tasks. In a developing plantation colony no German official doubted what those tasks

were: bringing the colonized people under control, securing German claims
to land and recruiting plantation labourers.

Control: Forced Labour
New Guineans built thousands of bridges, moved millions of tonnes of
soil and excavated numerous hillsides under German rule. The German
roads were military and commercial arteries designed to open the colony
to police patrols, labour recruiters, traders and planters. In New Britain
and New Ireland forced labour spread with the incorporation of the villages
into direct rule through *luluais*, who were expected to supply the men for
government work; on the mainland forced labour preceded the *luluais*, the
first of whom were not appointed until 1905, and was performed by prisoners captured in punitive expeditions as well as by local villagers. The
people of Siar Island near Madang, who never reconciled themselves to
the government and refused to believe the talk of the Lutheran missionaries,
had to be repeatedly dragooned into wielding picks and shovels for the
Germans. New Guinean dislike of the corvée could be fierce. To Vagira
of Tamanairik in the inland Gazelle Peninsula, an opponent of the Germans
who once threatened to eat Albert Hahl, was said to have killed a man
for doing roadwork for the whites, and resentment of forced labour appears
to have been among the motives of those Bainings who murdered ten Catholic missionaries in 1904.[18]

Forced labour was made statutory by a regulation of 18 November 1903
which required New Guineans to work up to four weeks a year on roads
and government plantations and in times of war and natural disaster, but
Hahl saw it only as the first stage of direct rule, a temporary measure which
would in time be superseded by the levy of a head-tax. When the head-tax
was eventually imposed Hahl wanted it to be easy to collect, lucrative and
not the occasion of bloody resistance to the administration, and for these
reasons he decided in 1903 to delay its introduction for a few years.[19] His
strategy for the government of the New Guineans was planned in advance:
first establish government stations as visible centres of German authority,
then appoint *luluais* and impose forced labour, then replace forced labour
with a tax in cash in order to integrate the New Guineans into the expatriate
economy as producers of copra and plantation labourers. Within a few years
Hahl began to emphasize the protective role of government, shielding the
villager from the excessive demands of the labour recruiter, but initially
he aimed above all at opening the country to the white man.

Control: the Luluai
Hahl's *luluais* were village policemen, responsible for rounding up carriers
and road-workers for the *kiap* or negotiating with the labour recruiter;
and they were minor magistrates as well, authorized to arbitrate in village
disputes and impose small penalties. Justice dispensed by *luluais*, men with

obligations to clans whose membership might or might not coincide with their 'administrative units', was apt to be arbitrary and Hahl delimited their magisterial responsibilities in 1903. In '*A vartulag tadap ra umana luluai* ', a proclamation in the Kuanua language of the Tolai, *luluais* were instructed to confine their judgments to disputes about pigs, money, shell-money or produce and to refer cases involving adultery, divorce, land, inter-village warfare or serious crimes such as murder and rape to the district office at Kokopo. They were to fine people in German marks, not in shell-money, and to hand over the proceeds to the authorities rather than using it to enrich themselves. In a further regulation of 1904, '*A vartulag ure ra varbean kai ra tarei*', *luluais* were specifically denied authority to deal with marriages and a native marriage law for the Gazelle Peninsula and the Duke of Yorks was proclaimed, defining legal grounds for divorce and providing imprisonment of up to six months for both parties guilty of adultery and for Christians committing bigamy. The German authorities were to be responsible for pronouncing divorces.[20]

The subordinate officials in the German colonial administration were less willing than Hahl to trust *luluais*, and more likely to rely on a strong detachment of police when making arrests, giving orders and delivering summonses. Hahl thought the position of the *luluais* was being disregarded and that involving them in the 'business of the judicial and administrative service' was unpopular among the field staff, but he could do little to change the attitude of officers on patrol. The *luluais* of the Madang area, as described by the district officer in 1909, were much weaker than Hahl envisaged: they lacked all authority in matters of criminal justice and were allowed to settle only those disputes which did not concern the whole village community. They were primarily intended to 'maintain the prestige of the government in the village', and the task of the assistants or *tultuls* who were by then being appointed by the Germans was to keep the district officer informed and to supervise forced labour.[21] The *luluai* in German New Guinea was always much more a village policeman than a village magistrate. He was, as C. D. Rowley says, the official who 'acted as an agent of the police, assisted in tax collection, organised forced labour and labour in lieu of tax; and the man of prestige to whom the recruiter had to pay "head money" when he wanted young men to sign on as labourers'.[22]

Leadership in the New Guinean village was much more complicated than the theory of the *luluai* system allowed for, and in practice the German officer in the bush, ignorant of the true facts and relying on information supplied by *luluais* who were interested parties, had little alternative but to side with one group of people against another. From the *luluai*'s point of view, the visit of the police was an opportunity to make use of the government for his own purposes, whether the issue be warfare, sorcery, women, land or pigs.

A government expedition to southern New Ireland in 1905, unremarkable in itself, may serve as an illustration. Lamassa Island off the coast of southern New Ireland had a population in 1905 of about ninety people. Their forebears had probably settled there sometime between 1840 and

1875, preferring to be safe even on a coral island without fresh water rather than live in constant fear of hill raids on the coast of the main island. Some among the Lamassans were the remnant population from another village close by, abandoned after most of its men lost their lives while hunting; others were recent immigrants from Mimias on the east coast of New Ireland. The government *luluai* was To Puang, a man of about forty who had been born in Mioko in the Duke of York Islands and became a sailor in Queensland even before the German flag was raised. He kept his links with Mioko, storing his shell-money treasure there and his experience abroad had given him a good command of Pidgin. The Lamassans also called two other men '*luluais*': To Puang's younger brother, Ponake, and Ponake's brother-in-law, Surrumm, who had brought his three wives from Mimias and was accepted as being in charge of the Mimias people of the village. Each of the three '*luluais*' owned the outward symbol of big man authority in that part of New Ireland, a *mon* or large planked canoe built by specialist craftsmen.

Seventeen kilometres to the south lay Lambom Island, the home of about a hundred people who were traditional trading partners with Lamassa, exchanging women in marriage as well as goods. To Puang himself had once acquired an extra wife from Lambom, a girl called Tinmandunlik, but sent her back after the two wives quarrelled. Lambom—and in this it was typical of hundreds of 'villages' in New Guinea—was not really a single village but a number of dispersed hamlets. In Lambom's case people lived in four hamlets, each with its own men's house for unmarried youths, yet the government recognized only one official *luluai*, a man called To Kulau. Administrative convenience in colonial Papua and New Guinea often dictated the creation of an artificial village community where none had existed before. The relationship between these offshore islanders and the hill peoples was not one of never-ending warfare, but of war and peace at different times in a long history of contact. In times of peace, Lamassa and Lambom supplied the hill villagers with coconuts and seawater, much valued for its salt and carried in long bamboo vessels, in return for spears, baskets and belts.[23]

When District Officer Kornmajer took twenty police from Kokopo to Lamassa in January 1905, he did so in response to reports that escaped labourers from New Britain had been killed and eaten in southern New Ireland and that mountain warriors were raiding the islands near Cape St George. Before he had a chance to explain why he had come, the Lamassa people asked for help in their dispute with Lambom, following allegations that a Lamassa man was working sorcery on Lambom women; then when he revealed the purpose of his visit, everybody hastened to complain about the big man To Kabar and his murderous raids on them while they worked in their gardens on the mainland of New Ireland. Two men with fresh spear wounds were exhibited as proof.

Kornmajer now took the *luluai* To Puang south to Lambom, but as the *Seestern* entered the harbour no one was to be seen. The houses were deserted. The Lambom people had hidden across the channel on New Ireland, their men armed with spears and ready to fight the police, and took much persuading to emerge from their hiding-places. Kornmajer thought they were afraid of government retribution for their dispute over sorcery, but other evidence suggests that they may have been responsible for killing escaped labourers. They had good reason to fear the police, perhaps, but soon realized that Kornmajer did not suspect them of any wrong-doing. On the contrary, he wanted to hear more stories about the bad hill people led by To Kabar, and they were happy to satisfy him. Not long before, he was told, To Kabar's people had killed Lambom women working in a taro field on the mainland.

The complaints of the Lamassa people about To Kabar now seemed confirmed and Kornmajer decided 'to take action against him with armed force'. With a knowledgeable guide from Lambom, the *Seestern* sailed to the east coast so that the party could approach To Kabar's village unnoticed. After hours of strenuous marching up hill-tracks and wading in the pouring rain through river beds, the expedition emerged below the village, to be met by a hail of stones and spears. 'We now stormed the village', wrote Kornmajer, '6 natives fell in the struggle. The village itself had been evacuated by the time we arrived. In the pursuit of the natives by the police troop 2 further kanakas were killed'. With night coming, the steep gullies were no place to be chasing warriors and he prudently decided that the punishment was 'adequate atonement', although he was careful to burn down the village before leaving the next morning.

To Puang and To Kulau, the government *luluais*, had seen the caps and sticks belonging to *luluais* in Tolai communities with whom they traded, and they asked Kornmajer for the same badges of office. Soon afterwards To Kulau, complete with the government's cap and stick, visited To Kabar and concluded peace with him. No record remains of what was said on that occasion but it is tempting to speculate that To Kulau represented himself as a powerful man who could call on his allies in the government at Kokopo and would not tolerate any more attacks on his people.

Kornmajer was typical of the German district officer in New Guinea in depending entirely for information on people who were immediately affected by his decisions, and in siding with one group of people against another who had no opportunity to present their side of the case before being confronted by armed police. In this incident the Lamassa and Lambom people, some of whom may have killed labourers, appear to have been eager to damn To Kabar in the eyes of the Germans once the cue was given; equally, they were not sure what to tell the district officer until he made his desires known. The Lambom islanders assumed he had come to punish them and must have been relieved at their unexpected good fortune when he said he was there 'to help them against their enemy To Kabar'.[24]

Joining forces with the government against enemies was an attractive proposition to many New Guinean communities. As German rule spread, villagers would often ask the local district officer to appoint a *luluai* and a couple of *tultuls*. Such appointments brought prestige to a village and offered it the option of exploiting the police as allies. The extension of colonial order was part conquest and part the result of the constant search for strong and reliable allies by New Guinea's village peoples. As the district officer in Madang said when asked by Berlin whether the New Guineans were satisfied with the colonial administration, 'opinion among the natives differs': those who were losing the wars welcomed the government, those who were winning them would have liked to shake it off.[25]

A few New Guinean communities made peace with the Germans by ostentatious displays of breaking and burning spears, clubs, bows and arrows, possibly in the expectation that the government would reciprocate by making no further demands for land and labour. The police sergeant in Madang from 1905 to 1908, Bernard Frommund, recalled a huge gathering of people 'from northern districts' at the district office. They had broken their weapons and packed them in baskets ready for burning and expected the Germans to do the same. The big men made speeches saying that they would fight the Germans no more, and District Officer Stuckhardt replied that he would always stand by their side. From the Germans, the colonial power intent on subjecting all villagers to central authority, the response to this unilateral disarmament was cynical: 'We too put a few old rusted and useless rifles on the fire'.[26]

The 'police-soldier', as the Germans called him, wore a uniform of shirt, trousers and cap, and a belt with a cartridge bag. Twice a week he practised sharpshooting at different targets with his M/88 rifle, and on patrol he carried a side-arm as well. At all other times his arms were kept under lock and key, almost certainly because the Germans did not want firearms to find their way into the hands of the villagers. The supply of arms and ammunition to the New Guineans was forbidden but, at least in the New Guinea islands, many communities had old Sniders and other rifles stored away, the legacy of the labour trade.

As German plantings expanded, New Guineans in widely separated areas of the colony decided to contest by force of arms the Germans' occupation of land. In the Gazelle Peninsula of New Britain, the struggle between the colonizers and the colonized over land led to the brutal murder of a planter's wife and child and equally brutal retaliation by the Germans; in the Witu Islands off west New Britain government military action was employed to confirm the land claims of the Neu Guinea Compagnie; and in Madang, the Yam and Bilbil peoples conspired to expel the foreigners from the land altogether.

Three hours' walk inland from the German capital of Kokopo a planter called Rudolf Wolff had bought 320 hectares of land. The land was at the foot of Vunakokor, a mountainous cone of volcanic origin, and Wolff obtained it from two big men of the Paparatava, a people whose rich domains covered the valleys beneath Vunakokor. His wife Hedwig joined him on the plantation in 1900 and gave birth to a son in November 1901. Wolff employed about forty Buka labourers on the plantation and a few village girls to do the washing, and bought copra, taro, fruit and vegetables from people in nearby villages such as Wairiki and Tamanairik. Apart from

152°00'E · WATOM I. · MAKADA I. · 152°30'E · DUKE OF YORK I. · Nodup · Kabakada · RABAUL · Vunakamkambi · Malaguna · ULU I. · MIOKO I. · 4°15'S · Kabaira · MATUPIT I. · Rakunai · VULCAN I. · Barawon · Raluana · KOKOPO (Herbertshöhe) · Ralum · Vunamami · Kinigunan · Bitarebarebe · Vunapope · Tamalili · Tingenavudu · Ulagunan · Toma · Takabur · (Mt.) Vunakokor · Paparatava · Tamanairik · Malakuna · Kabanga · Wairiki · Viveren · Londip · 0 10 20 kms

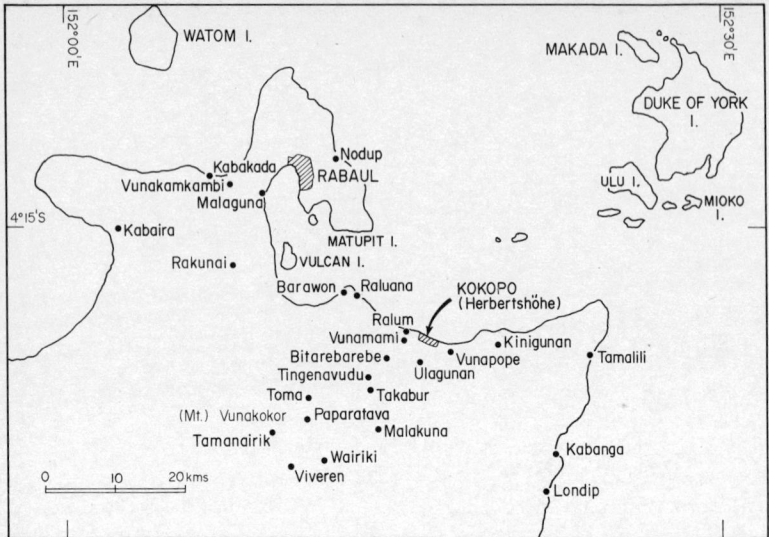

The Eastern Gazelle Peninsula of New Britain (Neu Pommern)

the murder of a labourer by To Vagira's people in Tamanairik, relations between the settler and his neighbours were peaceful.

One of the men who had parted with land, To Kilan, began to have second thoughts when Wolff started to extend his plantation from the valley floor up to the mountain, clearing the bush from an area which To Kilan hoped to make his last resting-place. To Kilan did not want to be buried in a white man's plantation and let it be known that he would not be satisfied until the land was returned. He sent back the trade goods received as payment from Wolff, complained bitterly about him to a missionary and thrust his spear deeply in the ground as a sign that he would kill the planter if the issue were not settled. He visited To Vagira who arranged for a meeting of warriors from Paparatava, Tamanairik, Viveren and Rapui and supported their decision to attack the whites; then, as a feint, To Kilan went to the plantation and assured Wolff that he accepted the price for the land and was a friend again.

On the day of the murders, 3 April 1902, Wolff was at work in the plantation when people from Paparatava and Tamanairik came to the house to sell copra, taro, eggs and a pig. As his wife bargained for the goods, To Kilan's son, To Manmaduk, hit her over the head with an axe. Others drove spears into her, attacked the servants and grabbed the baby from his pram, killing him with an axe-blow and throwing his body on to the back verandah. Wolff rode back to his house to be met by a Buka labourer who said: 'Master, kanaka, kanaka', and to find his house full of warriors:

One native was kneeling beside the bathroom with a gun, another in
the kitchen; a third was kneeling in front of my home underneath the
front verandah, all three taking aim. My wife lay beneath, propped
up against the bottom steps . . . on the right hand side as one comes
down the stairs. Next to her my child lay, completely pale. Blood was
streaming over my wife's face, her hair falling over it. I saw no traces
of blood on the child. I stopped and called out to my wife: 'Hedwig!'
She made no sign of life, and neither did my child. I wanted to get
into the house up the stairs where my wife lay . . . I now saw many
Paparatava in my house taking no notice of me. There was a terrible
din in the house.[27]

Wolff raised the alarm down on the coast in Kokopo. Hahl lay ill with
black-water fever, and the responsibility for taking action fell on the
Imperial Magistrate, who immediately took his police into the hills. This
was to be no ordinary punitive action. A white woman and her baby lay
murdered and the expatriates of the Gazelle Peninsula feared a general
Tolai uprising. In the following days the Germans organized forces on
an unprecedented scale, sending thousands of plantation labourers to
destroy the Paparatava gardens and reinforcing the police troop of eighty
men with an extra sixty ex-police. The hill Tolai were outnumbered and
outgunned. Short of ammunition, they melted buckshot from captured
hunting rifles in order to make lead plugs and adapted Mauser cartridges
for their old Snider weapons, but they were no match for the improvised
army which marched from the coast. Scores of Tolai were killed, about
eighty to a hundred altogether, and others were imprisoned. Acting Governor Hahl, by now sufficiently recovered from fever to issue orders, personally dispatched a detachment of friendly Tolai to seek out one of the fugitives and authorized them to shoot the enemy. The reserve of ex-police,
after doing 'good service', began to wreak such havoc that it was disarmed
and disbanded. Resistance ended in June 1902 when police shot dead To
Vagira, who was said to have struck out with a stone even as he lay dying
and whose head, like that of To Kilan, was carried in triumph to Kokopo.[28]

The people of Paparatava forfeited half their land to the colonial government and, together with the villagers of Wairiki, Tamanairik and Viveren,
were put to work building the strategic roads designed to prevent further
resistance to German rule. To symbolize their dominance the Germans,
protected by an armed guard of forty police, celebrated the German
Empress's birthday on 22 October 1902 at the new Toma police post on
the peak near Paparatava, now accessible on the mountain road constructed
by forced labour. Two thousand people from the area danced in a *singsing*
to mark the making of peace with the Germans.[29]

Most settlers supported the government's uncompromising stand.
Richard Parkinson, a veteran of battles with the Tolai, thought leniency
only made the villagers 'cheeky' and created the need for 'double severity'.[30]
But Father Johann Eberlein, a Sacred Heart missionary who knew many
of the villagers killed in the Paparatava affair, accused the government of
organizing an indiscriminate massacre. In an article published in the

Kölnische Volkszeitung and quoted in other German newspapers Eberlein claimed that the police had been instructed to shoot everything that moved; *luluais* who had no connection with Paparatava and innocent women and children had been shot dead; and the reserves had acted like a band of assassins. According to the Social Democrats' paper *Vorwärts*, a 'completely anarchic situation' had developed in which 'numerous innocent people were butchered' and conditions resembled those of King Leopold's Congo.[31]

The official defence of the Paparatava expeditions, based on the view that an extreme threat to white settlement deserved extreme countermeasures, could not hide the fact that the Germans had exacted ferocious revenge for the deaths at the inland plantation. Fritz Rose in the Colonial Department argued that the best answer to newspaper critics was to point to the 'treachery and cruelty' of the attack on Wolff's plantation, so shocking that the government in Kokopo was duty-bound in the interests of the security of the whites 'to atone for the murder with pitiless rigour'. Albert Hahl, about to leave Germany after his promotion from acting governor to governor, denounced Eberlein's account as false and incomplete, concealing the extent of the inland people's movement of opposition and ignoring the military position faced by a weak government in Kokopo. All those villagers who participated in the armed resistance to the Germans after the murders were 'guilty' in Hahl's opinion and, while the reserves were indeed ill-disciplined, this was only 'natural' for a force of men out of practice. As for the orders given to the police, they were to shoot 'armed enemy natives only if they did not stop', not everyone in sight.[32]

Paparatava was a turning-point in the history of the Germans in the Gazelle Peninsula, the last occasion on which they engaged in armed conflict with the Tolai. The Germans had not hesitated to use the villagers against each other. Like the hostilities of the 1890s, the Paparatava engagements were between small groups of allied Tolai warriors on one side and Germans together with their allies on the other. Europeans, part-Europeans, islanders from elsewhere in the Bismarck Archipelago and the German Solomons, Tolai villagers from the coast and non-Tolai, Taulil people from neighbouring valleys: these were the men, all foreigners to the inland Tolai, who united to destroy their mountain fastnesses. Without New Guinean allies, said Hahl, the Germans would not have been able to assert mastery over the inland peoples. Paparatava demonstrated the way in which the Germans were gradually to extend control over the villages of New Guinea, not simply by force of arms but by alliances with New Guineans who joined in punitive expeditions for purposes of their own, to defeat an enemy or just to enjoy the fight with its promise of rape and rapine. Where the conflict ended in the confiscation of land, the Germans kept the land for themselves rather than distributing it among their allies.

The Neu Guinea Compagnie included the entire Witu Islands group west of New Britain in its sweeping land purchases of the late 1890s. Many islanders died in the smallpox epidemics of 1894 and 1895—by one estimate, over half the population—and in the deserted villages there remained flourishing stands of coconut palms, source of the copra which labourers loaded into the NGC schooners at Peter Hansen's trading station on the main island of Garove. Hansen settled in the Witu Islands in the 1880s, became a trader for the Company when he ran short of money and was supplying his employers with 250 tons of copra a year by 1900. He was a Dane who lived the reckless life of the island trader, fighting in local wars and taking local women to his bed. Besides Bohiko from Ontong Java who had borne him six children, Hansen had an additional eight Witu Islands wives by 1904, some of them 'maries belong fight' given to him by grateful warriors for help against enemies, or as prizes of war. In about 1899, for example, he was said to have joined the Balangori people in their hostilities with the Lama, shooting a famous spear-thrower and cutting off his arm so that the Balangori could eat it and acquire the skill. On that occasion the Lama people gave him the dead man's wife, Maluki, the Balangori presented him with a woman called Golulu, and he acquired two more women as well. Women were useful to him because they climbed trees to collect coconuts in a society in which such work was beneath the dignity of a man.[33]

While Hansen was away in Sydney in November 1900, islanders attacked his trading post on Garove, stole pigs and killed nine of his labourers cutting copra in the bush. Soon afterwards Vingoru islanders plundered his trading station on neighbouring Mundua Island. The warriors who murdered Hansen's labourers were from the Lama people, enemies of his on previous occasions, and their actions were almost certainly those of men exacting vengeance in a continuing feud. This time Hansen had new allies to assist him in counter-raids, not the Balangori people but the Imperial Judge, Wilhelm Stuckhardt, his police and the German naval cruiser *Cormoran*, whose combined efforts resulted in the deaths of about fifteen islanders, the arrest of four and the destruction of numerous villages and canoes. For the Neu Guinea Compagnie, which came into full possession of the island group over the next two years, the value of Witu lay in trade copra, seed coconuts needed to expand plantings in Kaiser Wilhelmsland, and rich plantation land.[34]

Like villagers elsewhere the Witu people fully understood what they had done by selling land to Europeans only when men came to clear bush and lay down plantations. The work was so well advanced on the Witu group by 1903 that Governor Hahl sent an official commission to mark out the boundaries of indigenous reservations, as had been done in the Gazelle Peninsula. Many people apparently took this visit as a sign that they would lose all their land, those east of Mundua even toying with the idea of killing the land surveyors. On the morning of 11 November 1903, Peter Hansen was at work in the plantation and an engineer employed by the NGC on its Witu Islands steamer, *Meto*, was cleaning parts of the ship's engine on shore. The engineer, Doell, noticed that one of the ship's crew was missing, went in search of him, came upon the man asleep on the deck of the *Meto*, and hit him with a stick. Kiliu, as the man was called, was enraged and with a gun from Hansen's house he shot Doell dead. After killing another German, two Chinese and ten labourers on the station the islanders grabbed what weapons and ammunition they could, reassembled the *Meto*'s engine and steamed away in the direction of the Willaumez Peninsula in west New Britain. A trader on Mundua was speared in the arm but escaped in his boat to safety at Kokopo.

The Germans pursued the islanders to west New Britain and burned a village where they suspected the fugitives had stayed, but could not find them among 'the many natural hiding-places on Willaumez'. They had to be satisfied with killing about twenty-five warriors in battles on Garove and Mundua, and the last of the population which had fled to west New Britain, including many people from the Meto district on Garove, were not to return to their island home until 1905. In the meantime the NGC began to exploit the island intensively, backed by the small guard of police who were stationed on Garove; and after all the islands had been surveyed and the indigenous reservations demarcated the Company reported that nothing more stood in the way of a 'prosperous development of this most valuable possession'.[35]

Governor Hahl blamed Peter Hansen for the uprising. Islanders accused him of rape, cruelty to his labourers, keeping people prisoners until he was paid a ransom in pigs, turtle shells and dogs' teeth, and of having deceived sellers of land by telling them that he was buying only the coco-nuts, not the soil in which the palms grew. Hansen was a man of such insistent sexual appetite that no father dared bring his young daughter to the trading post for fear that she might join the harem. The explanation for the unrest advanced by Hansen himself—that people feared losing land—was officially discounted, yet Hahl had to admit that most witnesses to the events were dead and that 'complete clarity about the detailed causes of the uprising' was impossible to obtain.[36] Both interpretations probably held true: the islanders resented Hansen's cavalier treatment of their prop-erty, whether it be copra, pigs or women, and they saw the land surveyors as land robbers.

The Germans remained vigilant. Seven Witu islanders were arrested and sentenced to a year's hard labour in 1905 for spreading the perceptive rumour that the English would expel the Germans from Garove after destroying the German fleet.[37] The reward of control in the small island group, whose population was about 2200 in 1913, was land and copra for the NGC. Copra from the village groves and plantations of the Witu islands provided a third of the Company's copra exports in 1905-06 and plantations grew to cover 30 per cent of the islands' land surface by 1913.

On the same day on which the Witu Islander, Baleki, was executed for his part in the troubles, 17 September 1904, three men from the island of Siar near the German district office at Madang were also put to death. A month before, a military court under District Judge Knake had sentenced Mas, Majan, Amang, Kenang, Jjai and Matua to capital punishment for offences against paragraph 8 of the Prussian law on the state of siege of

Villagers of Aua, Western Islands, in the late 1890s: the Western Islanders were
the only Para-Micronesians in Papua New Guinea and their traditional
architecture was unique

Plantation labourers receive rations

A group of young Tolai men, about 1890: the pipes,
leather belts and loin-cloths show the people's rapid
adoption of Western goods

Making a road on the Gazelle Peninsula, about 1900

4 June 1851. A firing squad of police on Siar Island shot the six Madang men at 5 p.m. on 17 August 1904.[38]

The Madang executions were the Germans' response to a determined attempt by the Yam people, who occupied the islands of Kranket, Biliau, Siar and Panutibun outside Madang harbour, to drive out the foreigners who had been taking more and more of their land ever since Jan Kubary 'bought' virtually the entire coast of Astrolabe Bay in the 1880s. Imperial land ordinances of 1902 and 1903 had given German colonial governors new powers to forbid the acquisition of native land by colonists and even, in rare circumstances, to expropriate land already held by Europeans. But Hahl was already battling the NGC over labour policy and had no intention of preventing it from expanding plantations in the Madang district.

Early plans for the war against the whites were for an alliance between the Yam and islanders of Yabob and Bilbil to the south, but the Yabob and Bilbil defected, leaving about eighty Yam warriors from Kranket and Siar to make the assault. They crossed in their canoes to the German settlement on 26 July and presented the district officer with gifts of fruit, intending to kill him shortly thereafter. With a beach-head established the warriors would then rush upon the unsuspecting whites in the town and kill all of them except women and children. But the Yam had been betrayed by one of their own men, Nalon of Biliau village, described by the district officer as 'one of those characters who obtrude themselves on every newly arrived white, tell him everything possible and in the way that the person wants to hear it'.[39] Confronted with armed police who started firing, the warriors fled back across the harbour.

No European had been injured. Most saw nothing. Yet panic understandably ensued, with nervous Europeans arming themselves with sticks of dynamite and imagining new conspiracies. They appealed to Kokopo for help, and when Acting Governor Knake reached Madang on 16 August he declared a state of war. The District Officer Wilhelm Stuckhardt wanted to deport the Siar and Bilbil from their island homes permanently, and in the case of the Bilbil, Governor Hahl supported him. As the leading conspirators, in Hahl's view, they deserved 'severe punishment'.[40]

The Bilbil had fled to the Rai coast, where they made the most of their traditional trading contacts. Every year canoes laden with the pots which they specialized in making visited the coast to the south-east; now again they loaded their canoes with pottery and on reaching the village of Singor, held a great feast, inviting the hill peoples to select earthenware vessels and assist them against the police. The strategy worked. Frustrated by days of fruitless searching on an expedition in October 1904, the police sergeant Beyer promised a reward for every Bilbil fugitive delivered to the authorities. None was handed over. Everywhere Beyer went he received information about the whereabouts of the Bilbil, all of it false. Only once did he happen to encounter his quarry and that was on a mountain in the middle of the night. Chasing the Bilbil in the dark the police opened fire 'from time to time', though 'whether anybody was hit could not be established'.

Finally a group of villagers promised to take Beyer to the Bilbil, hastening to explain that the trip would take two or three days, but Beyer was tired of being told 'manifold lies' by the Rai coast villagers and refused to go on another goose-chase.[41]

Not until after July 1905 did the Bilbil people leave their hideouts on the Rai coast and settle on the south side of the Gogol River where the authorities could contact them. Stuckhardt demanded fifteen men for three years' work in Kokopo but was offered only four, who were sent back with the message from the district office that hostilities would be resumed. The police then surprised the Bilbil, killing nine, and submission to German rule was finally forthcoming. They were resettled on the coast at a place chosen by the Germans.[42]

The peoples of Astrolabe Bay and the Rai coast were noted for what Hahl called 'passive resistance' to European demands. Villagers from the Gogol River in Alexishafen were building roads by 1907 but they frequently deserted in large groups and had to be recaptured. Few people were yet prepared to offer themselves freely as contract labourers. Of 534 mainland recruits obtained by the Neu Guinea Compagnie in 1907, only twenty-six came from the Madang area and in 1908, the figure was eight out of 497. Land remained a source of bitter resentment. The reserves took years to survey and even when the boundaries had been marked, people wanted their land back. At Bogadjim in the south of Astrolabe Bay the NGC had taken so much land that the reserves were one to two hours' walk from the villages and were often plundered by plantation labourers.[43]

Hahl attempted to conciliate the people by guaranteeing land reserves of one hectare per person and by allowing the Bilbil to be repatriated in 1907, but too much land had been taken. Sustained by beliefs that the time was near when the whites would be expelled and their wealth distributed among the blacks, the Madang peoples never reconciled themselves to the German presence.[44]

Control and Labour

Just as vital to the plantation colony as land was cheap labour. But in a colony where, despite land alienation, most villagers enjoyed access to garden land and had enough to eat, labourers had rarely been driven to seek plantation work by hunger or economic necessity. Work on contract provided adventure, travel and a useful supply of European goods and was for most New Guineans a matter of choice. Trying to recruit on the southeast coast of New Ireland in 1900 the governor was told that nobody was available because the village was at war and at Lihir Island people asked him why they should go to Kaiser Wilhelmsland when they had food in abundance at home. *Singsings* in New Ireland were the dread of every European employer, according to District Officer Boluminski, and he deplored the influence which such 'strenuous pleasures' had on the New Irelanders' desire to work. Around Madang, which had been settled by Europeans since 1892, recruiting was still virtually impossible as late as

1901, though a few villagers agreed to spend a month in Kokopo 'in order to see the place'. Most people refused to sign on for another decade. Recruits could be obtained from the Huon Gulf in the early years of imperial rule but they demanded payment in their own currency, perfectly formed boars' teeth. In the west of Kaiser Wilhelmsland the people of Warapu Island told a German district officer in 1905 that they did not want to work in Madang any more because the pay was bad. In the Admiralty Islands, still without a government station in 1909, many recruits working on the Hernsheim plantations were physically undeveloped boys, sent by their villages because full-grown warriors were needed to fight local wars.[45]

The Germans diminished this New Guinean independence be extending control. *Luluais* were made responsible for ensuring that young men of the village signed on, villagers were required to build roads and later to earn cash in order to pay the head-tax, and most coastal districts of the Old Protectorate became much safer for labour recruiters. As communities and as individuals, New Guineans differed in their attitude towards contract work, some liking it, others having to be dragooned under threat of punishment. A few, Tolai especially, managed to avoid dreary plantation work altogether by becoming police, personal servants, boat's crew, and mission catechists. But for all coastal New Guineans the obligation to work for the colonial masters became increasingly difficult to avoid, and between 1900 and 1914 the number of New Guineans employed either casually or on contract in the Old Protectorate rose from about 3000 to about 20 000.

Control was meant to produce labourers. Apart from Simpsonhafen government station in Blanche Bay, three new government stations were established between 1904 and 1906, in southern New Ireland, Bougainville and the west coast of mainland New Guinea, each designed to bring more villagers into the labour force. For southern New Ireland, Namatanai was chosen because the east coast was more densely populated and, with its stretches of fertile flat land between sea and mountains, more suited to plantations than the west. The station was intended 'to guarantee the safety of settlers and missionaries', to 'further the development of the country by building roads', 'to support labour recruitment and return escaped labourers to their masters' and to extend direct rule through *luluais*. The district officer was granted police and judicial powers over New Guineans but not over whites and possessed a permanent force of thirty police. In two years from the founding of the station in August 1904, the Germans, pressing north and south, brought the coastal villages of central and southern New Ireland under direct rule and imposed road-building duties upon them. Once subject to the government, the coastal villagers appealed for police help against their enemies inland. In 1905 the police were suppressing warfare of this kind in the Muliama area, about ninety kilometres from Namatanai; in 1906 they were doing the same a further sixty kilometres south near Mimias, where a bush big man called Geges threatened to kill all supporters of the government and destroy their homes. For two *luluais* whom the government had chosen, he reserved special treatment: they were to be killed and eaten, and out of their *luluai* caps he would feed pigs. In an attack on Geges's village on 15 March 1906 the government forces killed nine men for the loss of none.[46]

Visiting Lambom in 1906, Acting Governor Emil Krauss found that almost all the men had already worked for the whites in Samoa, New Britain or Kaiser Wilhelmsland. The experience of To Kulau's village was almost certainly common for southern New Ireland. Out of a population probably somewhat greater than the 14 250 counted in 1914, recruiters had taken over 2500 labourers to the Kokopo control station from 1887 to 1903, and in 1905, 464 southern New Irelanders signed on to work in the Bismarck Archipelago and Samoa. Control added to this labour force by eventually increasing the numbers enlisting on contract and by creating a supply of day labourers. Local workers employed breaking and carrying stones to build a bridge at Namatanai in 1906 received one stick of tobacco a week as payment, which cost the government five *Pfennige* (in the sterling of the time, a little over a halfpenny) and the district officer predicted that a planter settling there could get all the labourers he needed at a monthly cost of three marks each. The attraction of this cheap labour brought the first European plantation to Namatanai in 1907.[47]

In Bougainville the government station, founded in September 1905, was put on the east coast at Kieta. *Reichstag* deputies being asked to approve expenditure on an officer-in-charge, a white police sergeant and fifty police in Bougainville were informed that the island was 'the most densely populated part of the Protectorate' and that a station would put a stop to inter-tribal wars and 'facilitate the recruiting of labourers'. The 'special task' of Kieta station, said Hahl, was to increase labour recruiting in the German Solomons, which were the most important source of workers for the Bismarck Archipelago and Samoa. Pacification and recruiting went hand in hand. In Buka, also part of the Kieta district, Hahl thought intervention in local wars was 'essential in the interests of recruitment' and when two Buka big men, Magara and Nebot, complained about the raids of a warrior called Cohe, the Germans destroyed Cohe's villages. In gratitude for help from their German allies Magara and Nebot presented a dozen men to the government for training as police. Buka men had served in the German police since the 1880s and by 1905 numerous ex-police were living in the villages, especially around Hanahan in the north-east and on Buka Passage, where they had become unofficial *luluais* enforcing loyalty to the Germans.[48]

The Bougainvilleans were much less pro-German. Labour recruiters were hindered by warfare and the concentration of the population in the mountains, where people had not forgotten their kinsmen who had died of malaria in coastal districts. The recruiter going inland had to start climbing within a few kilometres of the coast in many parts of Bougainville because he was already in the foothills of the Crown Prince and Emperor Ranges which dominate the island. Seven separate battles were fought with the mountain villagers of the Nasioi, the people living closest to Kieta, before they submitted and provided the men regularly demanded for public works. Nasioi spears, their shafts intricately decorated and points barbed with sharp pieces of turtleshell or bone from flying foxes, were traded to other peoples of Bougainville: Torau-speaking people of the east coast, descendants of immigrants from Alu Island; the Siwai and Buin of the south; people on Buka Passage speaking the Halia language of Buka; and still more, about nineteen language-groups in all.[49] Such spears were probably hurled at the police by the warriors of a place called Tangone who resisted the Germans in 1906. Dwas, their leader, was preventing people from doing forced labour and threatened to shoot police who ventured into his village. Led by allies from the nearby village of Toboroi, the Kieta station officer August Döllinger took a police sergeant and twenty-five police to Tangone in March 1906 in an attempt to arrest Dwas. The sergeant later reported that while he went to the upper part of the village with the police

> the natives who had served as guides lit a fire in the lower part of the village. According to the police and the natives five men and two women were shot dead in the houses, shootings which I did not see; whether the native Dwas was among those killed has not yet been established.[50]

Dwas, in fact, survived the combined onslaught of Toboroi warriors and government police, but submitted to German rule in May 1906. Further south people dared not work on the Kieta road for fear that enemies would pillage their homes, a situation which provoked another expedition under Döllinger, this time to a place the Germans called Tsiwo. Only partly in control of his police and guides as before, Döllinger was unsure whether two people had been killed or five. By 1908 the centralized authority of Kieta station was becoming widely recognized in Bougainville and the east coast road, constructed by forced labour, stretched for sixty-five kilometres and over 148 bridges.[51]

While the Bougainvilleans broke stones, German officials at a new government station at Aitape in western Kaiser Wilhelmsland were given the task of bringing colonial order to the coast between the Dutch border and the mouth of the Sepik River. Aitape station, under Hans Rodatz, was to prove for the first time that mainland villagers would sign on in large numbers, but initial resistance was fierce and Governor Hahl reinforced the station with a schooner and extra police in 1907. Aitape district then surprised the Germans by providing over 700 contract labourers in a year.[52]

By 1907 Hahl was beginning to see the fruits of his policy of opening New Guinea to the white planter. Over half the copra exported from the Old Protectorate still came from traders but plantations were being rapidly laid down. Since 1901 the area of cultivated plantation land had grown from about 4500 to 15 829 hectares; the number of labourers under indenture was up from about 3400 to 7000; and copra exports, worth less than 800 000 marks in 1903, were now valued at over 1 800 000 marks. Roads were spreading out from government stations in the Gazelle Peninsula, northern and southern New Ireland, Bougainville and on the mainland at Madang and Aitape. The planter in his homestead was safer from attack than ever before, his claim to the land backed by the district office and its police, while the labour recruiter ventured into new recruiting areas in the knowledge that the government stood behind him.

Equally important was the marked improvement in New Guinea's shipping communications with overseas markets, since cheap freights were vital for prosperous plantations. Until 1905 merchants in German New Guinea could export their copra and island products in a number of ways: by chartering vessels to sail to Europe, by transhipping exports to Europe in Sydney or by paying Norddeutscher Lloyd to carry cargo to Europe via the Far East. In all cases shipping was expensive because merchants had to bring their copra to Kokopo in the first place, and because, although competition between Norddeutscher Lloyd and Burns Philp was reducing freights to Sydney, the Australian domestic market for copra was small. Copra which went to Sydney had to be reloaded on to vessels bound for Antwerp, Bremen, Liverpool and other European ports. After negotiations with all the leading firms in German New Guinea, Norddeutscher Lloyd proposed a mutually advantageous deal: if all exporters in the colony promised to give their outward cargo exclusively to that company, it would provide an inter-island shipping service. The deal was agreed, and from October 1905 Norddeutscher Lloyd coastal steamers took copra from outstations to its newly built pier and store at Simpsonhafen on the site of modern Rabaul, where larger vessels called regularly to take on cargo for Europe.[53]

The prospects of copra planters were transformed. Burns Philp was forced out of the carrying trade to and from German New Guinea and Sydney lost its importance as an entrepot for the colony. Export products began to be stored on the spot in New Britain, a commission trade appeared and Germany's share in the colony's foreign trade rose from 29 per cent in 1905 to 62 per cent by 1912. Norddeutscher Lloyd had won the undying gratitude of Governor Hahl, who was soon insisting that the German government should substantially increase the subsidy of 275 000 marks paid to the shipping company for maintaining a service to New Guinea.

Hahl's colonial policy was now clear. To establish control he would not hesitate to use police troops against rebellious warriors. To entrench control he would depend upon *luluais* with circumscribed magisterial powers, men who were answerable to German officials. To keep pace with the expanding frontier of German planters and missionaries he would add to the decentralized network of government stations. Land would continue to pass into European hands as freehold under regulations which, while they put an end to the era of outrageous land claims, still permitted settlers to buy large holdings provided that they left enough for villagers' houses and gardens. For the sake of peace between colonizers and colonized Hahl would create further native land reserves. Labour would flow on to the plantations as the country was made safe for labour recruiters. Shipping within the colony and between New Guinea and European markets would be facilitated by generous state subsidies to Norddeutscher Lloyd. And for finances the colony would mainly depend, as before, on the imperial grant from Berlin.

On two parts of this colonial policy, however, events were forcing Hahl to change his attitude. Even as his encouragement of the labour recruiters showed signs of success he began to fear depopulation and suggested that 'Chinese field labourers' be used 'so as to relieve exhausted recruiting areas'.[54] It was an idea that was to absorb much of his energy in his remaining years as governor.

At the same time Hahl felt the first effects of budget cutbacks in Berlin, following *Reichstag* attacks on his administration. 1906 was a year of colonial scandals in Germany, as *Reichstag* deputies led by the Centre Party member Matthias Erzberger brought to light the cruelties and inefficiencies of a colonial policy which had caused two major rebellions in German East Africa and German South-West Africa. In discussing German New Guinea's annual budget, which in previous years passed through the *Reichstag* almost without comment, Erzberger expressed his opposition to spending 10 000 marks to assist the settlement of German farmers from Queensland and argued that imperial expenditure in New Guinea was extravagant:

> The colony's own income is 330,000 marks and the imperial grant this year is 1,168,963 marks. Seventy-five per cent of the entire expenditure of this colony has to be met by the tax-paying German people. For one farmer settled in New Guinea there is an annual imperial subsidy of 22,000 marks ... can Germany spend 1,200,000 marks every year because of fifty-two farmers in New Guinea and Kaiser Wilhelmsland? In my opinion the time has come for imperial expenditures to be restricted in view of the negligible economic importance which the colony possesses.

The *Reichstag* resolved to strike the 10 000 marks off the budget on the grounds that subsidizing settlers was a 'dangerous experiment' and reduced the imperial subsidy accordingly.[55]

Small as it was, the reduction was a warning of things to come. In the wake of the colonial scandals the German government under Bernhard von Bülow as Chancellor attempted to reform colonial administration, first by appointing as Colonial Director a banker and management expert called Bernhard Dernburg, then by replacing the Colonial Department of the Foreign Office with an independent *Reich* Colonial Office under Dernburg as Colonial Secretary. Dernburg, an anglophile, stood for a new idea in German colonial administration, or at least for one which had had no influence on German rule in the largest African colonies, the idea that colonial subjects were assets to be protected rather than pests to be exterminated. Treated humanely, the colonized peoples would join the common task of economic development. In some colonies, East Africa and Cameroun for example, Dernburg saw Germany's best hope in peasant agriculture rather than German plantations. He also wanted a scientific colonialism, in which German officials took the best of European expertise in agriculture, animal husbandry, medicine and construction techniques to the overseas possessions of the *Reich*. The Hamburg *Kolonialinstitut*, founded in 1908 to train colonial officials, embodied just this view.

These ideas were reactions to the corruption, patronage and brutality of German colonial rule in Africa. They had little impact in New Guinea, where Hahl already accepted broad principles of trusteeship. What mattered for New Guinea was not the rhetoric of reform but the rigorous economies which Dernburg imposed on colonial governments, for it was part of the Dernburg creed of efficiency to make colonies pay for themselves out of local revenue. Hahl, who believed that a plantation colony was better spared the burden of customs duties, could see by 1907 that he would have to increase duties substantially in order to compensate for a declining imperial grant. Without the financial independence he wanted, Hahl now faced the prospect of bitter confrontations with settlers who would be paying more in tax, and they were not likely to share his enthusiasm for preventing depopulation.

5
Extending the Colonial Order 1907-1914

When the price of copra boomed in the early 1880s Europeans in the New Guinea islands multiplied their trading posts; when it boomed again between 1906 and 1914 they laid down plantations. Backed by the colonial state, they now had the promise of land, labour and protection. The area of land planted, the number of indentured labourers, the pace of recruiting, the population of European planters and plantation managers: all more than doubled in the eight years before the war. And the value of copra exports from the Old Protectorate of German New Guinea increased sharply from under one and a half million marks to over six million. By the time the Australians reached Rabaul in September 1914 German New Guinea ranked among the leading copra-producing countries of the Pacific.

From the original plantation centres around Madang, the Gazelle Peninsula and northern New Ireland the planters spread to central New Ireland, eastern Bougainville, along the coast of the mainland from Finschhafen to Aitape and to islands such as Umboi, the Witu group and the Western atolls. They went where the rain was reliable, the land was flat, rich and well-drained and anchorages were protected. The largest plantation firm, the Neu Guinea Compagnie, had 8288 of its 138 000 hectares under coconut palms, rubber, cacao and sisal by 1913. Planters grew coffee, cotton, kapok, lemon grass, maize and taro in small quantities but copra was king: 93 per cent of cultivated plantation land in the New Guinea Islands and almost 80 per cent on the mainland was under coconut palms in 1913. The village producer remained vital to the export economy of the colony and 'native copra' accounted for 'by far the biggest proportion' of tonnage as late as 1909, but the trend was towards plantation copra and by the last year of German rule it probably predominated.[1]

Control, as Governor Hahl admitted, followed rather than preceded the scores of planters who came to New Guinea. Lacking uncontrolled areas legislation like that later used by the Australians to restrain the European adventurer, the Germans spent much of their time dealing with clashes on the colonial frontier. A more rapid conquest, Hahl said in 1911, would have spared both 'the gallant Europeans' and the villagers 'much blood and arduous sacrifices'. As it was, money from Berlin was so short that

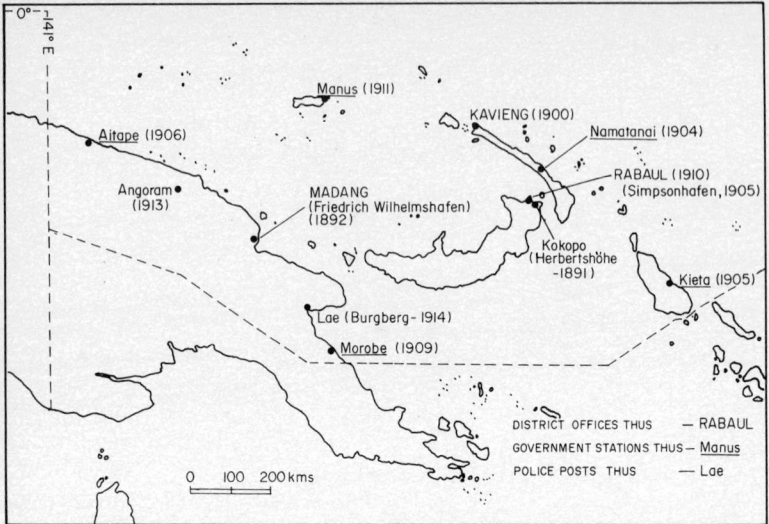

Centres of Government Administration, 1914

the first new government station after Aitape in 1906 was Morobe three years later, and the only other major station established before the war was at Manus (1911). The police posts at Angoram and Lae came in the last year of German rule. From district offices at Rabaul, Kavieng and Madang, government stations at Kieta, Namatanai, Aitape, Morobe and Manus and the police post at Kokopo, the German colonial administration in 1913 reckoned its control extended over the Gazelle Peninsula 'apart from the mountainous inner core', the Duke of York Islands, New Ireland, New Hanover, a coastal strip in the Admiralty Islands, the Western Islands, Buka and Bougainville with the exception of the interior mountains, the 'coastal fringe' of mainland New Guinea and the mountains of the Waria River region. Much of New Britain and almost all of the interior of the mainland remained uncontrolled by the Germans and unknown to them, and even in the supposedly pacified districts the Germans did not rule out the possibility of further trouble.[2]

Governor Hahl accepted as inevitable that police would have to kill villagers for the sake of colonial order. In October 1912, for example, soon after the discovery of a second conspiracy against the Germans in Madang, the police were fighting warriors in the lower Ramu; villagers near Aitape were offering armed resistance to the Germans; the Wampar people of the Markham Valley were resuming attacks on vulnerable neighbours; and the police were engaged in battles with islanders on New Hanover. Hahl told Berlin that the best analogy with the situation in New Guinea was the advance of the whites against the Indians in the American West: 'These bloody conflicts are regrettable but in themselves quite natural occurrences like those which have always and everywhere accompanied the struggle with savagery'.[3] Pacification was Hahl's first priority and 75 per cent of the spending on the police, government steamer and officials was for the protection of the colonists.

Control proved slower to establish, more complicated to maintain and less effective than Hahl anticipated. In the Huon Gulf, the Rai coast, the north coast of New Britain, the Admiralty Islands and southern New Ireland the effect of controlling coastal villagers and recruiting them for plantations in large numbers was to expose their homes to the attacks of inland peoples. On the Aitape coast villages were simply too big and their warriors too numerous for fifty police to manage. On the coast between the mouth of the Ramu and Hansa Bay and also in southern New Ireland, government-appointed *luluais* and *tultuls* took up arms against the Germans. It was an unstable colonial order which the Germans bequeathed to the Australians in 1914, and the first reaction of a 'great number of native labourers' on hearing of the Germans' defeat was to desert.[4]

Aitape district was an object lesson in the limits of German power. It was 'very difficult for the station to gain any influence or to achieve recognition of its authority', according to the annual report for 1907-1908. The Germans were 'openly challenged to fight and the troop was exposed to ridicule'.[5] Among a number of punitive expeditions led by Hans Rodatz against coastal, island and hinterland peoples in the district was an expedition in June 1908 against the Sissano, the most powerful group on the Aitape coast, capable of putting a thousand men under arms from eight villages. Sissano women also joined in battle, carrying and collecting arrows to be handed to warriors and removing the dead and wounded. Arrow-heads in this part of New Guinea were polished bird-bones with barbs, and when an arrow found its mark the shaft fell away leaving the sharp bone lodged in the wound; any Sissano man who cried in pain as this bone was withdrawn invited contempt for his weakness. Hearing from a trader that the Sissano had killed fifteen neighbouring villagers Rodatz demanded that the culprits surrender and when no one appeared he took his police to the area, pursuing the Sissano into the sago swamps:

> We came upon a lagoon-like river, very deep and muddy. A narrow half-rotten tree-trunk lay across it. I tried to walk over it but was just as unable to do so as the trader Schultz accompanying me. Time was not to be lost and tools for building a raft not available. So I sent the troop under its under-officers over alone to continue the chase and stayed with Schultz on this side of the bank.

The police killed three people before Rodatz abandoned the exercise, sending word to the warriors to return to their villages and stop fighting. Within a few days many of the hostile Sissano were again cutting copra for sale to the trader and Rodatz was congratulating himself on having 'shown the kanakas that they would be discovered by the troop even in the bush and sago swamp'. But as Rodatz was to learn, a successful pursuit was the merest beginning of control.[6]

To the east of Aitape near what is now the town of Wewak Rodatz's police intervened to protect the landholdings of the Catholic Society of the Divine Word (SVD) mission, active in New Guinea since its establishment on Tumleo Island near Aitape in 1896. The missionaries on Yuo Island had bought land on the coastline opposite in order to lay down a copra plantation, believing the Yuo Islanders who sold it to be the true owners. But on the night of 31 October 1908 mountain villagers burnt the SVD's plantation sheds to the ground and soon afterwards the mission was threatened with drastic reprisals unless it abandoned Bogim Harbour. Government intelligence about the affair was as slight as ever: Hahl was 'rather sure' that the Momoken people were involved and suspected the Yuo Islanders of originating the trouble, while the missionaries accused the inland Potui people, an accusation which officials were unable to substantiate. In any case German officials and the police landed at Bogim Harbour a few weeks later, climbed to a hill village, which they found deserted, and set fire to it. Like a blind giant, the colonial power thrashed out in the general direction of the enemy without really knowing who he was.[7]

One thing alone was clear. The coastal villages of the Aitape district, banded together in large communities for protection against marauders from the hills, were strong enough to modify the terms on which they accepted the colonial government. Jealous of their monopoly of trade with the Europeans, and commanding the routes inland from the coast, they did not hesitate to steal trade-boxes from inlanders returning from plantation work. Of 1253 recruits entered in the control books at Aitape between 1906 and the end of 1910 only 142 came from the hinterland, which the Germans knew to be heavily populated, and from 1911 onwards the number of men in this district signing indentures hardly increased. Hahl called in the Navy to visit Aitape coast in 1908 and was still doing so five years later, when he asked the *Condor* to go to all the important settlements from the Dutch border to the mouth of the Sepik River. Villagers near Aitape, resenting the constant claims of recruiters and government, had murdered a policeman catching escaped labourers and a *tultul* trying to enforce compulsory road-work, and then confronted the investigating official with 'open resistance'.[8]

Gold was the lure which attracted a German police post to Morobe. Miners had been panning for alluvial gold in Northern Papua since the 1890s and as the deposits became exhausted had moved north across the eighth parallel of south latitude, which was the official but unsurveyed border between Australian Papua and German New Guinea. When Governor Hahl went to the border in March 1908 he met a number of gold prospectors, all in German New Guinea according to his reckoning yet themselves claiming to be in Papua and producing certificates of miner's rights to prove it. The Australian authorities had even appointed village constables on the German side of the border. News of the 'drastic action' by the Germans 'to assert their claim to portions of the disputed area' spurred Australia into forming a Mixed Boundary Commission with Germany. As the first officer in charge at Morobe Hahl chose a man with long experience as a gold prospector in Australia, Hans Klink, who began building the station on a steep hill overlooking the islands and reefs of Morobe Harbour in July 1909. By 1911 the settlement looked like German government stations elsewhere in New Guinea: a few wooden houses for the Europeans and a cluster of bush houses for the gaol, store, barracks, native hospital and quarters for married police. Nearby was the Ongga Mission of the Neuendettelsau Lutherans and at the mouth of the Waria River was their Zaka mission, where Karl Mailänder and his Yabim and Kotte assistants from the Huon Gulf, strangers here, struggled with the complexities of the Zia language.[9]

Unlike Wau and Bulolo after the rich gold strikes of the 1920s, Morobe did not become the centre of a gold-mining industry. A few prospectors continued to sluice and pan on the German side of the Waria River Valley but Klink doubted whether ' "pioneers" such as gold-miners and people of similar adventurous occupations' did much to open up the country and thought they exercised 'a certain terrorism' over the villagers. In the upper reaches of the Waria at large mountain villages near Garaina, where Klink went in October 1910, people asked him if he was English and were relieved to learn he was not: they recited the names of numerous relatives shot dead by the 'English' on two previous visits. German prospectors could be equally aggressive. The miner Friedrich Hardin, after taking eight labourers up the Waria in April 1910 and returning in June with four, was found guilty by the Madang District Court of striking, kicking and thrashing his labourers and of supplying natives with ammunition. One of Hardin's party had deserted and subsequently died at the hands of mountain warriors, another disappeared and a third, whose decomposed body was later found, remained behind because he was too ill to walk back to the coast. Hardin was found guilty of mistreating these men but not of causing their deaths. He paid small fines.[10]

The people of the mountainous upper Waria region were the only inland inhabitants of mainland German New Guinea to come under administrative control before 1914. Klink had appointed a *luluai* in Garaina by 1911 and brought many inlanders to the Morobe station via the long track down to the coast at Sipoma and then south-east through Paiewa. By restraining hostilities between the coastal and mountain peoples the Germans hoped to allow labour recruiters safe access to the untouched populations living on the ridges above the Waria and its tributaries, and in 1913 Hahl cited the district as one where recruiters had taken virtually all the active young men. Villagers in the upper Waria told the Australians in 1915 'that, before, the German Police Master used to come up with about 60 Police boys— surround a village and capture all the young boys and take them for the New Guinea Company recruiter'. Having been compelled by the Germans to consolidate scattered dwellings into single villages, 'the reason being that if any kanakas were wanted the village could be surrounded', the people of the Waria began rebuilding in the bush as soon as German rule came to an end.[11]

The mighty Sepik River, disgorging its brown mud into the Bismarck

Sea near the Schouten Islands, remained unvisited by the Germans for twenty-one years after the NGC expedition of 1887. Then, in August 1908, the Company sent labour recruiters 100 kilometres upstream. A government expedition followed in November 1908 and in 1909 Hahl ascended the river on board S.M.S. *Cormoran* on a trip designed to show the flag, begin peaceful barter with the inhabitants, and produce a navigation chart. 'For the Governor', the commander of the *Cormoran* said, 'the first consideration in the further opening of the river basin is whether natives from there can be recruited as manpower' and he thought their physical fitness generally corresponded with expectations. Labour was the Germans' prime objective in the Sepik but they could not fail to be impressed with the richly decorated canoes, the sailing poles set with cassowary feathers, the cooking vessels whose decoration resembled 'modern European handicraft' and Sepik houses, among 'the most impressive buildings of natives in the colony'.[12]

German recruiters worked the lower reaches of the Sepik in the years before the war and on one of the few rises on the banks of that part of the river the government built the Angoram police post in September 1913. Sepik labour recruiting in German times can have been little influenced by government regulations because even the Madang district officer, Ernst Berghausen, took villagers by force. In December 1913, beginning a stay of two years in the Sepik, the anthropologist Richard Thurnwald described in his diary the violent progress of Berghausen up the Sepik as far as Malu near Ambunti. Heavily addicted to morphine, Berghausen was said to have recruited wherever he was not sick with fever or stupefied. He was unknown to the river people and none volunteered to go with him, so he used police to fetch recruits 'whether they resisted or not':

> He locked the recruited people in the dark, cramped store room of the steamer 'Kolonialgesellschaft'. Like an old slave trader, he had 17 people cooped up there . . . Forced recruiting is suitable after fighting. But when conditions are peaceful the people become irritated and many of the murders of the last few years which have taken place in the region of this district office are in part no doubt attributable to this ill-considered and blunt procedure.

Travelling upstream Thurnwald encountered villagers planning to avenge the loss of kinsmen by eating the 'two white pigs' who had abducted them.[13]

It was Berghausen who brought colonial order to the coast north-west of Madang from Alexishafen to the mouth of the Ramu River. The thick bush which covered what had once been the NGC plantation at Dugumor near Hatzfeldthafen was a reminder that the Germans had not returned to this favoured locality, with its rich soils and convenient anchorage, since warriors drove them away in 1891. SVD missionaries settled at Potsdamhafen on the coast opposite the smoking volcano on Manam Island in 1899 and the NGC laid down plantations along the edge of Hansa Bay, but in 1910 no Europeans lived on the long stretch of coast from Bogia south-east to Megiar near Cape Croisilles.

The impetus to extend control came from an alleged conspiracy of the Kamasina, Kumani and Kosakosa peoples. First betrayed by a man from Sepa village near Bogia, the plan was to intercept the district officer and police on a march from Potsdamhafen to Madang (one account specified Tobenam as the place of attack) and, after killing them, to light a fire on an offshore island which would be the signal for a general uprising against the Catholic missionaries and all other Europeans in Bogia, Potsdamhafen and on the plantations of Hansa Bay. If the NGC steamer were to arrive with reinforcements, the conspirators intended to blow it up with dynamite from the Company store. Like the failed Madang revolt of 1904, the Potsdamhafen conspiracy aimed at murdering all Europeans. Its causes almost certainly lay in resentment at the relentless campaign against abortion and infanticide being waged by the Catholic missionaries, who prompted the authorities to arrest four women and to burn a house belonging to people accused of killing babies. The Germans arrested a man called Mamagal in February 1910 and gathered information but at Hahl's urging Berghausen did not proceed with a punitive expedition against the Potsdamhafen villages. Instead he took twenty police on a major patrol along the whole coastline from Cape Croisilles north-west via Bogia to Hansa Bay. Hahl wanted the permanent control created by appointing *luluais*, not the temporary success of 'suppression by force of arms'.[14] At village after village Berghausen would arrive, persuade one man to accompany the party back to Madang in order to learn Pidgin, or if there were Pidgin speakers already, install a *luluai* and a couple of *tultuls*. At Tokain a man who agreed to go to Madang was promised appointment as *luluai*. Everywhere, Berghausen ordered the planting of twenty coconut palms for every able-bodied man in the village and in places closer to Madang he conscripted men for labour on road-building. His reception differed from community to community. At Sarang village, on the coast opposite Karkar Island, women and children were not afraid of him and he was entertained with a *singsing*; at Malas, about ten kilometres away, people had always refused to go with the labour recruiters and much persuasion was necessary before they spoke to the district officer and offered a man to learn Pidgin; in the mountains behind Malas the people fled before Berghausen could establish contact; in the hostile Potsdamhafen villages men agreed to make peace.

But Berghausen's troubles were not over. After three days in Madang all the men who had come to learn Pidgin fled on seeing the Norddeutscher Lloyd postal steamer *Prinz Waldemar*, having heard a rumour that they would be taken to Rabaul and never return. Found on Sarang Island, they were brought yet again to the German district centre. More seriously, 'unrest flared up again' in September 1910 and German marines, complete with the imperial flag, were sent to march through the Hansa Bay and Potsdamhafen villages. Further east the Tobenam and Kaiten people sent Berghausen a message that, far from making peace, they would kill him if he pursued them. Long-standing enemies of the Germans, the Tobenam and Kaiten had killed a Malay bird-of-paradise hunter in 1908 and been punished by the loss of valuable dancing drums and sea-going canoes. Their 'derisive message had to be answered if the natives were not to gain the impression that the government was weak', Berghausen thought, and with *luluais* from nearby villages on board to watch, S.M.S. light cruiser *Nürnberg* fired shells at Kaiten.

By mid-1911 Berghausen was more confident. The Tobenam and Kaiten people of Hatzfeldthafen had made peace. The Kamasina, Kosokosa and other Potsdamhafen peoples had planted over 2000 coconut palms, paid the first levy of the head-tax willingly and welcomed home the prisoner Mamagal and the four women gaoled for a year for infanticide. Eight men from Malala village east of Hatzfeldthafen had come back from their first contract as police and were proving 'good supporters of the government'. Five communities on Manam Island now had *luluais*. To Berghausen it was a 'gratifying picture of progress' as Pidgin learners returned to their villages to become *luluais* and *tultuls*, forced labourers toiled at building the coast road, villagers paid tax, day labourers enlisted for local plantations and indentured labourers departed for plantations elsewhere in the colony.[15]

In the New Guinea islands the small settler used the copra trade as a springboard to investment in plantations. On the mainland he became a bird-of-paradise hunter or sent 'shoot-boys' into the jungle to hunt for him, profiting from the rapid rise in the European prices of the bird-of-paradise, crown dove, cassowary and heron after 1909. From that year, the first in which bird skins and plumes were exported to Europe to adorn women's hats, they were second only to copra as exports from the Old Protectorate, rising in value to 14 per cent of all exports in 1913. By Hahl's estimation, the bird trade financed fifteen plantation undertakings on the coast of Kaiser Wilhelmsland between 1909 and 1914.[16]

Hahl did not always avenge the violent deaths of white adventurers in remote country, but his general rule was to exact retribution for every murder of a white person, however much it was invited by the victim's foolhardiness. Otherwise, he feared, white prestige would suffer and the mastery of the Germans come under threat. The bird-of-paradise hunters greatly complicated the government's task of extending control because they penetrated further inland than district officers and frequently clashed with bush peoples, whom the government then thought it had to punish. Deep in the bush, with no knowledge of local languages and no reliable information, the German district officer was an easy target for villagers eager to manipulate the masters to their own advantage.

When a hunter called Richard was killed in the hinterland of the Herzog mountains in the Markham Valley region in January 1911, Berghausen took forty-six police from Morobe on a punitive expedition. A Buang man had brought the news of Richard's death, and on reaching the territory of the Buang on 31 January at a place called Busamang Berghausen received a warm welcome from men who were itching to deal a blow against their Wampar enemies:

> On 1 February we then advanced against the Wamba [Wampar] people, leaving all our packs behind. We were accompanied by over 400 Buang

people armed with spears, bows and arrows, wooden swords and shields. As we arrived in Wamba territory crowds of natives gathered in the villages and performed war dances. We advanced to a high mountain summit near the largest of the Wamba villages; there the Wamba people went directly into the attack against us from two sides, in long lines and behind shields the height of a man. They were thrown back and dispersed in a battle lasting almost three hours. The big Wamba village came under fire and was reduced to ashes. The Wamba people have perhaps 40 dead. The friendly Buang people joined in the battle ... Part of the bodies of the Wamba people were consumed by the Buang people in spite of my prohibition. I did not have the power to stop it in populated territory far from the coast.[17]

Best described as a Buang war party assisted by the police, the expedition against the Wampar saw Buangs and Germans making use of each other in achieving common political ends. The Buangs were delighted to have the police guns on their side and the Germans were willing to believe partisan information and exploit traditional rivalries in order to avenge the death of a white man who had strayed far beyond the German pale.

In the case of Peterson, a bird-of-paradise hunter killed in 1912 by villagers five days' march inland from Madang, the district officer admitted that the man had taken an 'imprudent risk' venturing so far from the coast. But principle demanded that the guilty be punished, and in June 1912 the police undertook a patrol far into the mountains, where they arrested the alleged murderers, burnt villages and killed at least five men. The effort strained the meagre resources of the district administration and District Officer Scholz suggested to Hahl that he restrict bird-hunting to within sixteen hours' march from the coast. A few weeks later, warriors on the upper Ramu proved Scholz's point by spearing to death the hunter Mikulicz, who had stayed behind in his tent while six of his seven 'shootboys' went in search of the brilliantly plumaged bird they called kumul.[18]

Soon afterwards came news that villagers of Kagam, Gorak and Aringer in the lower Ramu River region had killed more bird-of-paradise hunters, three Chinese and eleven New Guineans in all. Boroi and Kaian, places close to the mouth of the Ramu, also seemed implicated and Hahl decided that the Ramu would be a good testing ground for the new and untried expeditionary troop. Formed in 1911 as a mobile force of trained police to open up the country, the troop numbered 114 in August 1912 at the start of its four-month patrol inland from Hansa Bay to punish the murderers and bring the region under government influence. Hahl declared a state of war in the lower Ramu 'for the duration of military operations' and authorized the German captain in charge to sentence New Guineans to death without the usual governor's approval required by the native criminal code. By November 1912 the expeditionary troops had killed at least twenty people. Scores of men, women and children were taken prisoner and kept at the German camp at Kagam until released or transferred to Kokopo. Captain Prey sentenced sixteen people to three years' exile from their homes, recommending that they be given 'strict training and work', and a further two to five years' hard labour. A man called Isar was to serve

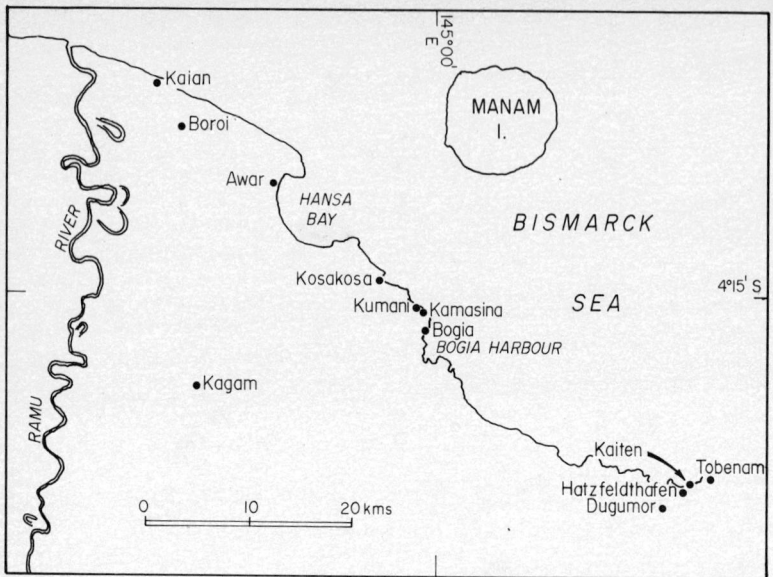

The coast from Tobenam to the mouth of the Ramu River, Kaiser Wilhelmsland

an additional five years for ignoring a German order to surrender arms. 'It is very remarkable how unbelievably suspicious all natives here are', wrote Prey:

> Not one word from me do they trust. I now have friendly communication with six places. But I have been able to force this situation only by seizing people, handcuffing them, taking them with me and sending them back with gifts. I had to resort to this means because I needed information at all costs.

Even on the coast, supposedly under control, the Germans' influence was limited. Villagers between Awar and the mouth of the Ramu, said to be head-hunters, refused to provide carriers and Prey vowed to punish and replace their *luluais* and *tultuls*. A few kilometres inland, in the sago swamps and lagoons on the eastern side of the Ramu, the Boroi people issued a challenge to Prey, warning him that if the police tried to reach the river islands they would be speared and thrown to the crocodiles. Prey and the police, expected to approach Boroi along the coast, took the overland route instead, killed five people and arrested others but were unable to find the rest of the Boroi population, who had fled deep into the swamps beyond the government's reach.[19]

Prey depicted the Ramu expedition as a success which confirmed the reports of bird-of-paradise hunters that the inland of Kaiser Wilhelmsland was densely populated and demonstrated its potential as a source of the

plantation labourers 'so urgently needed'.[20] With enough police, he thought,
the government could begin to open up the New Guinea mainland within
six months and complete the main part of the job within two or three years.
Prey spoke from ignorance. He had gone no further than forty kilometres
from the coast and knew nothing about the interior. But he expressed the
hope of Governor Hahl that the Ramu and Markham River valleys would
be the gateways by which the Germans would enter a populous hinterland
and replenish the labour supply. Before Hahl left New Guinea in April
1914 plans existed for government stations on the upper Markham and
middle Ramu, and a police post was established at Lae shortly before the
outbreak of World War I.

The Manus, Matankor and Usiai peoples of the Admiralty Islands, numbering about 13 000, maintained a fierce independence of the government
until the last years of German rule. Two Europeans were killed in 1900,
another in 1901 and the Hamilton Pearling Company's lugger *Corea* was
attacked in 1903. Three crew were killed together with the captain William
Howard, who ignored the advice of the sailor Tokalulu to 'look out good
Billy, plenty Kanaka he stop ship'.[21] Manus warriors on Big Ndrova Island
off the south-east tip of Manus Island sank another Hamilton boat, the
Wild Colonial, in January 1904, threw the crew overboard and took eighty
rifles as booty. Reporting on the naval expedition which followed, Commander Kirchhoff did not doubt that the:

> cruiser's longer stay, the destruction of many villages and of a great
> part of their canoe fleet, as well as the shooting of several of their
> people, have instilled in the natives, who all know the reasons for this
> action to punish them, with a salutary fear which will deter them for
> a while from crime against the life and property of the whites . . .[22]

Such gruff talk may have impressed Kaiser Wilhelm II, an avid reader
of naval reports, but it was self-delusion. The Admiralty Islanders were
far too absorbed in trading and fighting with each other to be impressed
by men-of-war. They treated the Germans as intruders who were to be
imitated, ignored, plundered or killed, not as men who deserved respect
or obedience. When canoes were destroyed, the Manus built new ones and
carved new alligator heads on the bowsprits. Along the north coast of Manus
Island, where each offshore people had their own trading partners in a
particular bush community, local trade at markets was far more important
to the islanders than trade with Europeans. If a European idea looked useful,
the islanders adopted it: after seeing the Hamilton Pearling Company's
copra drying shed at Komuli in the St Andrew group, one man returned
to his village and made a replica for himself; the people of Loniu on Los
Negros Island, possessing no guns, carved intricate wooden imitations
instead. But few islanders were attracted by the European idea of plantation
labour. As elsewhere in New Guinea, the Germans' interventions often
benefited one group of villagers at the expense of another. Complaints by
Matankor people on Baluan Island about a Manus pirate called Barbi on
Rambutyo led to the arrest of ten of Barbi's men in November 1907; and

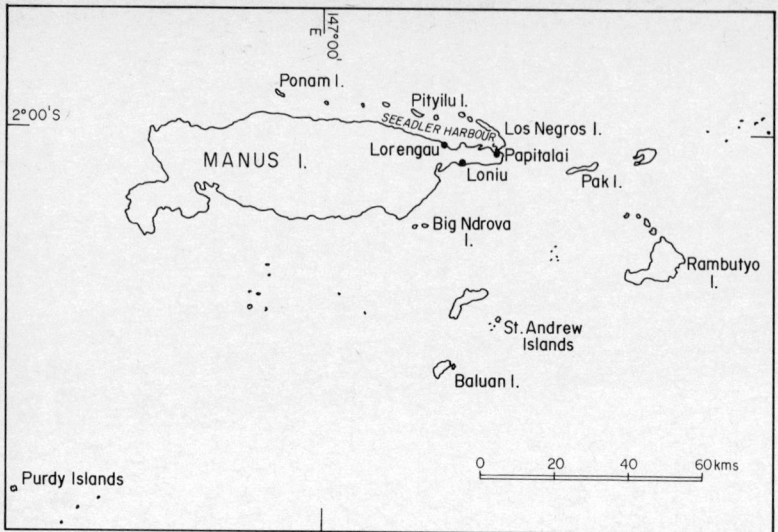

The Admiralty Islands

on Los Negros, where the Papitalai were a Manus people and the Loniu belonged to the Matankor, the protests of the Papitalai about the Loniu were so frequent that one district officer called them a 'constant item on the programme of native matters awaiting settlement in the Admiralty Islands'.[23]

Hernsheim & Co., with five trading posts and plantations in the group by 1909, were caught in the middle of the local conflicts. Their labourers ate sago, obtainable only through village trade, and the men sent to get it were Admiralty Islanders with guns in their hands. Unsurprisingly, the Hernsheim *saksak* trade did not proceed without violence and on one occasion Usiai warriors killed an entire boat's crew. The Japanese trader Komine Isokichi, then laying down a plantation for Hernsheims' on Ponam Island, barely escaped with his life in 1909 when inland people of Manus Island enticed him into the interior with the offer of selling him a signalling drum. Ambushed en route, he threw off his attackers with deft ju-jitsu and fled to his schooner on the coast. A punitive expedition into the mountains of the south-east, one of many undertaken by the Germans in the Admiralties since the coming of imperial rule, burnt down a village, shot pigs and encountered none of the enemy.

The Admiralty Islanders had begun to experiment with European wage labour from about 1907 onwards, and the Germans had managed to disarm a few communities. The guns which the Rambutyo Islanders surrendered to the Germans in 1909, all carefully lubricated with palm oil and in good condition, were booty from previous attacks on trading schooners. Like the Paparatava people of the Gazelle Peninsula in the troubles of 1902, the Rambutyo Islanders had adapted small-calibre revolver cartridges for use in rifles. Pak was the first of the Admiralty Islands to make peace when Sapon and Simio, appointed as *luluais* in 1909, persuaded their kinsmen to sell all weapons including obsidian spears to the local Chinese trader and to build a road. Flanked by ditches for drainage, this first Pak road was modelled on the roads which Sapon and Simio had seen on a visit to New Britain.[24]

The colonial budget had provided for a government station in the Admiralties as early as 1903 but the funds approved were inadequate and nothing further was done. As Hernsheims' plantations expanded and the colony grew shorter of labour, however, officials pressed Berlin more urgently for a station, the only guarantee of the peace which would allow recruiters into the villages and put an end to warfare between rival peoples. Instead of bringing the Admiralties under control, the *Reichstag* was told in 1911, visiting expeditions had driven the population inland and intensified resistance.[25] For its trade copra, plantation land and labourers the Admiralty group was finally occupied permanently by German government forces in October 1911, the new station of Manus at Seeadler Harbour having jurisdiction over the valuable Western Islands as well. Within two years the number of Admiralty Islanders signing on as labourers had risen from 320 to 823.

The New Guinean's purpose in the colonial state was to buy simple manufactures, toil as an indentured labourer and defray the cost of colonial administration. Hahl was determined to impose control on southern Bougainville inland from Buin, for example, for the sake of its 'numerous people (about 12-15 000) with their need for goods and potential to work and pay taxes'. After an unsuccessful expedition in 1913 a force of police and German marines landed at Buin in February 1914. A naval telegram told the familiar story of deaths, presumed deaths and fired villages typical of the German extension of control:

> Landing corps with government officer and Kieta police troop has carried out a six-day expedition. Demonstration in SW Bougainville and simultaneous punitive expedition, local feud suppressed. Three natives shot dead in reciprocal attack, allegedly another three as well. Two villages burnt down. No injuries to the troops, morale excellent.[26]

The Germans planned a police post for southern Bougainville in 1915.

On the Gazelle Peninsula of New Britain the Germans faced a unique situation. The Tolai, whose villages stood in the heart of the Old Protectorate's principal planting district and who had been directly ruled longer than any other New Guineans, managed to work proportionately less for the Europeans than villagers in many other controlled areas. Their cash income from trading as coconut producers and market gardeners gave them relative immunity from the pressure of the head-tax and the lure of plantation wages. Of 30 752 Tolai counted by the Germans in 1910 only 1095 adult men, a tenth of the adult male population, were working as indentured labourers or soldiers, and 763 of them were employed close to home in the Gazelle Peninsula or the Duke of York Islands. Others had entered into short contracts of a few months on local plantations. The increased head-taxes of that year were 'willingly paid' and in the whole Gazelle Peninsula there were only two cases of villagers having to commute the cash tax into work. When they worked for the colonizers the Tolai preferred to do so as servants, police, or skilled labourers rather than in the plantation lines.[27]

The Germans were too weak to impose the control which Hahl wanted. In 1914 the government postulated the existence in inland New Britain of 15 000 people who were still uncontacted by the Germans. Hahl asked in 1911, 1912 and, again, in 1913 for a doubling of police strength in the expeditionary troop. Berlin refused him on each occasion. Unable to penetrate new areas, the Germans were carrying out what Hahl called 'the most serious despoliation of the people in the opened and pacified regions', and in the last two years of German rule the government began to lose its grip on people who were supposed to be under its complete domination.[28]

'Lyssa jingle lurker lutation ability = scholz'. With this coded telegraphic message District Officer Scholz informed Berlin in September 1912 that 'unrest broken out in Friedrich Wilhelmshafen ringleaders caught peace restored without bloodshed'. It was the second conspiracy of the Madang peoples in eight years. The time chosen for the attack was the night after the visit of the steamer *Coblenz*, when all the whites would be sleeping off their heavy drinking, and the first target was to be the district office with its store of arms. Then all the whites, with the possible exception of the women, were to be killed. Such at least was the unsolicited evidence of the *tultul* Tagari of Bilbil, who said the plan was dropped after the Germans posted extra sentries in response to signs of unrest, but it was enough to cause the arrest of suspects, the despatch of a warship to Astrolabe Bay and wholesale deportations. The peoples of Siar, Biliau, Panutibun and Yabob, together with half the Kranket Islanders, were exiled to the Rai coast while the remaining Kranket people were sent north to Megiar on the mainland coast opposite Karkar Island. In the following year the number of recruits at Madang more than doubled, from 935 in 1912 to 1955 in 1913, and exiles were almost certainly among them.[29]

On New Hanover and New Ireland the Germans met 'unprecedented resistance': trouble from 'recalcitrant natives, mostly absconders and former labourers' and in the mountains of southern New Ireland an uprising of numerous villages threatening to attack plantations and kill planters. The Chinese small settlers on the west coast fled in boats to Rabaul. Soon afterwards, in December 1913, ninety-two police, fifty-one carriers and five European officers of the expeditionary troop marched through the disaffected villages. The rest of the Old Protectorate was left with local forces alone, a situation Hahl thought dangerous at a time when the pressure of labour recruiting was making unrest likely elsewhere. In appealing once again for more police and more European officers he pointed to southern New Britain, Manus, the Kieta district and mainland New Guinea as areas where similar conflicts could be expected as recruiters sought new men for the labour lines.[30]

Police were hard to get in the last years of German rule and district officers in Rabaul and Kavieng began conscripting a few village men for the police force. Hahl was so impressed by the fact that these demands went unchallenged that he proposed a general conscription measure by which all male villagers between the ages of sixteen and thirty would become liable to call-up for service as police on three-year indentures. His aim was to fill the ranks of the police without competing with the planters for labour. Indeed, planters could anticipate easier recruiting of men who did not want to be conscripted. The Colonial Office approved the conscription ordinance in September 1913.[31]

Control produced labourers for the colony, more and more of them. Recruiters signed on 8713 recruits in 1908 and 1909; 14 132 in 1910 and 1911; 19 093 in 1912 and 1913, a total of 41 938. Most came from the enumerated population of the Old Protectorate, numbering a mere 152 075 at the beginning of 1914, perhaps an eighth of the total population. Hundreds of thousands of villagers lived in the highlands of New Guinea in ignorance of the German presence. Every recruiting district listed by the Germans offered more labourers in 1913 than five years before: the Gazelle Peninsula, the rest of New Britain, the Witu Islands, southern New Ireland, northern New Ireland and the Nusa Strait, New Hanover, Emira and Mussau, the Western Islands, the Admiralty group, the islands east of New Ireland, Nissan, Pinipel, the Carterets and Mortlocks, Buka, Bougainville, Madang, Aitape and Morobe. By then 19 000 New Guineans were in some fixed relationship of service to Europeans. About 15 000 were labourers on plantations, 1500 were household servants (more than one for every European), 900 were on plantations in Samoa, 814 were police stationed in New Guinea and in the Carolines and Marshalls, 380 were government labourers, 300 worked in trade-stores, warehouses and so on, and 100 were boat's crew. A colonial society founded on the labour of a native underclass had been formed in New Guinea and was to be preserved in all its essential characteristics by the Australians.

Head-tax, Recruiting and the Work Experience

Governor Hahl proposed an annual tax of five marks for every able-bodied man in controlled areas in 1905, levied it for the first time in northern New Ireland and New Hanover in 1906 and issued a head-tax ordinance in 1907. Communities which paid tax were freed from forced labour. German experience in Africa was used as a guide: the Colonial Department added a clause to Hahl's draft ordinance enabling *luluais* to be paid up to a tenth of the returns, arguing that tax collection in German East Africa would be impossible without paying chiefs a proportion, and it vetoed Hahl's proposal to hire out tax defaulters as wage labourers until their debt was paid. In effect, Hahl was suggesting a form of forced labour for private employers. Such a scheme had failed in German East Africa, and so the

New Guinea ordinance was amended to allow tax defaulters to work off their tax by labouring for the government at a rate to be fixed by district officers: in 1910 the government itself fixed the rate at one mark for six days' work. Such defaulters had to pay the costs incurred when the government could recover the money only by force.[32]

Like poll taxes in other plantation colonies, the German head-tax in New Guinea was intended to swell the labour lines with men who had no alternative but to offer themselves as wage labourers, and a specific inducement was provided by freeing from tax any New Guinean employed for ten months of the fiscal year. Solving the labour question, a naval commander reported in 1907, depended on 'awakening the desire to work or creating a certain compulsion to work', a compulsion which he thought was being felt by New Guinea villagers who had to pay the head-tax. Hahl expected the head-tax to persuade villagers to sign more three-year labour indentures. Yet Hahl claimed to have been surprised by the actual effects of the tax: instead of going away to plantations the villager worked close to home for a few months as a day labourer and was eager 'not to earn the tax by working for the European in future, but to pay it from the proceeds of his increasing income from cultivation. The latter, so far as one can tell, has been more stimulated by the pressure of tax than by official directions and obligations to plant'. According to Hahl, the head-tax was encouraging the villager to become a cash cropper and day labourer, not a long-term indentured labourer.[33]

The effects of the head-tax differed from place to place, depending on people's access to money through trade. The villagers of Vunamami near Kokopo welcomed the tax because it replaced the hated roadwork, but the inland people of Tatavana, only a few kilometres away, possessed few coconut palms and in 1908 and 1909 they had to pay the tax by building the Barawon road for a month. The Sulka and Mengen people, immigrants from the south who had settled near St George's Channel, were also short of copra and worked in plantations to raise the tax-money, while in the Baining mountains villagers depended on selling taro or their own labour. Wealthier in coconut palms than their countrymen inland, the coastal Tolai paid the tax without difficulty, in the first year with all sorts of coins accumulated from past trading and thereafter in one-mark pieces, the currency of present income.[34]

The tax created pools of day labour in New Ireland and Bougainville. Hahl told the Colonial Office that 'an abundant selection' of day labourers were available in the Namatanai and Kieta districts 'in view of the tax payments of the natives'. At both places the Berlin finance group, W. Mertens & Co., which owned two plantation companies in Samoa, selected the first European plantation sites and was soon followed by other investors attracted by cheap labour. The Bismarck-Archipel-Gesellschaft explained to prospective shareholders that the Melanesians were cheaper to employ than almost all other workers in the tropics. Everything—recruitment wages, food—could be had for only fifty-eight *Pfennige* a day per head, and for even less in those parts of the archipelago where it was possible to employ local villagers on piece work or for the day. These already favourable conditions, said the company, had been improved by the head-tax which was inducing New Guineans to seek work with Europeans or make more copra.[35]

The Germans did not use the head-tax to create a labour force as crudely as the Australians were to do. When graduated rates of tax were introduced in 1910—five, seven and ten marks—the Germans distinguished between different communities' ability to pay. Of the people near Rabaul, for example, the district officer noted that they could afford to pay ten marks per man because they could so easily sell products to Europeans and take daily jobs with Norddeutscher Lloyd, whereas the Taulil, who were a day's journey from the nearest trading post and had raised less than half their tax in 1908, were to be freed from tax altogether and required to construct a bridle-path instead. For the Duke of York Islanders, who were not especially wealthy in land or coconut palms but did not have to maintain roads, the intermediate rate of seven marks was struck. Under Australian rule many villagers had to pay the maximum rate of ten shillings regardless of their economic circumstances. A lieutenant in the Australian Naval and Military Expeditionary Force at Kokopo in 1915 described the head-tax in this way: 'Every nigger pays a tax of 10/- per year which they have to be chased for, it seems rather like highway robbery but it is a German custom & of course we are supposed to be administering their laws'. In at least one instance the Germans used the head-tax directly (and illegally) as a way of compelling villagers to work for a planter: the Rabaul district officer told the *luluais* of Unea Island in the Witu group in 1913 that he expected punctual payment of the ten marks head-tax and that everyone who could not pay in cash would be assigned to two months' work on the NGC plantation nearby.[36]

A recruit from the Finschhafen area called Mojuc wrote to his brother Ngibatu in 1910:

> You know I left because the people in the village wanted to give me a wife. But I would like to see the wide world first before I marry and settle down.[37]

Motives such as this must have driven many other villagers to sign on for work as news of the Germans' presence placed village life in new perspective. Experience in the 'wide world' of the colonizers brought status to the labourer returning to his village, where as a Pidgin speaker he might be made a *luluai* or *tultul*. Much less certain is whether one of the main attractions of plantation work for many villagers was the prospect of never going hungry: plantation rations were meagre, but information on what people ate in the villages hardly exists. Obviously, many recruits signed indentures with their eyes on the trade-box which they would carry home three years later, and the Germans consistently used a display of largesse in recruiting.

Iron tools superior to those supplied by traders encouraged the first four recruits to leave the village of Leitere in western Kaiser Wilhelmsland in

1905. After three years so few young men remained in the village that its houses were falling into ruin. People in newly opened areas, like the New Irelanders in the day of the Queensland labour trade, had no conception that enlisting would mean absence from home for two or three years. To overcome suspicion, the NGC adopted the practice of sending the first recruits back after only a few months, laden with European goods. Where recruiting occurred peacefully the payment of a fee to the relatives of recruits was universal. The recruiter would arrive in the village, display his goods like a travelling salesman, inspect the young men and women offered, pick out the strongest and then pay for each according to the negotiated price in loincloths, shirts, matches, bangles, axes and knives. Advances were also paid to the recruits themselves. In many villages recruiters had to reckon with traditional preferences for a particular destination known and liked by the people, for Queen Emma's plantation at Ralum in New Britain, the Neu Guinea Compagnie's at Madang or the DHPG plantations in Samoa, for example.[38]

By the nature of the recruiting business the use of force and intimidation, though not as widespread as in the days of wholesale kidnapping, was inevitable. The big companies employed their own recruiters and professional self-employed recruiters received cash for every recruit delivered to an employer. The government paid eighty marks and other employers 100 marks per head. When the professional recruiters entered Kaiser Wilhelmsland in about 1908 a government official complained that they caused 'the most enraged confusion' in the villages, presumably because they employed more violent methods than the NGC recruiters with a permanent interest in the villagers' willingness to enlist. The recruiter who knocked out a man's front teeth in anger at getting no men was not exceptional, as shown by the ruthless recruiting of the Forsayth company and the DHPG in the last few years of German rule, when convictions for recruiting crimes increased. Nor was it anything but normal for armed black recruiters to be sent unaccompanied into inland villages while the whites waited in the boats or on the beach. As a New Guinean revealingly testified to the Kavieng district officer in a recruiting case, the 'other boys carried weapons as usual'. On some occasions New Guinean recruiters roamed the bush for months at a time.[39]

In a colony where the white man as government officer could walk into the village and tell the *luluai* he wanted twenty or thirty men for road-work immediately, the white man as private recruiter may have been seen by many people as possessing similar authority. For all the ingenuity which New Guinea villagers displayed in manipulating the Europeans for their own advantage, many village people undoubtedly felt themselves powerless against white demands. After Governor Hahl visited the Lutheran mission station at Sattelberg near Finschhafen about 1913, for example, he took a man called Lokicne back to Rabaul to take delivery of some goats for the mission, and then promptly forgot all about him. Lokicne wrote to his kinsfolk:

The Master Mahler came and said I was to work for him. As I did not know what I should do he signed me on and I am therefore here and nothing has happened about the goats . . . The whites say we Papuans are liars but they also lie themselves. I now have to pay for their lies by staying here three years.

A New Guinean hospital orderly in Kokopo wrote in 1914: 'My time was up and I wanted to return home. But Dr Steincke lengthened my time of service and so I have to stay . . .'[40]

Once on the plantation the new recruit was subject to an unfamiliar regimen of European work discipline, enforced by corporal punishment, fines and imprisonment. The shell-horn would sound at 5.30 a.m. to muster the labourers from their grass huts for the morning's work and again at 11 a.m. to signal a two-hour break in the heat of the day. Afternoon work was from 1 p.m. until dusk at 6 p.m., the stronger clearing land and collecting coconuts, the weaker cutting copra. The same hours applied to the more strenuous work on the roads. 'Disobedience' and mass desertions were commonest among recruits from districts with little previous experience of the Europeans.

The Germans flogged village men for misdemeanours which ranged from 'laziness and cheekiness', 'slovenliness' and 'loitering' to the more precisely defined offences of 'lighting a grass fire', 'pilfering food' and 'stealing coconuts'. Police, who were also indentured labourers, were sometimes flogged for having dirty rifles. The entries in the punishment book of the Rabaul government stables for a single day, 29 January 1913, show that the Germans took regular beating of labourers for granted:

> Wankili 15293, 15 strokes, because he left work for a long period and attended to his private affairs.
> Eweke 26905, 10 strokes, because, when admonished, he used insolent expressions
> Naringara 24383, 10 strokes because he did not do the work assigned to him . . .
> Omi 24286, confinement on three Sundays, because he left alone the workers given to him to supervise, went to another house and hid there. Omi did not obey the order to come out and did not open the door . . .[41]

When the Australians prohibited corporal punishment by private employers in 1915, German planters protested that

> as soon as the natives get aware of this change of the regulations, it will be impossible to keep up the absolutely necessary discipline among the labourers and the boys will neglect their work to such an extent that the lucrativeness of all plantations is questioned . . .

Employers, it was claimed, would lose all their authority 'if the labourers know that they are no more entitled to flog a boy'.[42] Most Germans in German New Guinea, Governor Hahl included, believed that whites had to flog blacks if they were to remain in command. (And many Australians in New Guinea would later take the same view.) Under the indenture system, the labourer was akin to the property of his employer for as long as his indenture lasted: it was illegal to employ escaped labourers and Europeans were required to hand them over to the authorities. The ten marks paid by an employer for each absconder captured by the police could be deducted from the absconder's wages, equivalent in value to six or eight weeks' work. The labourer who ran away from work in German New Guinea bore the cost of his own arrest.[43]

The New Guinean recruit's chances of surviving his years on a plantation in the Old Protectorate improved in the decade before the war. Whereas, for example, one in every eight indentured labourers had died under contract in the Gazelle Peninsula and the Duke of York Islands between 1887 and 1903, the official figure for 5100 labourers in the Gazelle Peninsula in 1910 and 1911 was fewer than one in forty deaths per year. Other plantation districts probably remained less healthy than this, however, and villagers who signed on were everywhere prey to epidemics. After severe outbreaks of dysentery, malaria and beriberi at Madang in 1907, attributed by Hahl to insufficient medical facilities for the labourers and bad drinking water, the Colonial Office requested the NGC to build another isolation room for dysentery patients and send a second medical assistant. In the Gazelle Peninsula hospitals of a primitive kind were run by the two largest private employers of labour, the NGC and E. E. Forsayth G.m.b.H. as well as by the government. Employers were supposed to pay for the medical treatment of labourers made sick through working and of those with venereal disease but otherwise their responsibilities ended after a labourer had been ill for six weeks, when he could be sacked. New recruits incapable of work were sent home at the employer's expense, either immediately or after medical care paid for by the government. As always in colonial New Guinea, a vast gap yawned between the theory of government regulations and the practice of men on the spot: technically only 'healthy' people who were 'adequately developed physically and not decrepit' were eligible for recruitment as labourers; in fact many recruiters took whomever they could get, including children and sick people, for the doctor at the labour office would frequently pass recruits as 'fit' simply because they had already come hundreds of kilometres from home.[44]

Hahl was a frustrated man in the last years of his governorship. Under attack from the *Reichstag* for failing to develop the colony quickly enough, he complained that no other German colony had had to pay for its own exploration and pacification, the pre-conditions of rapid development. In German South-West Africa 2500 German soldiers and 500 Africans were available to enforce German colonial supremacy; in German East Africa the Europeans commanded a force of 2500 African and Arab soldiers in addition to 2200 police; in German New Guinea no such *Schutztruppe* existed. Fewer than 600 police carried the government's guns in the Old Protectorate in 1913: fifty each at Rabaul, Kavieng, Namatanai, Manus, Aitape and Morobe, 120 at Madang, 120 in the expeditionary troop and seven at Kokopo. Many more were needed to guarantee government control but the *Reichstag* would not vote funds for them. Hahl did not fear a general uprising: split into numerous small groups, the New Guineans could not have organized one, and in any case many villages valued the Germans as allies, protectors and suppliers of European wealth. Yet the New Guineans' very diversity made the task of controlling them unexpectedly laborious for the Germans. Pacification, said Hahl, was only the beginning: 'much more difficult than suppressing the low standing tribes' was incorporating them into a system of government, teaching them 'regular work' and making them conscious of their duties towards the state. With some impatience, Hahl wondered whether a country as large and fertile as German New Guinea could depend for its development on 'half a million natives' whose capacity to survive 'under the pressure of the new conditions of life' was still an open question. He had no faith in the New Guineans as developers of their own land.[45]

In muted form, Hahl echoed the Social Darwinism which had become common in German colonial theorizing. On a trip to mainland New Guinea in 1890 the journalist Hugo Zöller gave typical expression to this way of thinking when he asked whether it was better for the New Guineans to die out or to be saved from extinction by working for the Germans under a system of forced labour which would add their efforts to the civilizing of New Guinea: 'world history showed that primitive peoples who did not roll with the wheel of their times were crushed by it'.[46] Hahl did not believe in such crude inevitabilities. Most of the time he was sure that, treated properly, the New Guinean population would survive colonization. He fought an endless battle with planters to secure that proper treatment. But in his view New Guinea did not belong to the New Guineans. Its ultimate destiny was to become a truly Asian colony of the German Empire, populated by millions of Asian peasants.

6

Depopulation and the Planters

Depopulation was the issue which divided Governor Hahl and the planters in German New Guinea. Hahl wanted colonization without genocide, believing that the New Guineans were more use alive than dead. They were an asset, worth preserving as labourers and trading partners, and need not disappear from the face of the earth so long as the colonial administration intervened to protect them. 'In fact', he wrote,

> there is for generations to come no more rewarding task than to bring about growth in the native population. Their cultural improvement must keep pace with it. But if training a people to be capable of buying goods seems a goal worth striving for in the island territory, for New Guinea it should be training a people to be a workforce. The means are to eliminate the blood feud and establish state order, suppress abortion, combat disease, impart simple school instruction, set up specialist schools at the headquarters of government stations. The assumption behind this is that the tribes are in fact capable of survival.[1]

Though they might survive, the New Guineans were too few to satisfy Hahl. In his vision of the future, German New Guinea was to become another Malay Peninsula, North Borneo or Fiji, home to Chinese, Tagalog, Malay and Indian peasants whose small-holdings would give the colony an economic competitiveness beyond the capabilities of the Melanesians. The Germans would be the 'educators, masters, colonisers' who would teach the Asians to be 'industrious New Guineans'. For a start the Asians might be encouraged to settle in southern New Ireland with its space for 'many tens of thousands', its 'pacified and organized' inhabitants and its fertile, well-watered lands suited to small farms. Hahl's concern for the survival of the New Guineans did not extend to a desire that they should remain the predominant population in the colony. They would not become extinct, but they would be at the bottom of an hierarchical society with Germans as the master class at the top and the Asians in the middle.[2]

Hahl's stand against depopulation was bound to anger planters because it entailed a series of measures which made labour more expensive and less easy to procure: prohibitions on recruiting certain classes of labour, women for example, and on recruiting anybody in districts deemed to be in danger of population decline; stricter labour legislation, including more nutritious and more expensive rations for workers on the plantations; the encouragement of village cash cropping, a threat to the labour recruiter because it put money in the hands of the villager at home; village improvement schemes financed with the proceeds of the head-tax; and official pressure on planters to import costly Asian indentured labour. The planters were to block some of these schemes, others they could only delay; but when Hahl left New Guinea in 1914 they agreed that his 'philanthropic ideas greatly checked the development of the possessions'.[3]

It is ironic that Hahl should have been castigated by German settlers for hindering development. Nothing mattered to him more than the economic progress of the colony. He was preoccupied by the problems of realizing New Guinea's potential in copra, timber, minerals, tobacco, rubber and jute, and tireless in efforts to attract capital investment by large concerns such as Norddeutscher Lloyd. In a ten-year programme for German New Guinea, prepared for Berlin in 1907, Hahl stressed that New Guinea had wealth waiting to be unlocked, and called for better shipping, small railways in the Gazelle Peninsula and northern New Ireland, a radio link between New Britain and Yap in the Carolines, an agricultural experimental service based on the Botanic Gardens at Rabaul and a programme of geological exploration. He could write of New Guinea:

> The country exhibits an abundance of fertile soil with high rainfall and a good supply of water. But the population is sparse, of inferior quality and diminishing; malaria and dysentery are present everywhere; high freight rates have to be paid in accordance with the great distance from commercial entrepots.[4]

For Hahl the New Guinean people were a resource, like land or rainfall, a resource of 'inferior quality' but not to be wasted carelessly. He was a labour-conservationist. 'The administration's endeavour', said the New Guinea budget proposal to the *Reichstag* in 1911, 'must be directed towards maintaining for the protectorate the basis of all economic development: its labour force, that is, its native population', an objective which could be reached by attacking those diseases causing population decline.[5]

Like most of his contemporaries, Hahl did not doubt that villagers were sickening and dying under the impact of Western disease and new styles of life. The evidence appeared overwhelming. Demographers now know that the decline in Pacific Island populations, where it occurred at all, was rarely as severe as Europeans imagined at the time. In societies where women and children frequently fled into the bush at the approach of Europeans, census takers could be misled into underestimating the number of inhabitants and producing spuriously exact statistics revealing the depopulation which they expected to find. German censuses in New Guinea were no exception and must have been considerably distorted by the fact that the district officer who came to count people also came to collect tax. Hahl thought the New Irelanders were declining in numbers, for example, and told settlers in 1903 that recruiting results were poor in New Ireland because no more people were left to offer. Women, for whom New Ireland was especially prized by settlers, were thought to be leaving the villages so rapidly that the fertility of the population was endangered. New Ireland's villages might well have been home to fewer people in 1914 than in 1884—the evidence is uncertain—but any fall in population was probably less than Hahl feared. Yet in the case of the atoll dwellers on the western and eastern fringes of the protectorate, Hahl was not chasing a phantom in his efforts to stop depopulation. In the Polynesian outliers of German New Guinea, in Ontong Java (German to 1900 and British thereafter) and in the Western Islands of the Bismarck Archipelago populations indisputably decreased. Hahl understandably assumed that, unless he took action, other parts of the colony might also be drained of inhabitants and potential labourers.

Wuvulu and Aua are coral atolls forming the most westerly extrusions of a submerged plateau stretching from the Admiralty Islands. Their inhabitants, like atoll dwellers elsewhere in New Guinea, paid a heavy price for living on unusually fertile islands, thick with the palms which attracted traders, and for having been isolated from the diseases of Europe and Melanesia. The Wuvulu and Aua spoke the same language, traded goods and exchanged wives with each other, and cultivated taro in ways which reminded visitors of the Gilbertese and the Ponapeans. They looked like Micronesians, built houses with planks as Micronesians did and obeyed the orders of high chiefs. Remarkably, they were free of malaria until the end of the nineteenth century.

For years Europeans encountered a hostile reception on the two atolls. Wuvulu people refused to go with Ludwig Kärnbach when he came to recruit for the NGC in 1893, they killed a trader called Schielkopf who landed with some Buka men to establish a post for Hernsheims' in 1896 and, by massing on the beach with spears and clubs, they prevented two more traders from coming ashore in 1899. Finally the islanders of the nearby Ninigo group, whose chief Hallokonin knew the Wuvulu, persuaded them to accept the presence of the trader Louis Voaden in 1900. Labourers from Aitape probably were the carriers of the malaria which now spread swiftly through the Wuvulu population, transmitted by the anopheles mosquitoes which abounded on the island. 'Slender, powerful, beautiful people', a German anthropologist wrote, 'became gaunt, hollow-cheeked, sick people with fat distended stomachs, suffering from anaemia and with swollen spleens like enlarged navels'. Great villages were reduced to a few miserable houses. Perhaps 500 people died in an unidentified epidemic about 1902, and the Wuvulu population shrank from over 1000 to under 600 by 1906.[6]

A more extraordinary fate befell the Aua. They too distrusted the foreigners and took to arms when two Hernsheim traders settled on Aua in 1903. An uneasy peace made between the two sides disappeared after the trader Otto Reimers flogged Tallemanu, the son of the high chief Wunia. As he lay dying in February 1904, Wunia resolved that the white man should die too and commanded his people to perform the killing. Standing unarmed on the verandah of his house to buy copra, Reimers

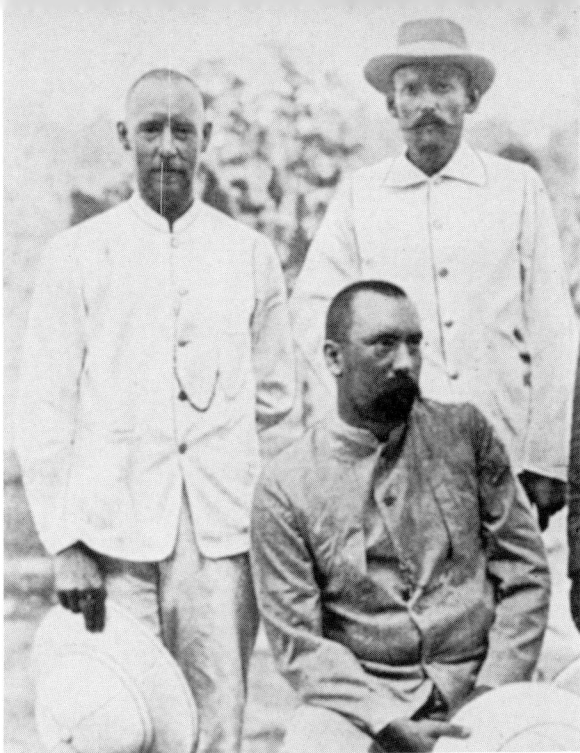

The Ramu Expedition, 1899: standing, left to right: Hans
Klink (first *kiap* at Morobe), Hans Rodatz (first *kiap* at
Aitape); seated: Karl Lauterbach (botanist, leader)

The Police Troop at Madang, about 1910

An ocean-going canoe, Ali Island, in the early 1890s

The German light cruiser *Cormoran* of 1600 tonnes, a steam-sail vessel in New Guinea waters from about 1901 until 1914

was grabbed from behind, speared to death and dismembered. The people of the Baraavu district of Aua, who were responsible for the murder, now feared retribution from the government and on seeing a schooner sailing towards the island a few weeks later, they fled across the water in the direction of Ninigo. They took a grave risk because their canoes, unlike the large sailing outriggers of the Ninigo people, were ill-adapted to rough seas. A storm blew up, many canoes sank and about 370 men, women and children drowned. In that single catastrophe probably two in every five Aua died. Governor Hahl arrested the man who was supposed to have thrown the fatal spear in July 1904 but took no further action against the Aua 'since the core of the people had perished at sea'. Perhaps as many as 1000 strong at the turn of the century, the Aua numbered fewer than 500 in 1906.[7]

As people died in the Western Islands the small atoll archipelago became one of the richest sources of copra in New Guinea, a personal fiefdom of the Hamburg adventurer Heinrich Rudoph Wahlen, who left Hernsheim & Co. in 1903 to become a trader on his own account. Wahlen acquired the entire Ninigo group of islands, fifty-six in all, as well as much of the Hermit Group, and the government did not hesitate to confirm his occupation of a further 1000 hectares of Aua and Wuvulu in 1906, more than half the area of those atolls, in view of the 'quite extraordinary decline in the population' and the 'not inconsiderable stocks of coconut palms which the natives do not need for their subsistence'. Acting Governor Krauss thought plantations would be good for the sickly Wuvulu people because marshy land would have to be drained before planting.[8]

Wahlen grew rich from the palms left by a declining population. In the Hermits he built an imposing two-storey house on the highest point of the island of Maron, eighty metres above sea level. From its verandahs he looked down to his labourers' huts on the beach and across the water to the palm-covered islets which formed the ring of the atoll. He installed an underground water tank, lit his house with electricity and furnished it with the memorabilia of his world trips. It all showed what 'German industriousness and German sense of order and beauty' could create from the wilderness, wrote Paul Ebert, commander of S.M.S. *Cormoran*.[9] While his Western Islands enterprise grew to rank with Hernsheim & Co. in size, Wahlen extended his plantation interests throughout the Bismarck Archipelago by becoming a major shareholder in E. E. Forsayth G.m.b.H. after it was sold by Queen Emma and, from 1911, its managing director in the colony. As the master and monopolist of the Western Islands, Wahlen was the direct beneficiary of depopulation, the man who took what the dead left behind, and he became a fierce opponent of Governor Hahl's efforts to prevent the New Guineans from dying out.

Like the people of the Western Islands, the Polynesians of Nuguria, the Tasmans and Mortlocks in the east of the colony declined in numbers under German rule. The Nuguria population, reduced by half to about ninety persons in the influenza epidemic of 1892, fell to perhaps fifty after 1900. The Tasman Islands, bought by Queen Emma in 1886, supported a population of between 200 and 300 at the turn of the century, but when the Germans gave the cap and stick of the *luluai* to Wialli in 1906 the count finished short of 100. Not long before, thirty Tasman Islanders died from an epidemic said to be carried by the local trader's Melanesian labourers. The home of the Mortlock Islanders was also acquired by Queen Emma in the 1880s at a time when they were more than sixty strong; photographed by Richard Parkinson in about 1905, the surviving islanders were no more numerous than a large family, consisting of six women, six men and five children. At least in the atolls, the depopulation predicted by Hahl was actually taking place.[10]

The Asian Solution

Fear and ambition lay behind Hahl's advocacy of Asian immigration. He was afraid that the villagers of New Guinea would waste away unless Asian indentured labourers relieved 'exhausted recruiting areas' and he aspired to initiate colonization in New Guinea on a scale which would do justice to Germany's international importance. Deeply impressed by the size and sophistication of the Dutch East Indies, he spoke of 'only ten thousand people' as the basis for a new, Asian future in Germany's Melanesian possession.[11] For a start, he tried to attract skilled Asian tradesmen to German New Guinea. Under a scheme instituted in 1901, tailors, shoemakers, barbers and carpenters were offered low taxes, peasant cultivators received small plots of land on lease and poor labourers travelled free on condition that they repaid the fare either in cash or labour. A minor scandal interrupted the scheme in 1902, when the Germans flogged ten Chinese tradesmen from Singapore who refused to work on a Sunday. At the suggestion of the German consul in Singapore, who could think of no other way of circumventing British objections to the migration of indentured labourers to German New Guinea, the Chinese had been illegally recruited, being taken on board a German merchant vessel as temporary 'crew'. Questioned by the British authorities, the German consul lied, claiming that he thought the tradesmen were free emigrants. The Germans acted quickly to forestall international criticism by abolishing flogging of Chinese in January 1903, so that when the German consul finally apologized to the British for the incident nearly a year later, he was able to refer to this change in the law of German New Guinea, adding that the magistrate who ordered the punishment had been reproved for his 'grave error in judgement'. Hahl, a man who believed that the lazy labourer deserved a good beating with the stick, reserved the right to restore corporal punishment of Chinese in the future.[12]

Hahl imposed few restrictions on the Chinese, numbering scores rather than hundreds, who continued to reach New Guinea as indentured labourers and free emigrants. He was convinced that mass Chinese migration would come once employers imported large numbers of Chinese labourers: free settlers would follow their indentured countrymen. Hahl repeatedly implored plantation firms to introduce Asians on indenture, and just as often they ignored him, baulking at the expense. Attempts to settle

Malays in western Kaiser Wilhelmsland failed, but by 1914 thirty-two Chinese had taken advantage of Hahl's leasehold scheme and become planters on modest plots of land. Chinese free emigrants came and went from New Guinea in a constant stream, earning money as carpenters, blacksmiths, tailors, shoemakers, saddlers, mechanics, cooks and servants and on board coastal vessels as stewards, stokers and engineers. The Rabaul Chinese quarter, a few streets of simple trade-stores, owed its foundation to an arrangement between Governor Hahl and Ah Tam, a shipwright and merchant who had lived in the Gazelle Peninsula since the 1880s. Ah Tam was permitted to employ three Japanese prostitutes in his drinking saloon at Matupit in 1904 on condition that the girls submit to regular medical examinations, Hahl having decided that suppressing prostitution was impracticable. A few years later Hahl granted him a lease of land at Rabaul, in return for which he undertook to import Chinese men as 'carpenters, cooks and coolies' and Chinese women as wives. Unless their jobs took them elsewhere in New Guinea, all Chinese were supposed to live in Rabaul's Chinatown. Free labourers often graduated from working on the Rabaul wharves to positions as trading agents and traders on their own account, and by 1914 fewer than one in seven of 1377 Chinese in the Old Protectorate were labourers. Among the remaining 'non-native coloured population' of about 350 the main groups were Malays (163), working as police, overseers, servants, clerks and bird-of-paradise hunters, and Japanese (about 100) who appear to have been skilled tradesmen, overseers and labourers.[13]

However, New Guinea did not become a favourite destination for Chinese emigrants after the founding of Chinatown, as Hahl hoped, and did not benefit from Germany's negotiations with China and the Netherlands over the coolie question. Germany was a newcomer to the vast Asian labour market and, unlike France, Britain and the Netherlands, it had no treaty with China governing the emigration and employment of Chinese in colonial territories. The Chinese authorities preferred to delay the signing of a treaty with Germany indefinitely because they were then able to negotiate separately over each recruitment of coolies for the German colonies in the Pacific and to extract concessions on each occasion. The Sino-German treaty talks which began in 1909 were never successfully concluded. Whether or not a treaty existed, Chinese indentured labourers would not have flocked to New Guinea, but Hahl resented the fact that Berlin made no special effort to woo the Chinese. As Colonial Secretary from 1911, Wilhelm Solf, former governor of German Samoa, wanted to keep the legal status of Chinese in New Guinea as a bargaining counter which he could produce at the right moment in order to persuade China to allow more coolies into the Samoan plantations. When China demanded a special concession, he would promote the Chinese in New Guinea from 'natives' to 'Europeans' in the eyes of the law. Clever as this stratagem might have seemed to the Colonial Secretary, however, to Hahl it looked as if his old rival from the Pacific was playing with New Guinea's economic progress at a time when the colony needed immediate mass immigration.

The Berlin view prevailed over Hahl's protests and Chinese remained 'natives' until the Australian occupation.[14]

The flow of Indonesians to German Pacific possessions dried up in 1900. The Dutch were happy to let their colonial subjects go to French Indo-China, New Caledonia and British North Borneo but consistently refused German requests for labour. Hahl hoped to see Javanese joining Chinese in that relief army of labourers who would solve the planters' labour problems at the same time as they saved the New Guinean villages from excessive recruiting and depopulation. In the long run even the plentiful flow of labour from the inland areas of New Britain and mainland New Guinea would not be enough, he told Berlin in 1913, and the colonial administration had a duty to provide a substitute which would allow people in pacified areas to be unyoked from their work burden and improved in health and civilization. The sentiments were fine, but could not create the substitute labour force Hahl wanted. The Dutch rejected an application for 1000 coolies to work for E. E. Forsayth G.m.b.H. in 1913 and when the German government complained to the Hague, they put an end to years of negotiations by stating flatly that no coolies from their territories were to go to German colonies in the Pacific. Long after leaving New Guinea Hahl continued to believe that, with its 'dwindling native population', the colony could not do without the immigration and settlement of people 'accustomed to the tropics and eager to work' no matter where they came from. For the failure of his Asian solution he blamed the influence of the White Australia policy on settlers in German New Guinea.[15]

The Politics of Colonial Policy

By giving the villagers enough land to live on, by restraining labour recruiters and by extending government control Hahl sought to husband the apparently disappearing resource of people in New Guinea. Beyond that, he planned to check the ravages of disease and revitalize village society by sending doctors, agricultural extension officers and teachers into the villages. To succeed, he needed money and a measure of support from settlers, neither of which was forthcoming in useful amounts. Settler opposition and a parsimonious metropolis would combine to render much of his population policy a dead letter.

The bitterest conflicts between the colonizers and the colonized in German New Guinea were fought over the spread of plantations, yet Hahl did not believe that New Guinea villagers were short of land. He could see no 'land problem in the sense of land scarcity or difficult legal regulation'. The village population was small, 'a rich selection of fertile land' was therefore available for settlers and his task was to keep a balance between the legitimate interests of villagers and settlers. On the one hand, villagers needed sufficient land to propagate themselves and be 'fit for work'; on the other, land for plantations had to pass into European ownership as freehold property 'in order to guarantee the possibility of mortgage credit' and attract capital to an isolated tropical colony. His experiences in the Gazelle Peninsula in the 1890s had taught Hahl the political necessity of creating native land reserves in cases where villagers felt threatened by expanding plantations, and he proceeded to set aside numerous reserves in the colony's plantation districts. He even persuaded the German government to enact an expropriation ordinance for the German colonies in 1903, giving the authorities the right to repossess native land in European hands. The ordinance was emasculated after protests by the German Colonial Society, and so Hahl relied on a series of local regulations to give him the power to authorize European land acquisitions and delineate reserves. In areas such as the Duke of York Islands, where village land was scarce, the administration refused to approve European purchases and on one occasion sentenced a German planter to gaol for a day for altering the borders of his property in an attempt to defraud local landowners. Where land was deemed to be plentiful, as in many other parts of the colony, planters were encouraged to buy.[16]

Official information for prospective investors in 1912 stressed the abundance of land for European occupation, and spoke of 'large tracts of uncultivated land available in almost any part of the colony'. In theory, a planter had to abide by strict improvement conditions. He had to prove he had capital of 20 000 marks for every 100 hectares of land purchased and to start cultivating within one year of taking possession, bringing three-quarters of the area under cultivation within fifteen years.[17] In theory, too, reserves were supposed to include one hectare per person. What mattered in practice, however, was the speed of surveying. German New Guinea's surveyors were chronically slow and, as the settler community grew, planters often became squatters on land to which they had no legal rights. Confident that the legal transfer of their properties would not take place for years to come, many planters cleared and cultivated two or three times the area to which they were entitled. Land speculation was not the problem. At a time of high copra prices planters were keen to improve their estates. The problem which the Germans left the Australians to solve was rather one of squatting on unsurveyed land.[18]

The threat to the New Guineans' survival came not from their loss of land, Hahl thought, but from excessive labour recruiting. He wanted to control recruiting, 'close particularly exhausted regions', open new districts to the recruiters, guard workers' health, spread the burden of toil widely over the population and improve working conditions. Settlers objected from the beginning. At a meeting with settlers at the hotel 'Zum Fürsten Bismarck' in Kokopo in June 1903 Hahl suggested that more men would sign on and fewer escape if employers treated them humanely. Planters and traders favoured force and punishment. The representative of Octave Mouton & Co. demanded to know how the government proposed to stop workers from deserting, called for Sunday work as a punishment for 'continual laziness' and wanted disciplinary authority over labourers extended to all employers. Hahl replied that desertions were so frequent that a great part of the Protectorate's armed forces would have to be employed chasing deserters if the government assumed responsibility in the matter. As for punishment, he was against giving illiterate traders or runaway sailors the right to flog New Guineans and insisted that, unless an employer was properly authorized to impose penal sanctions, he should bring every case to the authorities. This was wishful thinking on Hahl's part: one settler remarked that hardly a planter or trader in the colony would not be guilty of having struck his labourers. For difficulty in getting labour, settlers and officials blamed each other. Recruiters from New Britain could not persuade Buka and Bougainville men to sign on, according to leading settlers, because the villagers feared the government doctor in Kokopo: the Buka bore a grudge for the operations previously performed by the NGC doctor, especially those for venereal disease involving circumcision and scarring of the genital organs. The government doctor disagreed: the Buka did not want to come because of the dysentery rife in Matupit and the working of labourers on Sundays. He appealed to employers to consider the climate when recruiting. People brought from malaria-free areas died 'like flies' and their deaths hindered recruiting more than circumcision.[19]

The settlers were a force which Hahl could not ignore. They founded a Bismarck Archipelago branch of the German Colonial Society in 1903 in order to 'further colonial interests' and a Planters' Association, representing independent planters, in the following year.[20] Meanwhile Hahl was required by imperial statute to convene a Government Council, consisting of the governor as chairman, four officials and five unofficials. The Council's powers were only advisory but, by providing a public platform for the large trading and plantation companies, it exercised considerable influence over Hahl, who preferred not to act against concerted opposition from settlers. Employers were able to use the Council to modify and delay regulations likely to increase the cost of labour, a constant source of dispute, and they clashed repeatedly with Hahl in their efforts to prevent labour reforms.

The long dispute over labour reforms first centred on the issue of recruiting women from New Ireland. During 1906 settlers on the Government Council twice opposed an official proposal that recruiters be prohibited from signing on women in northern and central New Ireland, arguing that it would impede the flow of labourers from the villages and fail to achieve its purpose of adding to the population. The Council resolved merely to make inquiries. In 1907 the Council adopted a suggestion of the Planters' Association that labour contracts should have a normal minimum length of three years. Hahl protested against coercing labourers but yielded to the planters nevertheless by proclaiming three years, neither more nor less, as the period which the government would normally approve for the 'initial recruitment of a native'. This was done, the Colonial Office noted, 'in the interest of the employers, who are not to be expected to pay the high costs of recruiting when people are bound for too short a time'.[21]

Working through the Government Council and the Colonial Office, settlers then forced changes in Hahl's proposed new labour ordinance and delayed its promulgation for a year. The Council was against giving the government the right to inspect plantations and permit contracts shorter than three years, and objected strongly to planned increases in recruiting fees, a doubling from five to ten marks for every labourer recruited 'overseas' and a new charge of one mark for each year worked by a labourer recruited 'overland'. In resisting higher fees the six unofficial members of the Council were joined by the Bismarck Archipelago branch of the German Colonial Society and by the NGC's directors in Berlin, who sent a representative to the Colonial Office in the Wilhelmstrasse to complain personally. The NGC wanted to raise extra capital, said the Company man, and if recruiting fees went up investors would hardly get the impression that the government was prepared to spring to the Company's aid. A few years before, the colonial bureaucrats in Berlin had overridden Hahl to guarantee the NGC a monopoly of labour on the mainland. Now again they did what the Company said, and told Hahl not to burden the plantation firms. Except for the minor fee for overland recruits, no increases were made.[22]

With or without the fees, Hahl's administration faced a financial crisis in 1908. The times of generous imperial grants for the colony had gone, destroyed by the colonial scandals of 1906 and the reconstruction of German colonial administration along lines of efficiency. Bernhard Dernburg had been chosen as Colonial Secretary, in charge of the new Colonial Office, for his ability to economize in running Germany's overseas possessions, and he lived up to his reputation. It was obvious, he told the *Reichstag* in 1908, that for as long as the *Reich* cared for the colonies like a good father, governors would have no desire to seek revenue elsewhere; they would depend on the *Reichstag* and the Colonial Office instead, and that was not in the interest of 'thrifty, self-confident management'.[23]

Of all the German colonies in Africa and the Pacific, German New Guinea depended most on imperial subsidies and therefore stood to lose most from Dernburg's 'era of reform'. Dernburg proceeded to change the financial administration of the German colonies so that they would become increasingly self-supporting. German Togo already paid for itself, and from 1909 Samoa, East Africa, South-West Africa and Cameroun were made to follow suit. For Samoa financial independence was no burden because its mature plantation economy generated lucrative revenues from customs duties and poll taxes. In the case of the African colonies, what Dernburg took away with one hand he gave back with the other. A new law of 1908 permitted colonies to raise loans in their own right for 'extraordinary purposes', meaning long-term capital works, especially railway construction. A railway boom followed as the *Reichstag* approved vastly increased loan expenditure in the years to the war, a total of 282 million marks altogether. Even tiny Togo, with a population smaller than New Guinea's, received over eleven million marks in loans for railways and roads, and in German Cameroun the German government secured both interest and amortization payments on the colony's public debt. In German East Africa loan income in 1914 was 50 per cent higher than ordinary revenue. A few per cent of the money which banks lent to the African colonies would have fulfilled Hahl's dreams for New Guinea, but Melanesia was not railway country, and no one would lend money for purposes such as exploration, pacification and medical services. East Africa, South-West Africa and Cameroun also benefited from having separate military budgets, which the *Reich* either paid in full or generously subsidized. Not a single mark was lent to New Guinea, and it had no military budgets, paying its expensive military bills from the same budget which provided for all the other responsibilities of the administration. Nor was there a New Guinea lobby in the *Reichstag*, like that for German East Africa, clamouring for more expenditure. As the Colonial Secretary Wilhelm Solf was to admit in 1912, New Guinea was the Cinderella colony.[24]

In July 1908, without warning, Hahl imposed export duties on copra, trepang, turtleshell and bird hides and feathers, doubled the import duty on spirits and introduced a general *ad valorem* tax on all imports. The settlers were appalled. Planters and traders found the new impost of ten marks on every tonne of copra especially obnoxious, and the unofficial majority of the Government Council resigned in protest in February 1909. Unpopular with the settlers, Hahl was equally under siege from the *Reichstag*. Members of the Budget Commission of the *Reichstag* vied with each other to show how savings could be made on Hahl's administration and two even asked Dernburg what the government steamer *Seestern* was used for. The Centre Party tied the New Guinea budget to the question of imperial subsidies for Norddeutscher Lloyd, refusing to vote for more money to go to the shipping company unless New Guinea 'made sacrifices'. In negotiations between the Budget Commission and the Colonial Office a deal was agreed. The New Guinea budget lost 15 per cent of its proposed allocation of 1 064 835 marks, the Centre Party ensured that the shipping subsidy bill passed and Norddeutscher Lloyd could look forward to receiving 700 000 marks a year for its New Guinea service instead of 275 000. At the same time the German government required Norddeutscher Lloyd to guarantee cheap freight rates for New Guinea copra bound for Europe, not more than fifty-five marks a tonne.[25]

Hahl's government had to sustain successive falls in the imperial subsidy, from 1 159 000 marks for the Old Protectorate in 1906 to 759 000 marks for the whole colony of German New Guinea, including the Island Territory in Micronesia, in 1911. Phosphate revenues from the new mines at Nauru and Angaur helped a little. The *Reichstag* transferred 62 000 marks from the Island Territory to the Old Protectorate in the budget of 1909 and from 1910 the budgets of the two parts of the colony were treated as one in order to boost New Guinea's revenue. But the administration's income for the whole colony was scarcely more in 1911 than five years before. Hahl lacked money for everything. He could not afford control, far less schemes to forestall depopulation.

The effect of financial stringency in New Guinea was that Hahl could proceed, as far as funds allowed, with the politically acceptable elements of his colonial policy, extending control and opening new districts to labour recruiters, while having to delay, emasculate or abandon plans to protect villagers from the deleterious effects of colonization. He was caught between *Reichstag* and settlers. Eager to discuss issues such as the threatened extinction of the bird-of-paradise, most *Reichstag* deputies had no understanding of Hahl's concern to preserve the New Guinean people and no desire to spend money on New Guinea until it was too late. As for the settlers, it was to them that Hahl had to turn for the extra marks he needed, men who were determined to make New Guinea a colony where the black man would not be spared in serving the whites.

While the *Reichstag* cut funds Hahl struggled against the settlers to put the 1909 labour ordinance on the statute book. Not for the last time in colonial Papua New Guinea, rations were especially contentious. Abuses were rife. The NGC used the legal minimum rations for recruits on board ship, when they were at rest, as the exact measure of how much to give labourers working ten hours a day on the plantations, with the result that labourers were often taken to hospital suffering from malnutrition. The protein diet of many workers came in the form of salted fish imported in sacks from Hong Kong and stored in hot, corrugated iron sheds or as barrels of indigestible meat in brine with bones and fat.[26]

A comparatively generous plantation firm, Queen Emma's E. E. Forsayth & Co., gave each labourer one and a half lbs (680 grams) of rice or six lbs of fruit and vegetables a day plus one lb (454 grams) of fish or meat a week, either fresh or imported. The problem was that no law existed to stipulate rations on plantations. On the basis of medical evidence Hahl proposed to increase rations to 750 grams of rice a day and the same amount of fish or meat a week, and to oblige employers to give the food to labourers on plantations as well as on the recruiting vessels. E. E. Forsayth & Co. objected with a string of arguments which must have been wearily familiar to Hahl: costs would rise; few labourers even in Germany would have 750 grams of meat a week; every planter found it was in his own interest to feed labourers well; labourers could complain about bad food if they wished and planters be charged with breach of contract; Forsayth & Co.'s labourers had free fruit to eat and bought pigs from local villagers; too much meat was no good for labourers anyway because it made their cuts and sores heal slowly. The Bismarck-Archipel-Gesellschaft estimated that the cost of feeding their 400 labourers would rise by 41 per cent and total business expenses for the current year by 15 per cent. Hahl relented a little under this pressure by fixing the final rice ration at 625 instead of 750 grams but he refused to reduce the meat ration even after representations by the head office of the Bismarck-Archipel-Gesellschaft in Berlin induced the Colonial Office to order a further inquiry. This time the investigating doctor, Dr Born, concluded that the new rations were themselves far too little and that a labourer of fifty-five kilograms, an average New Guinean weight, needed 760 grams of rice and 150 grams of meat a day to remain properly nourished while doing moderately energetic work. Even if he ate meat only on the days he worked the labourer thus required 900 instead of 750 grams a week. It was under-nourishment, Born said, which created the 'alarming lack of resistance of many plantation workers to various diseases like dysentery and pneumonia' and he reported hearing visiting doctors express astonishment and anger at the famished appearance of many labourers. Born's recommendation went with Hahl's approval to Berlin, but the Colonial Office did nothing more than inform the Bismarck-Archipel-Gesellschaft. Rations were not increased as a result, and remained at the 1909 level until the end of German rule. Each labourer was also to get eighteen grams of tobacco, a clay-pipe and twenty-five grams of soap once a week, a loincloth every month, a blanket, and an eating bowl, the cost of all of which could be taken from the labourer's wages. Except for the tobacco and pipe these were all new requirements. German New Guinea was no paradise for the indentured labourer before or after 1909. The meat ration, for example, was a quarter of that which Queensland employers had been required to give Pacific Islanders in the days of the Queensland labour trade.[27]

Hahl won minor victories over the employers in the 1909 labour legislation. The law now offered minimal protection to the labourer on the plantation by prescribing what he should be given to eat and by allowing officials to inspect plantations. For the first time regulations governed the employment of men who, after signing indentures, travelled from home on land rather than on board a recruiting vessel. Administration officials could now act on complaints made by labourers. Previously only employers' grievances had been dealt with on the spot, while dissatisfied labourers had been referred to the district courts, which for many of them were hundreds of kilometres away. Hahl thought reform vital: more labourers were working in outlying areas and posed a potential threat of unrest. Once again settlers in the newly reconstructed Government Council objected to reform, predicting a flood of workers' complaints unless the employer was by the official's side as he walked along the labour line. That confident Christian, the Methodist missionary Heinrich Fellmann, backed the employers, pointing out that New Guineans should get used to expressing themselves freely and openly and, as finally worded, the government's instructions to plantation inspectors insisted that inspections should at least begin in the presence of the employer.[28]

Having made concessions over working conditions, Hahl was now forced to compromise over selective recruiting, a policy which he regarded as vital if the population were to be preserved as a workforce for the future. By the time recruiters were prohibited from recruiting women in northern New Ireland, in January 1910, nearly four years had passed since the Government Council voted against the measure and over three years since it recommended further investigations. Meanwhile those investigations appeared to show beyond doubt what Hahl considered obvious, that the population of New Ireland was on the brink of serious decline. The Germans could not obtain exact statistical evidence of a fall in population, and the district officer at Kavieng even thought there were as many people in northern New Ireland in 1908 as in 1904, but counts of the existing population showed such a lack of women and children that a future fall seemed inevitable. A census of ninety-seven villages in central and southern New Ireland taken in 1907 gave total numbers as 12 189, of whom 56 per cent were males and 44 per cent females. Of 2564 families counted within a smaller area in central New Ireland more than half were said to be childless and only 146 to have more than two children; and this in villages where many older women claimed to have borne six or eight children. In central New Ireland, stretches of coast twenty kilometres long, where old men remembered many villages, now lay uninhabited, and a village leader near Kavieng told a government doctor in 1908 that he was afraid his people would soon die out. A census in northern New Ireland in 1909 produced 'quite distressing results'. Almost everywhere, from Bagail near Kavieng to Lamussong 140 kilometres down the coast, there were apparently fewer women than men in the villages.

The New Irelanders were dying out, the Germans thought, for three main reasons. The first was mere fantasy based on ignorance of inter-village marriage exchanges: a 'degeneration of the race' was said to be resulting from prolonged incest within mutually antagonistic villages. The others were matters of fact: widespread disease and the recruiting of women. Doctors frequently observed the characteristically enlarged spleens of malaria sufferers among the New Irelanders. Of 308 men and boys from ten villages near Kavieng, examined in 1907, 111 had such swellings and malaria was equally common in central New Ireland. Dysentery was rife in northern New Ireland though probably not, as one doctor believed, because people ate too much pork during feasts. The people also lacked resistance to pneumonia and other lung diseases, especially if they wore European clothes, and were often afflicted by a range of skin ailments from scabies to yaws. Such a pattern of disease, however, was common to many New Guinean communities. What seemed to make the crucial difference in New Ireland was the spread of gonorrhoea. New Guineans claimed that particular villages were notorious far and wide for having a large number of venereally infected women, and many women brought venereal disease back to New Ireland after service with the whites.

As the only part of the Old Protectorate where women could be persuaded to sign indentures, New Ireland was the colonists' principal source of cheap female labourers, household servants and concubines. In the three years 1905 to 1907 recruiters shipped 475 women from New Ireland for employment in the Gazelle Peninsula and the Madang area and a further 150 were at work elsewhere in the colony and in Samoa. Absent from home at the peak of reproductive age, often infected with venereal diseases producing sterility, such women bore few children when they returned to the village, if they returned at all. By taking women the recruiters facilitated the spread of venereal disease and lowered the fertility of the population, though whether the New Irelanders were in fact declining in German times remains uncertain. Hahl never doubted that they were a classic example of Pacific Islands depopulation, shrinking in numbers from year to year.[29]

Hahl's solution was to stop the recruiting of women and extend medical services. In the budget of 1910 he asked for a doctor and a native hospital for Namatanai and, on the grounds that New Ireland was 'by far the most important area for labour recruitment', the Colonial Office supported him.

'Everything', it agreed, 'must be done to check a further decline of its population'. Then Hahl tested settler opinion. He asked all companies, missions, and government stations what they thought of his proposal to forbid the recruiting of unmarried women and permit married women to sign on only with their husbands, the law to apply throughout the Old Protectorate. Opinions differed. The missions were in favour, and so were companies such as the DHPG and the Bismarck-Archipel-Gesellschaft which relied on New Ireland labour. Other companies, as well as government officials in Aitape and Madang, argued that stopping the flow of single women to the plantations would deter many men from entering indentures: in order to prevent homosexuality and attacks on village women, they said, male labourers had to be given opportunities for sex with plantation women, and young whites would have to turn to Malay or Japanese girls or even prostitutes if the proposal became law. Nothing could have revealed more clearly the extent of the sexual services which New Ireland women provided to men, black and white, on the plantations of German New Guinea. Hahl admitted that the measure would make some plantations less attractive destinations but he hoped a severe labour shortage might compel employers to import Asians, and the disadvantages for white men could be overcome by bringing in girls from Java.[30]

The Colonial Office, noting that European opinion was split on the issue, told Hahl to consult the Government Council yet again. Even on so fundamental a matter as depopulation, Berlin felt bound to listen to the settlers. The new Council, chosen in July 1909 after negotiations failed to revive the old one, represented the big New Britain firms as before except for the NGC, which sent a man to oppose Hahl at the meeting in December anyway. The motion which Hahl put to the meeting showed the concessions he had already made to the planters. A few months before he had feared immense damage if recruiters of women were simply diverted from New Ireland to other parts of New Guinea and insisted that any prohibition must be general. Now he proposed closing only northern New Ireland and New Hanover to recruiters of women, and during the meeting agreed to suggestions from Max Thiel of Hernsheim & Co. and Oskar Haesner of Norddeutscher Lloyd that New Hanover and the islands of New Ireland be kept open as sources of village women for the whites. That left northern New Ireland and the islands of the Nusa Straits. Hahl now depicted the measure as a way of encouraging labour recruiting in the long run by maintaining the population, an insurance policy for the future of the colony, and the Council voted to prohibit the recruiting of women in this reduced area. Married couples remained free to sign on and Hahl reserved the closure of southern New Ireland for a time when money was available for a medical service which would restore health. He saw little point in placing a cordon around areas where there was no doctor. Deprived of funds by politicians in the metropolis and opposed by settlers in the colony, Hahl had to settle for less than he originally wanted as a safeguard against depopulation.[31]

The settlers remained at odds with Hahl over population policy, criticizing him for closing recruiting areas, requiring Europeans to accompany recruiting expeditions, not insisting that New Guineans do their duty and for other distortions of the settlers' ideal of a proper colony, in which the colonized existed solely to toil for the colonizers. He was urged to conquer yet more recruiting districts, raise head-tax, stop the DHPG from taking New Guineans to Samoa and make forced labour available to private employers. But Hahl's policy was to move in the opposite direction. He imposed bans on taking away labourers from the atolls, the Nuguria, Mortlock, Tasman and Western Islands, as well as from Kapingamarangi in the southern Carolines, an island group administered from New Britain. First visited by a government official in April 1914, Kapingamarangi was the exclusive preserve of the Mouton company under a concession of 1902, its population of about 350 trading copra for the biscuits, sugar, tinned meat and other European commodities stocked by the Mouton trader.[32]

To convince settlers of the need for further restrictions Hahl embarked on a propaganda campaign, publicizing reports of depopulation and appealing for immediate action. Under a census of the Namatanai district in 1911, showing a serious fall in population in the previous four years, the official government gazette commented that, in order not to hasten the decline, all recruiting of women in southern New Ireland should cease, for it had been carried on at a faster pace since being forbidden in the north of the island. A medical report on central New Ireland, published later in 1911, made the same recommendation. From Bougainville the district officer reported a 'shocking decline' in the population of the controlled villages near Kieta and called for a doctor to be posted to the German Solomons while time remained to prevent loss of people in the 'very productive recruiting areas' of Buka and northern Bougainville. And a published census of the Witu Islands suggested that the percentage of recruits was extraordinarily high and, in the absence of exact figures, that the population seemed to be diminishing. Hahl told the Government Council in November 1911 that recruiting unmarried women would have to be outlawed not merely in northern New Ireland but everywhere in the colony, pointing out that no neighbouring colony tolerated the practice. In the face of further criticism from employers, a general prohibition eventually became law in 1913.[33]

Meantime Hahl debarred recruiters from two areas in New Britain, the migrant settlements on St George's Channel of the Sulka and Mengen people and a long strip of coast in western and southern New Britain from Cape Gloucester to Montagu Harbour. The settlements of the Sulka and Mengen, who had come north from their homes south of the Gazelle Peninsula, had been carefully cultivated by the government—even to the extent of acquiring land for them—and Hahl feared their disappearance if further recruiting were permitted. In west New Britain years of ruthless recruiting, especially by E. E. Forsayth G.m.b.H., had aroused such fear of the whites that many villagers fled inland. As the company also made a practice of employing 'all the arts of persuasion' to extend the contracts of these labourers, so that they were absent from home for six years or even longer, the government forbade contract extensions for people from this district already on the plantations. One recruiter for the company, Karl Münster, was sentenced to three months' gaol and fined 323 marks on a series of counts from kidnapping to assault. He had struck New Guineans out of anger at finding no recruits, brought six men on board by force, thrown his axe into a canoe to make it sink, shot at villagers to frighten them and stolen coconuts. By so intimidating people as to drive them into the bush, the Rabaul court noted, he had harmed both future labour recruiting and the spread of government control. Like other recruiters in the area Münster was undermining official authority. In west New Britain villagers tried to protect themselves from the attacks of white recruiters by saying that the *kiap* would help them, only to be told by the recruiters: 'me no afraid belong kiap, kiap and Doktor Hahl shit nothing'.[34]

Hahl resented this challenge and closed the region to recruiters without consulting the Government Council or the most affected company, H. R. Wahlen's E. E. Forsayth G.m.b.H., whose 306 workers from west New Britain represented almost a third of their plantation labour force on the island. The refugees should not fall victim to warlike mountain people, he told the Government Council afterwards, but must return to their villages and the basis of population increase, the family, must be restored. Government policy was, as the Rabaul district officer said, 'that the natives should be drawn into work ... But this must occur only to an extent consistent with the government's endeavours to preserve the natives, add to their numbers and civilize them'. On a trip to the closed district in January 1913 he explained to the villagers that recruiting would be properly conducted once it was permitted again, no one would be forced to sign on, but that it was his wish and in the interests of the New Guineans themselves for every unmarried man to work at least once for the whites.[35]

The campaign which E. E. Forsayth G.m.b.H. now mounted against the closure of the south coast of west New Britain was to broaden into a general attack on official population policy. Demanding 'New Pomeranians for the plantations of New Pomerania', the company reminded Hahl that it had pioneered the development of west New Britain as a source of labourers and needed to pay a regular dividend if it were to become an *Aktiengesellschaft*, a public company. From Hamburg it impressed upon the Colonial Office that in rejoicing over the coming of big capital to the Pacific Islands, the German government should remember that this was not predicated on a return of 5 or 6 per cent but in the hope of profits commensurate with the great risks involved—and in this calculation the risk of a change in the government's labour policy had not been considered. Referring to Hahl's encouragement of palm planting by the New Guineans, the company thought the idea of making the New Guineans into planters ignored the fact that 'these natives are idlers almost without exception unless they are in the service of Europeans'.[36]

Wahlen discussed the labour question personally with the Colonial Secretary in Berlin in November 1912, arguing that it should be treated by the government hand in hand with the plantation companies. Two and a half months later the major New Guinea interests in Hamburg, Forsayth G.m.b.H., Wahlen G.m.b.H., Hernsheim & Co. and the DHPG, combined in complaining to Berlin about the closure of west New Britain and pleaded for the larger financial grant needed from Germany to open new recruiting areas in the well populated districts of mainland New Guinea. 'The sooner means are approved for establishing new government stations in the region to be opened up', they said, 'the quicker will hopes be realised for an improvement of the labour situation'. Together with representatives of the NGC, Max Thiel of Hernsheim & Co. and Heinrich Rudolph Wahlen repeated those arguments in a meeting with the Colonial Secretary in April 1913. Meanwhile a Forsayth recruiter ignored the prohibition and broke the law by recruiting labourers for the company's Arawe plantation on the south coast of west New Britain from Rauto, sixty kilometres away. Who had the last say, a villager in Rauto asked the district officer, the *kiap* or the Forsayth company?[37]

Hahl anticipated the protests of E. E. Forsayth G.m.b.H., supplied Berlin with counter-arguments and was backed by the Colonial Secretary. Solf was no stranger to the aggressive settler. 'Whoever has not seen them with his own eyes or heard them with his own ears', he had written of Samoa years before, 'will not be able to believe what outrageous injustices are caused by the common selfishness of whites towards coloureds'.[38] Hahl proceeded to impose controls on recruiting by E. E. Forsayth G.m.b.H. and two other companies, requiring them to have every recruiting expedition accompanied by a white man. The armed black recruiters sent into the bush to get people from the villages were not careful observers of the niceties of German recruiting law. At the end of 1912 the story of how the black recruiters of the DHPG's ship *Samoa* had overpowered a woman and raped her was angering all the tribes of north-west New Britain, according to the Rabaul district officer, and would have hindered recruiting if an investigation had not been held. By putting the whole process into the hands of the whites, even the seeking out of inland villages, Hahl hoped to prevent such excesses, as far as this was 'possible at all'.[39]

Wahlen wanted investors to be confident in E. E. Forsayth G.m.b.H. when it became an *Aktiengesellschaft* and probably meant to give Hahl the occasion of issuing a reassuring statement on labour policy. He chose to organize the submission of a long memorandum to Hahl on the subject, signed by all the large plantation companies except the NGC and stating the planters' view of the black man's place in a German colony. The labour question, said the planters, was 'not so much a question for the natives as, above all, for the white planters', whereas the government viewed it 'almost exclusively from the natives' standpoint'. While doing everything to encourage settlers to lay down plantations the government worked against those settlers by failing to open up the country and provide labour at the same pace, the memorandum said. For planters in New Britain, where the oldest and biggest plantations were, New Ireland and Buka had been almost eliminated as sources of labour because of the new undertakings established there; yet knowing this the government had closed southern

New Britain to recruiters and, in forbidding labourers to renew contracts, had prevented New Guineans from serving Europeans at a time when every settler was having to stand up for the imposition of gentle pressure on the villagers to make them work; nearly all plantations in the Gazelle Peninsula, it was claimed, were so short of labour that copra could not be fully harvested. As for the government's assumption that imported coolies would be able to supply the needed labour, this the planters questioned, pointing to the failure of attempts to introduce Malays or Javanese and to the disadvantages of the industrious Chinese, who were said already to be creating unfortunate competition in the Chinese quarter of Rabaul. The Chinese in any case did less work on copra plantations and had to be paid much more than the Melanesian, according to the planters: it was the difference between having to pay over two marks for a Chinese each day and seventy-five *Pfennige* for a Melanesian, and the attempts of the government more or less to force planters to import coolies would ruin all copra plantations. Provided the release of land to new undertakings was kept within limits, the planters argued, the country itself would be able to supply all workers needed for years ahead. But first there would have to be a complete change in the government position on the treatment of New Guineans. In return for the blessings of the Europeans' economy and civilization the 'Negro' in New Guinea would have to offer an equivalent, 'which naturally can consist only in the performance of work'. While every male German was compelled to serve the Fatherland with two or three years in the army the government ruled out milder compulsion of the New Guineans. Was the 'Negro', the planters asked, to have it better than the German worker forced to work by the need for daily bread? Was he, who did not know anxiety about food, clothing and shelter 'in contrast to the hard struggle for existence in which we must all fight', to have the blessings of European progress fall effortlessly into his lap?

The planters complained that most district officers saw their main task as convincing the New Guineans that they had many rights but few duties: the government did not teach the villagers near Rabaul to offer themselves for work on loading and coaling ships; the frequent desertions by labourers would continue as long as the police did so little to catch them; and while firms were made to maintain roads, those for which New Guineans were responsible were in a terrible state. In the Rabaul and Matupit area many villagers were said to be showing the unpleasant effects of not being taught to obey the European. In the planters' opinion the ordinance forbidding New Guineans to act as independent labour recruiters amounted to a death-blow to successful recruiting, because in most cases villagers would flee if they saw a European recruiter coming, quite apart from the fact that Europeans were not equal to the exertions of penetrating the forests and mountains. The planters admitted that forcing the New Guineans to fulfil their duties would encounter political opposition in Germany and called instead for a 'gentle pressure' on them to work. In short, planters wanted a native policy which trained the villager to work and left the white settler free to exploit village labour.

Hahl was to reply to his critics at a meeting of the Government Council, but first he defended his policy to Berlin, conceding that settlers were short of labour and needed new recruiting areas and blaming lack of finance from Germany as the reason for delay. He stuck to his belief in restricting recruitment as a way of regenerating the labouring population. His chief opponent Wahlen, he thought, actually benefited from having recruiters excluded from the Western Islands, where people were more susceptible to the malaria of the larger islands. He rejected the idea of restricting government land sales: the beneficiaries would be Forsayths and the NGC, which would be able to sell their surplus land. And he defended the government's enforcement of labour law on the grounds that the employer in German New Guinea was in practice a magistrate as well as a manager, using his disciplinary powers to punish crimes, and should therefore be carefully watched by the authorities. What the planters meant by 'gentle pressure on the natives to work' Hahl did not know, though he suggested that it already existed in the form of direct taxes, forced labour on public works and the new system of conscripting men into the police.[40]

The New Britain planters knew it was useless to ask for forced labour for themselves. The issue had been raised before. In November 1911 a Forsayth representative on the Government Council proposed a system under which every young New Guinean would have to work on indenture for three years, and a special commission of the Council was later formed to examine such proposals. Hahl argued that the state could not go too far without arousing resistance and the Colonial Secretary, Solf, told Wahlen in 1912 that forced labour for private use was not to be considered. An inquiry into the possibility of forced labour, completed in 1913, showed how few men in controlled areas had still not worked for the whites, how insignificant were the reserves of people, how radically and comprehensively service for the Europeans had affected the population. Hahl explained this to the Government Council, estimating that 100 000 people had been recruited in the colony up to 1913, of whom he thought (too pessimistically) about 25 000 had died under indenture. In view of the *Reichstag*'s resolution of 8 March 1913 against forced labour in the colonies, and because he believed requisition of labour was much more injurious to population stocks than free recruiting, Hahl told Council members he assumed they no longer doubted that forced labour for private employers could not be introduced. In any case, said Hahl, so many villagers from controlled districts were on the plantations that forced labour would hardly add to their numbers. Few men in the Namatanai district had not already spent three or more years on contract; in the Kavieng district 30 per cent of all males from fourteen years of age upwards were in the service of whites; in Morobe the percentage of young men working was fifty or sixty and in newly-controlled Manus, of 490 unmarried men aged from eighteen to twenty-four years counted in a population of 6120, 240 had been recruits.[41]

The planters' demand for re-opening west New Britain to the recruiters was met from the beginning of 1914, but at the same time Hahl imposed restrictions in two new areas, the Tench Islands north of Kavieng and villages near Aitape. The Aitape communities, with a population of about 800, stood in the path of recruiters going inland. Having lost all their young men to the plantations, they had taken up arms against the government. Hahl thought the situation similar to that in west New Britain in 1912: the villagers must be collected together again, the young men must be able to return home and marriages must be made in order to maintain the population. He hoped a year's closure would be enough.[42]

Keeping recruiters out of villages cost Hahl's administration relatively little. He planned to do more to preserve the labouring population but it was not until 1912 that the *Reichstag* at last had a change of heart and increased the imperial grant. The Colonial Secretary agreed that New Guinea had been 'very shabbily treated' in colonial subsidies and Hahl hastened to prepare a comprehensive development plan for the 1913 budget, aimed at quickening the spread of control, making the administration more efficient, assisting the planter and reinvigorating village life. He called for an extra 1 348 000 marks to be spent over two years on a bigger, better-trained police force, more roads, more sailing vessels, improved land surveys, lighthouses, secretarial help for district offices, a forest officer, a veterinary quarantine station, an agricultural research station on the mainland to test new crops such as rice, sugar-cane, tobacco and hemp and another station to monitor copra cultivation, extended medical services and the appointment of agricultural extension officers to teach villagers how to grow good copra.[43]

Just when the *Reichstag* became willing to vote funds to New Guinea, however, the German colonies faced the competing claims of the German army. By 1912 the German High Command was expecting war and the government was scrambling to cut expenditure in the national budget in order to finance the raising of a massive force of troops. On 3 June 1912 the Chancellor, Theobald von Bethmann-Hollweg, ordered that grants to the colonies were to remain at their 1912 level until 1917 because of the new Army bills. The Colonial Office accepted the general principle but demurred in the case of New Guinea, which had been 'neglected by comparison with the other protectorates and retarded in its development as a result'. It asked for 700 000 marks more for New Guinea in 1913 than in the previous year, arguing that the colony of Old Cameroun was having to pay for the administrative costs of New Cameroun, acquired after the Morocco Crisis of 1912, and that if this were not so, the total colonial budget would be enough to subsidize German New Guinea. An enlarged colonial empire, in other words, was having to live on an unchanged subsidy. 'Old Cameroun', a Chancellery official noted, 'could spring to the aid of New Guinea if it did not have to bear the burden of the new acquisitions'.

The outcome of this bureaucratic dispute was a compromise. The Chancellor allowed New Guinea an extra 120 000 marks in the budget which went to the *Reichstag* in 1913 and the Budget Commission, now eager to develop the colony, added a further 91 000 marks, of which over half was for the agricultural research station on the mainland and the rest was for

medical care, including a hospital for New Guineans at Kieta. The 1914
budget also circumvented Bethmann-Hollweg's ruling. It increased the
imperial grant to New Guinea by 298 000 marks. Even so, Hahl had
received less than two fifths of his original request for development finance.
Armaments took precedence over colonies. Money which would have taken
years to spend on police patrols into the Markham Valley or the middle
Sepik was to pay instead for ten minutes' fighting in Flanders. By 1914
the revenues of the colony, buoyed up by lucrative customs duties and
head-taxes at a time of high copra prices, were beginning to match Hahl's
expectations. But his political problem remained the same. The more he
depended upon local revenue in the form of export duties on copra, the
more he needed to placate settlers on other matters. That is why he sought
so much financial aid from the metropolis.[44]

Hahl intended to ask for more imperial money in the budget of 1915
and to initiate a vast expansion of control in the colony, with government
stations or police posts in west New Britain, south Bougainville, New
Hanover, on the mainland coast at Wewak and Vanimo and on the Markham
and Ramu rivers by 1917. But in the meantime he had to turn to settlers
for revenue. He proposed new taxes and duties, plans of which went to
a committee of the Government Council, and before he left the colony
in April 1914 settlers were demanding their price for willingness to pay
the government's bills: concessions over population policy. As H. R.
Wahlen said amid the pleasantries of his speech at the Rabaul club farewell-
ing Hahl on behalf of the settlers, their difference with the governor had
been 'above all in recent times because of the labour question, in which
the settlers have a different viewpoint from Your Excellency...' Replying,
Hahl did not deny that he saw 'the solution of the most important economic
problem, that of the natives, with different eyes' and reiterated that 'all
progress depends on our relationship with the natives'.[45]

A revised labour ordinance, never enacted, was already coming under
fire from settlers in 1914. Many of the new clauses arose from the experience
of the previous five years: the prohibition on recruiting unmarried women
was to become permanent; a much more varied diet for labourers was to
be mandatory as government doctors recommended; the governor's right
to close a recruiting area by proclamation was expressly stated; and the
DHPG's special right to take New Guineans to Samoa was to be removed.
The most important new provision in Hahl's opinion was that all wages
were to be paid in cash rather than kind. Since employers made great savings
by reckoning labourers' goods at so-called 'native prices', which were considerably higher than the prices paid by whites for the same goods, this
innovation was among the first to be attacked in the Government Council
in March 1914, together with others which added to labour costs: the
reduction of the normal length of service from three years to two years,
for example, and the ban on deducting the cost of a labourer's clothes,
tobacco, soap, and matches from his wages. Under the draft ordinance the
labourer was to work nine hours a day instead of ten; only in pressing cases
was he to work in heavy rain; he was not to be given jobs beyond his physical

strength; he was to have three holidays a year as well as Sundays; he was to have the next day off if worked on holidays or Sundays; and he was to be provided by his employer with suitable cooking places, toilets, washing facilities and drinkable water. Women were not to be given work for two months after confinement. All these regulations were new and would almost certainly have been resisted by the planters if war had not intervened. Others they would have welcomed. Copying a German East African ordinance of 1913 Hahl planned to give employers the right to sack indentured labourers on virtually any pretext; the employers' complaints about labourers' escapes were to be met by a provision that repeated offenders could be imprisoned for up to a year with forced labour; and flogging remained, though now with a rope-end rather than a stick and confined to the labourers' buttocks.[46]

Planters were growing restive in the last year of German rule. The big companies' blast against Hahl in September 1913 was followed six months later by another from smaller planters in New Ireland and New Hanover, calling for government conscription of plantation hands, since the colony was suffering not from lack of labourers but from 'the natives' reluctance to work'. After the war German companies told the Australians that in 1914 'it was proposed to issue regulations to the effect that every fit and adult native shall be bound to serve at least six years within a certain period and age as labourer'. Whatever the truth of this claim, it is evidence of the wide gulf between Hahl and the settlers and their determination that his philosophy should not be perpetuated.[47]

Wahlen was right, said Hahl, to speak of a conflict between government and settlers. But the conflict was not over fundamentals. Whether New Guinea should be exploited for European benefit was not at issue. Rather was it a question of how far immediate exploitation of New Guinea's resources should be limited for the sake of future development. Like the planters, Hahl wanted control extended and new districts opened to the recruiters; unlike them, he also wanted to husband New Guinea's labour by systematically opening and closing villages to recruiters and by creating an alternative labour force in the form of Asian coolies.

For the employers, coolies were out of the question because of their high cost. Octave Mouton, a planter in New Britain, recalled that it 'was understood between us not to pay more than a certain amount, that is amongst the planters. The rule was not to pay less than four marks for a labourer, nor more than six marks' (a month). In 1909 each New Guinean labourer was reckoned by the government to cost most plantations no more than 150 marks a year or £7 10s in the sterling of the time, including the expenses of recruiting, food and wages paid in kind. No Asian labourer could be had so cheaply, and mass Asian immigration, blocked in any case by diplomatic obstacles, was desired by no one in the colony except Hahl himself.[48]

Hahl did not share the popular view that, inevitably, museums would soon be the only reminders of the vanished New Guinean race. The New Guineans were not doomed, he thought: they could be saved from depopulation by a strong and far-sighted colonial government. The government had to ensure that the colony's productiveness lasted whereas planters, he said, put immediate interests first, and in 1911 he was reminding them to take care lest New Guinea be short of labour in the 1920s. He was afraid that planters would squander New Guinea's labour resources in one generation of rapacious colonization and they interpreted his attempts to preserve 'existing stocks of labour' as a betrayal of white solidarity.[49] Yet Hahl shared the racist prejudices of his generation and in the 1930s accepted an official position in Hitler's *Reichskolonialbund*, a Nazi propaganda organization. The phrases he used about the people of New Guinea were those of the prudent stock breeder, worried about the depletion of his herds, and his whole aim was to ensure that the servile class in the colony reproduced itself for future generations of Germans. Little of Hahl's vision of a regenerated New Guinea survived practical politics and tight budgets. The settlers resisted him. The *Reichstag* ignored him until it was too late. And when the Australians landed at Rabaul in 1914 they found a colony dominated by planters.

7
The Missionaries

Villagers were fighting less, becoming accustomed to regular work and developing a taste for order, cleanliness and clothing. That was the conclusion reached by Germany's imperial commissioner Gustav von Oertzen when he reported to Bismarck on the influence of the Australasian Methodist Mission in the New Guinea Islands in 1885. But in the time to come, Oertzen said, church, school and language would be 'such important factors' that they should be exclusively in German hands. As a first step, German missionaries, practical men, should be dispatched to northeast New Guinea in order to forestall non-German mission societies and lay the foundations of civilization.[1]

Oertzen thought about missions as other German colonial administrators were to do. As far as government officials were concerned, the missions were there to serve German as well as Christian purposes, to colonize as well as evangelize and to teach the German version of European civilization; and the ideal missionary was one who concentrated on the practical task of opening up the country by teaching villagers to keep their gardens clean, operate sawmills, sail European vessels and offer themselves for plantation work.

If the Neu Guinea Compagnie had had its way, the only missionaries allowed into the colony would have been German-speakers sponsored by German mission societies; once in, the missionaries would have been required to support the colonial authorities, accustom the villagers to regular work and teach them 'manual skills, horticulture and farming'. As the NGC envisaged it, the messengers of Christ would be 'important for gaining mastery over the natives peacefully'. This colonial conception of the role of the missions had been popularized in Germany before the colonial era by Friedrich Fabri, Director of the Rhenish Mission Society and author of the influential pamphlet *Does Germany Need Colonies?* (1879). For Fabri successful colonization depended upon missionaries. They were the ones who would influence the 'mentality, intelligence and moral and religious conceptions of uncivilized, still barbaric peoples'; they alone were capable of regenerating such peoples by educating them to work. While planters, traders and officials would undertake the external education of the colonized people, the missionaries would work internally, ensuring a ready acceptance of European values.[2]

136

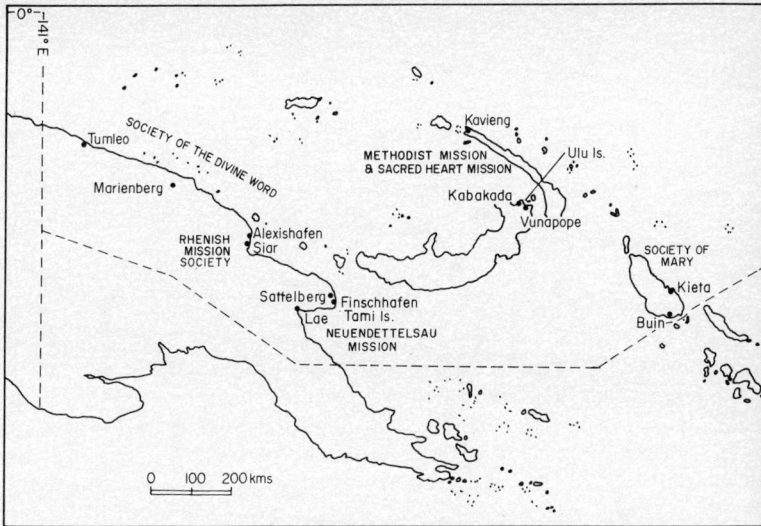

Christian Missions in the Old Protectorate

For two reasons Christian missions in New Guinea were not as German in language, nationality and purpose as officials would have liked. Men and women with French, Dutch, English, Samoan, Fijian and Tongan names easily outnumbered Germans in the mission field in the 1880s and 1890s. Throughout the German era the largest Catholic mission remained under the control of a French bishop, and the largest Protestant mission made only half-hearted attempts to recruit German staff.

To begin with, a foreign Protestant mission was entrenched in the heart of the colony's island district. When the flag went up in 1884, possibly a hundred Pacific Islanders and their wives from Fiji, Tonga and Samoa, together with a handful of Australians, had already served in the New Britain mission field of the Australasian Wesleyan Methodist Missionary Society. Germany could hardly expel the Methodists without international consequences, and did not consider doing so.

Second, the Catholic Church was a barrier to any thoroughgoing Germanization of missions. The Foreign Office in Berlin, for example, could not agree to exclude non-German mission societies from New Guinea, as the NGC wanted, because such a rule would have excluded all Catholic missionaries. No Catholic mission societies existed in Germany at the beginning of the colonial era. They were forbidden under the anti-Catholic laws of the *Kulturkampf*, which had the ironic effect of ensuring that most German Catholic missionaries were trained in France. As it happened, the fate of Catholic missions throughout the German colonial empire was determined by the arrival of a group of Sacred Heart missionaries in New

Guinea in 1888. Were they, as French Catholic missionaries, to be admitted to a German protectorate or not? It was a test case, and from his castle at Friedrichsruh Bismarck ruled that all Catholic missionaries, even Jesuits, should be allowed into German colonies in view of the fact that colonial administrations had the right to expel them at any time. As explained to the *Reichstag* in November 1889, the official policy was that while Catholic missions would be treated in exactly the same manner as German Protestant missions, the government was keen for Catholic missionaries to be of German nationality and to be under German control. The question would be seen as national rather than confessional.

Pope Leo XIII accepted the formulation and the Church strove to meet the German government half-way on the nationality issue. Rome chose a German-speaking mission, the Society of the Divine Word, for its new prefecture of Kaiser Wilhelmsland. It gave the German Solomon Islands, at first in the vicariate of the assertive Bishop Louis Couppé in New Britain, to the Marists in Samoa, who had proved more accommodating to German interests. At the request of the German authorities, it transferred Nauru from the 'British' vicariate of the Gilbert Islands to the 'German' vicariate of New Britain, and gradually replaced the French staff of the Sacred Heart Mission with Germans. But the Church left Couppé at his post and insisted on the Picpus Fathers, a French congregation, as the mission for a new field to be opened in New Guinea in 1914.

For its part, the German government relaxed its prohibitions on Catholic mission societies as the *Kulturkampf* came to an end during the 1890s. The Colonial Department, especially under its first director Paul Kayser, saw patriotic advantages in the 'nationalisation' of colonial missions and was in favour of allowing even the French congregations to come to Germany. Both French societies active in New Guinea received permission to train missionaries in Germany, the Sacred Heart opening a mission house at Hiltrup near Münster in 1896 and the Marists one at Meppen near Osnabrück in 1900. In the Marists' case, the German government specified that the seminary was for training 'German missionaries for Samoa and the German Solomon Islands'.[3]

Seven Christian missions worked in New Guinea in German times: the Methodists, who had reached the Duke of York Islands in 1875; the Catholic missionaries of the Sacred Heart (New Britain, 1882); the Neuendettelsau Lutherans (Finschhafen, 1886); the Lutherans of the Rhenish Mission Society (Bogadjim, 1887); the Catholic Holy Spirit Mission of the Society of the Divine Word (Aitape, 1896); the Catholic Society of Mary (German Shortland Islands, 1899); and the fundamentalist Protestants of the Liebenzell Mission (Manus, 1914). Of these only two came to German Melanesia for openly patriotic reasons: the Liebenzell missionaries, insignificant in the history of the colony, were financed by patriotic German army officers who wished to support a missionary in a German overseas territory; the Rhenish Mission Society, active in South-West Africa and an advocate of German annexation there, saw its Christian and patriotic duty combined in accepting the government's invitation to go to New Guinea.

The other five missions firmly put religious motives first. The Catholic missions, though happy to respond to official requests for priests, brothers and sisters of German origin, never accepted the idea of a colonial mission in which the missionary owed first loyalty to the German state. They might teach the villagers about things German, as the Society of the Divine Word missionaries did on the coast of the mainland, but their allegiance always belonged to the Church. The Neuendettelsau Lutherans, based in Bavaria, announced their principal object in going to New Guinea to be the preaching of Christ crucified and preferred to be left alone by the colonial authorities. The Methodists took their orders from Sydney and remained largely British colonial or Polynesian in attitude.

The Methodists
'Natives stark naked. Most unprepossessing': that had been the judgement of the founder of the Methodist mission, the Reverend George Brown, when he set foot on the soil of the Duke of York Islands in August 1875. He came with eight Fijians and two Samoans as mission teachers, who were followed a year later by a further seven Fijians under the Reverend Sailasa Naucukidi. From then onwards the character of Methodist evangelization in the New Guinea islands was set, a few Europeans, usually Australians, directing operations while Fijians and to a lesser extent Samoans and Tongans did most of the work of converting pagans. The tally in 1885 showed that three missionaries from Australia and thirty-eight South Sea Island teachers staffed the Methodist mission, which claimed 370 converts and 3000 attenders at church services.[4]

Mostly men of limited education and narrow outlook, the Australian and New Zealand Methodists identified Christianity with respectability as well as salvation. They were affronted by the dirt, nakedness and apparent disorder of the Melanesian village. The Reverend Benjamin Danks, reaching the Duke of Yorks from Sydney in 1878, found 'utter and complete degradation' stamped on the features of the first New Guinean he saw, a man 'covered with dirt and filth as though he had not been washed for years'. After three years' work, mostly at Kabakada on the north coast of the Gazelle Peninsula, Danks still regarded the 'natives of the New Britain group' as 'low and degraded beyond expression'. R. Heath Rickard, who served at the Duke of Yorks and at Raluana village in the Gazelle from 1882 to 1892, was struck by the New Guineans' apparent lack of purpose in life. Instead of 'meeting and seeing busy men hard driven in the struggle of life—and boys and girls already preparing for the strife', he wrote after eight months in New Guinea,

> we meet and see a multitude of natives roaming about, or making bubbles for the fun of seeing them explode, or laughing and talking life away as though it were purposeless; instead of Church bells at night, we hear the natives singing as they dance the night away; instead of the language which we learned from our mother's lips, we hear the chatter of an untrained tongue . . .

As far as Rickard could determine, the villager's day was 'generally spent in wandering about, except occasionally fishing or planting'. His colleague Isaac Rooney was less pessimistic. He thought the Duke of York Islanders 'degraded' but 'a very interesting people' nevertheless: 'They are born traders and very parsimonious. They would not give you a blade of grass. Everything has to be bought'.[5]

Soap, clothes and a neat appearance were the marks of the Methodist convert as much as his or her individual confession of penitence and profession of faith. 'His hair is not cut; he wears a waistcloth; and his very features are altered', wrote the New Zealander the Reverend John Crump of a new Tolai convert, and Danks exulted in the sight of his school pupils, all 'dressed, their hair combed and neatly dressed; faces bright and clean, all joyous and happy as they formed in line and marched to the church singing the songs taught them for the occasion by our teachers', a perfect contrast with the 'dirty crowd' of 'four or five hundred naked men and women' who looked on. Danks did not grudge the labour needed for this transformation, but he reminded his superiors in Sydney of the 'care, the watchfulness, the kindness, the patience, the forbearance' which he and his fellow missionaries had had to exercise 'in order to get this Jack-as-good-as-his-master crowd to attend school'. A strong sense of the good they were doing for others sustained the Methodists in their cause.[6]

With a typical concern for exact accounting, the Methodist Missionary Society of Australasia reckoned that it spent £67 333 15s 10d on the New Guinea Islands mission between 1875 and 1906. By then the mission was running 158 day-schools and claimed over 17 000 adherents; when the German flag was lowered eight years later it had over 200 schools and about 30 000 people came regularly to its services in churches in east New Britain, the Duke of Yorks and New Ireland.[7]

The German authorities were never impressed by the Methodist achievement. The 'churches' mentioned in mission reports, said one official in 1894, were nothing more than 'native huts', even the white missionaries were badly accommodated and the mission teachers were so poorly paid that they were driven to engage in trade. The commercial activities of South Sea Island mission teachers caused constant friction between mission and government in the Company period. All teachers supplemented their meagre annual stipend of from £7 10s to £12 by selling copra, turtleshell and shell-money to firms such as the DHPG, and some abandoned their vocation to become full-time traders. The Methodist mission teacher was a man who spent much of the day haggling with villagers for a livelihood or encouraging them to contribute large sums of money to the mission. Heath Rickard, who left New Guinea in 1892, embodied the two faults which German officials found most obnoxious in the Methodists: he insisted on trading and he never bothered to learn German.[8]

To appease the colonial government the Methodists appointed Heinrich Fellmann of the South German Conference of the Episcopal Methodist Church as Chairman of the mission in 1897, but Hahl remained impatient with the mission's progress in assuming a German character. For Hahl language and nationality were inseparable, and the battle against the use of English in German New Guinea was a matter of self-preservation. He foresaw the day when the 'English-speaking German colony' would want to unite with Australia, proposing that the Kuanua language of the Tolai be adopted as a lingua franca instead of the 'corrupted South Seas English' which every German settler was forced to learn in order to communicate with his servants. As for the Australian mission, its 'passive loyalty' was not enough for Hahl. He wanted to get rid of it and believed German Protestantism had a 'national duty' to replace the Australian Methodists in the Bismarck Archipelago.[9]

Hahl's patriotism achieved little. In vain, he asked Berlin for permission to refuse entry to any missionary who could not speak German. He impressed upon Fellmann the need for German-speaking missionaries and requested the Mission Board in Sydney to include German in training courses. But after a meeting with George Brown in 1905, Hahl realized that while the Methodists would persist in assurances of loyalty, their personnel would remain largely foreign-speaking. He was right. Five German missionaries joined the Methodists between 1906 and 1914 but negotiations to transfer the mission to the German branch of the church were never completed.[10]

Methodist evangelization centred on the village. Under the watchful eye of a Fijian, Samoan or Tongan teacher, the Methodist village was one where no one cooked, fetched water or picked coconuts on a Sunday and where even pagans did not dare break the Sabbath. Annual thank-offerings, church land planted with coconut palms and regular individual contributions were Methodist traditions. Villagers gave about 10 000 marks to the missions in 1898, when the most generous village was Vunamami in the Gazelle Peninsula, and the figure quadrupled by 1914. Together, Church and State in German New Guinea must have stripped some villages of their entire cash income.

Chronically short-staffed, the Methodists rapidly localized. As the flow of South Sea Islanders to the mission dwindled after 1900 the Methodists trained a new corps of New Guinean teachers. Promising village boys in one of the scores of Methodist village schools graduated to one of the three Circuit Training Institutions in New Britain and the Duke of Yorks or, from 1900, to George Brown College on Ulu Island. Here they lived as boarders, learning more about reading and writing and the Bible in the mornings and cutting grass or tending to their gardens in the afternoons. At separate girls' schools ministers' wives taught hygiene, sewing and other European domestic knowledge. By 1914 the Methodists had over 200 teachers, almost all New Guineans, and fifteen catechists in charge of groups of teachers. They were in New Guinea in part to rescue villagers from heathendom and in part to forestall Catholics. 'The aggressiveness of Roman Catholicism', said the chairman of the mission in 1910, made the question of Methodist expansion into the Admiralties, Buka, Bougainville and the major part of New Britain 'a very urgent one'. The sectarian struggle was fierce. Charges and counter-charges were the order of the day, and at Vunakamkambi in 1909 villagers of opposing denominations even began arming for war with spears, knives and iron rods. The fight was averted by the intervention of a Catholic missionary, Brother Weber, but he came to blows with a Fijian teacher, Titiko, who had threatened to kill a Catholic catechist. Weber was later acquitted on a charge of attempted murder and Titiko deported. The Methodists, like other missionaries, regarded prior occupation as the key to foiling their religious rivals. They multiplied the number of mission stations in northern New Ireland when the Catholics entered that district in 1912, just as the Marists were to do on Bougainville and Buka ten years later in response to the coming of the Methodists.[11]

The Sacred Heart Mission (Mission du Sacré-Coeur or MSC)

Continuous Catholic evangelization in Papua New Guinea dates from September 1882, when Fathers Navarre and Cramaille and Brother Fromm landed at Matupit in the Gazelle Peninsula for the Society of Missionaries of the Sacred Heart, the French order charged by the Holy See with the task of taking the Gospel to the vicariate of Melanesia and Micronesia. Initial progress was slow. The missionaries were washed out of their bamboo and grass hut at Nodup, a second hut at Kokopo burnt to the ground, Father Navarre was away for long periods organizing the Yule Island mission in British New Guinea, and it was not until 1889 that the apostolate took firm root under the capable leadership of Louis Couppé. Made bishop in 1890, Couppé dreamt of a community of Melanesians who had made a clean break from the paganism of the village, and he proceeded to buy unwanted children, orphans and slaves for his orphanages at Volavolo and Vunapope. The Fathers and Brothers looked after the boys; the Sisters, members of the Community of the Daughters of Our Lady of the Sacred Heart who arrived in New Britain in 1892, cared for the girls, teaching them to read, write and embroider and dressing them in beautiful clothes for First Communions.[12]

The Methodists accused the Catholics of conducting a trade in converts, and in June 1893 the Company Governor Georg Schmiele forbade Couppé to take 'free children' from their parents. Undaunted, Couppé appealed direct to Berlin, had the order rescinded and was left free to purchase more children as the core of the future Catholic villagers. During the 1890s the authorities progressively permitted the MSC to take abandoned children from labour recruiting vessels, to seek them elsewhere in the Bismarck Archipelago and to use its own boats in the work of collection. But Couppé proved to be more than a match for all who stood in the way of the Sacred Heart Mission, whether Methodists, Tolai villagers or German officials. He never resigned himself to official directives which he did not like. In an attempt to keep the competing missions apart, the colonial administration split the Gazelle Peninsula into Catholic and Methodist districts in 1891. Couppé responded with a concerted campaign against the arrangement, continuing to extend Catholic landholdings within the Methodist domain and bombarding Berlin with complaints. To an unsympathetic observer in the Colonial Department, Couppé appeared to have 'no great scrupulousness' in the methods he used to destroy the districts system, but the strategy worked. By the late 1890s the Kaiser himself was being briefed on the issue and Berlin was assuring the Vatican that the matter would be resolved. The districts were abolished in 1899.[13]

The Catholics proved superior to the Methodists in the race for the souls of the Tolai. They had far more European mission staff for a start, forty-five out of the forty-eight in the Bismarck Archipelago in 1899, and they were less concerned with reformed behaviour than the Methodists, who would not admit villagers to church membership without a period 'on trial'. They concentrated instead on displaying practical goodwill towards villagers, offering their services as mediators in disputes, interceding with officials on behalf of villagers and helping to protect Tolai land. The MSC claimed its first adult convert in 1895, had 1700 converts by the end of 1896 and, after a rush of baptisms, over 4000 a year later, far surpassing the number of Methodists so painstakingly won since 1875. Hahl, amazed at the speed of Catholic expansion, attributed it to a 'clever calculation' by many people that they would be better protected by the stronger mission. For the villager who wanted to keep all his coconuts for sale to a trader, the Catholic mission was cheaper because it demanded no annual donation; nor were there Catholic pastor-teachers in the village to check on the behaviour of individual Christians.[14]

The MSC worked from large mission stations, first at Volavolo on the north coast and Kinigunan near Kokopo, renamed Vunapope in honour of the Holy Father; then inland from Kokopo at Takabur (1895), Paparatava and St Otto (1898), with further settlements on the north coast at Vunakamkambi and Nodup (1898) and by 1900 four stations in the coastal Bainings district, Vunamarita, Ramandu, Nachunarep and St Paul, the converts' village several hours walk from the coast.

Mission plantations, hundreds of hectares in extent by the turn of the century, provoked a number of clashes with villagers, first at Vunakamkambi and in 1900 in the coastal Bainings, where the people of Livuan village competed with the mission for taro grown in the Baining Mountains. The most serious conflict occurred for different reasons at the mission's artificial village of St Paul in 1904. Here in the Baining Mountains, where the MSC had gathered together freed slaves and orphans for a new life as tillers of the soil, the dictatorial Father Matthäus Rascher issued orders, supervised the building of roads and dealt with moral lapses by beating people. The imperatives of Christian sexual morality troubled him. 'Here there is a heathen living with a Catholic woman', he had written in 1899,

> his first wife is living elsewhere. She does not want to come back and he does not want her to. The heathen wants to become a Catholic, comes every Sunday to Mass and has rejected all attempts by the Wesleyans to get him. So he wishes to be upright. Whether his first wife wants to become Catholic or not I do not know ... Can I marry

the heathen (after baptism) to the Catholic woman, even if the heathen woman said she wanted to be converted but not stay with her husband? I have chewed over these questions for a long time . . .[15]

Rascher did not want to be held responsible for encouraging adultery. At St Paul a few years later he refused permission for To Marias, a convert of Bainings origin, to leave his Christian wife for another woman; and when To Marias fled with his lover to a nearby village, Rascher had the two of them thrashed for their sins. To Marias, whose relatives lived nearby, vowed revenge upon the Catholic missionaries and gathered allies from all who resented the mission's presence.

The massacre of St Paul on 13 August 1904 was brief and bloody. To Marias, the adulterer, killed Rascher with a blast of buckshot in the right lung. Within minutes his co-conspirators had felled three brothers and five sisters with axes, and a tenth missionary died when the warriors murdered Father Rutten at the nearby station of Nachunarep. In the month that followed Bainings warriors fell to the bullets of the police on a number of occasions, the affair ending with the execution of seven men by a firing squad.[16]

Violent as it was, however, the St Paul massacre did little to interrupt the advance of MSC and was untypical of the mission's encounters with the people of the New Guinea islands. Villagers more commonly reacted with curiosity, tolerance and incomprehension. A priest newly arrived in a heathen village might find himself occupied for months or even years in simply getting established, building the mission station, learning the language, visiting people in their gardens and carrying a portable altar from place to place for the offering of masses which he knew the people did not understand.[17]

There were even places, such as central New Ireland, where latterday John the Baptists had already prepared the way for the priests. New Irelanders who had been indentured labourers on mission plantations in the Gazelle took the message back to coastal villages such as Bom, Rapito, Kurumut and Bisapu, where they led Sunday services in specially constructed prayer houses. Men such as Paranis of Bisapu and Sushut of Metanangas were mission labourers, then catechists in training at Vunapope and finally bearers of the gospel to their home villages. By the time Fathers Anton de Jong and Josef Abel established themselves on the west coast of central New Ireland in June 1902, a version of Catholic Christianity was already familiar to people of the area.

From there the MSC spread to the east coast when the government began building an official post at Namatanai in 1904 and by 1912 the mission was penetrating the Methodists' heartland in northern New Ireland. Forewarned of the arrival of the Catholics, the Methodists mobilized teams of new teachers to occupy villages along the north-east coast and in the offshore islands. Time, Father Gerhard Peekel recalled, was vital. Every day could mean the loss of a station to the Wesleyans, who had all the advantages of having been in the district beforehand: 'The Wesleyan mission was known in the land, indeed, in many places there lived boys and young men who . . . stood up for their church all the more resolutely'. The Catholics finally centred themselves in the Kara-speaking village of Lemakot, which had no Methodist teacher and provided access on a good path over the mountains to the Catholic village of Lemusmus.[18]

The catechists were the Catholic equivalent of Methodist teachers. One of them, August To Kadalama, accompanied Bishop Couppé to Europe in 1890 and learned to speak French, English and German. They were mediators between mission and village, teaching children in mission schools, calling the converts to morning and evening prayer, warning people against heathendom and Methodism, negotiating settlements in village disputes and introducing priests to new communities. Especially on Tabar, Lihir, Tanga and New Hanover they were the MSC's pioneer evangelizers. Like the Methodists, the MSC ordained no New Guineans before 1914. The role of the catechist was to be a faithful helper. He might prepare people for the sacraments but not administer them himself, except baptism for people on the point of death; he prayed with the European priests at Mass but did not officiate.[19]

The Neuendettelsau Lutheran Mission

The Protestants of mainland German New Guinea were Lutherans, first represented by a mission named after a village in the rolling hills of northern Bavaria. The impulse for a Lutheran mission in Kaiser Wilhelmsland came from Johann Flierl, a Neuendettelsau pastor working in the mid-1880s for the Immanuel Synod of the Lutheran Church in South Australia at a mission to the Aborigines. When Flierl suggested a New Guinea mission, his superiors in Germany were eager to embrace the idea, having been under pressure to send missionaries to the new African colonies. While Africa was out of the question for the small mission society, New Guinea clearly was not; the Christian people of Germany were demanding immediate evangelization of the newly acquired territories, the opening of a new field would encourage interest in missions and the Neuendettelsau mission, if it acted promptly, would be ahead of rivals. Flierl disembarked at Finschhafen in July 1886 and after a few months settled at Simbang, about an hour's walk away.

The attraction of Flierl and his fellow missionaries was Western wealth. On trading trips to Simbang, the people of the Tami Islands gazed covetously on the iron tools and cloth in the mission house and when Flierl suggested that they accept a missionary on their island home, they were pleased to agree. The soil of the Tami group being too rocky and coralline to nourish gardens, the Tami Islanders carved wooden figures, bowls, drums and headrests and wove sleeping mats from leaves, articles which they exchanged for food on long voyages to the Huon Gulf, Siassi, Umboi and west New Britain. Flierl wanted to convert these 'Phoenicians' of the Finschhafen coast so that the Gospel would be carried far and wide in

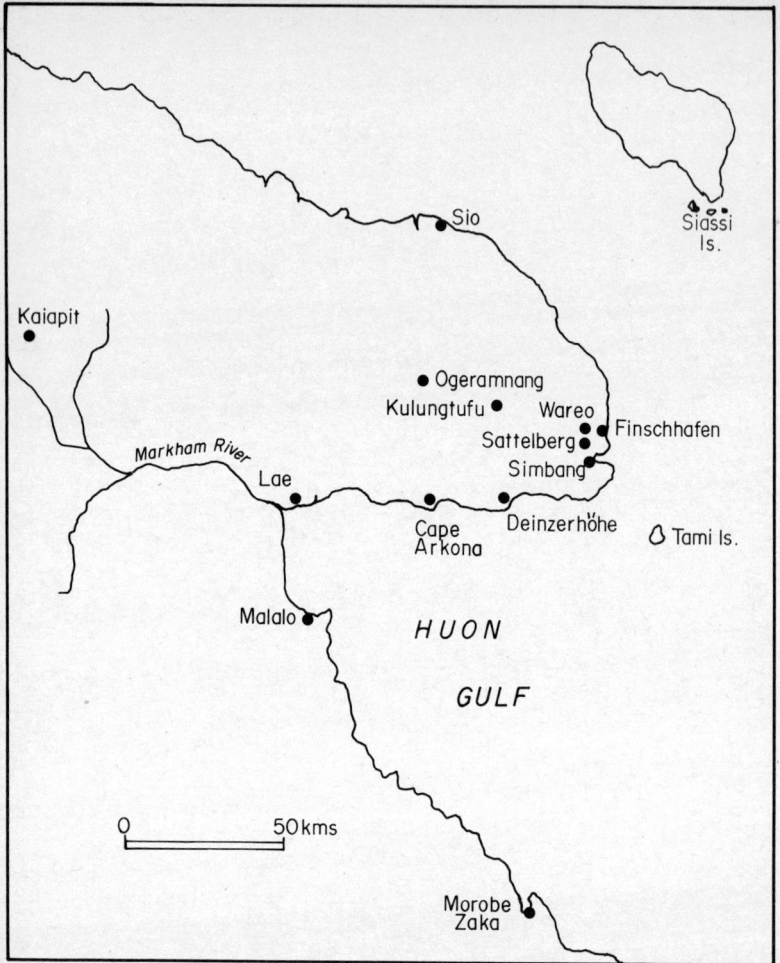

Neuendettelsau Mission Area, Kaiser Wilhelmsland

their double-masted canoes. They wanted his goods, and in 1889 they sent two great canoes to transport the missionary Karl Tremel to their home, where he was soon joined by Georg Bamler.

Flierl, though he recognized the economic motive behind the Tamis' welcome, could not help hoping that they would prove receptive to the Gospel. Yet by 1894 he was speaking of their contempt and hatred for God's Word and thought they were morally degraded by abortion and infanticide. Bamler and Tremel, not knowing what else to do, tried to make the Tami come to church services and listen to sermons delivered in

Pupils of the Rhenish Mission Society, Kranket Island, near Madang, about 1902

Pupils of a Sacred Heart Mission school on the Gazelle Peninsula

Joinery in the Divine Word Mission at Alexishafen

A Lutheran missionary, the Reverend Heinrich Zahn, 'preaching to the heathen': Zahn contributed a chapter on the Yabim people to Neuhauss's monumental *Deutsch-Neuguinea* (Berlin, 1911)

stumbling and unintelligible versions of the local language. Bamler complained that the Tami people would not

> sit behind each other, as we missionaries would have liked to see, and just as infrequently would they stand up during prayers. That was the cause of much dissension. In their opinion they were quite good and righteous enough. And they therefore did not want to continue going to church ... They said quite openly 'God's Word is for you whites; we are Tami, we have *our* customs'. . . some gave vent to their displeasure by spitting when they were called to church services.[20]

Tremel lectured people who did not come to church about their negligence and for a while, employing an economic sanction, the missionaries demanded church attendance as the price of trade. On Christmas Day 1892 the adults deliberately stayed away from church, saying they wanted tobacco and had to listen to God's Word incessantly without getting anything in return.

A further difficulty lay in the theology of Lutheran conversion. It was easy enough to translate the Ten Commandments, whose meaning was clear, but how was the missionary to explain the mysteries of the Crucifixion and Salvation? Konrad Vetter, who joined Flierl at Simbang in 1890, pointed out that since the villagers had no consciousness of sin they felt no need for a Saviour; knowing nothing of Hell, they did not strive to go to Heaven. Vetter was the first of the Neuendettelsau missionaries to propose a theology adapted to the situation of the New Guineans, one which stressed not that Christ died for their sins but that He would keep them safe from sorcerers. Protection from sorcery was a benefit which every villager understood.[21]

No converts were made until 1899 and then only two former school pupils in Simbang were baptized. One of them, Kamusanga, left his wife for another woman and was expelled from the Christian congregation for five years. Yet Flierl had laid the groundwork for a highly successful mission. By choosing to stay in the Finschhafen area when the Neu Guinea Compagnie was driven out by malaria in 1891, he ensured that the missionaries would not be associated with wholesale loss of village land to plantations, as occurred in Madang; and by building a hill station at Sattelberg in the mountains behind Finschhafen and staying there despite depredations by thieves, he created an unusually healthy mission centre and a base for the later evangelization of the densely populated mountain ranges to the west.

From the original three stations at Simbang, Tami and Sattelberg the Neuendettelsau Lutherans spread west from Finschhafen along the coast of the Huon Gulf to Deinzerhöhe (1899), Cape Arkona (1906) and Lae (1910), across to the south coast of the Huon Gulf at Malolo (1907) and the border with Papua at Morobe (1911), north as far as the Rai coast at Sio (1910) and to the Siassi Islands (1911). Around Finschhafen they founded a cluster of stations between 1902 and 1908, but their most remarkable achievement was to extend mission influence inland: to another mountain station at Wareo north of Sattelberg (1903) and then west to the Hube people of the interior of the Huon Peninsula, beginning with Kulungtufu (1908). After a dramatic peacemaking with the Wampar people who had been raiding coastal villages the Lutherans went from Lae up the Markham Valley to Gabmatzung (1911) and were at Kaiapit by 1917.

The initial conversions—of Yabim-speaking coastal villagers—came two or three at a time. Later, especially after the earthquake of September 1906, Kotte speakers in the Sattelberg district turned to the mission in a mass movement. Within little more than a year the Reverend Christian Keysser had baptized 200 villagers and hundreds more clamoured for the sprinkling of the water, so many that the mission called a halt to baptisms for fear of losing control of the congregation. The new church at Wareo, built to seat 550, could not accommodate the crowds who thronged to a baptismal ceremony in 1910.[22]

The Neuendettelsau Mission, isolated from plantation companies and government, became a kind of state within a state, organizing an alternative, church-based form of village government. Christianized villages, even where some inhabitants remained heathens, became theocracies under the rule of church elders and subject to the decisions of congregational meetings. The model for this development was the Sattelberg congregation, where for twenty years the Reverend Christian Keysser endeavoured to realize his vision of an organic Christian community in which secular and spiritual were one. At Sattelberg all villagers were compelled to live in the main settlements where they could be kept under church control; children had to attend school; pathways from place to place had to be kept in good condition so that people could go to church and also sell their garden produce; the village chief, called a *songang*, supervised communal work such as building houses or roads; the old decorations and valuables, previously signs of a man's wealth, were forbidden; brideprice was abolished and husbands were not allowed to beat their wives; heathen dancing was outlawed. To enforce the new order, the Sattelberg congregation and others before World War I imposed secular penalties including imprisonment, thrashing and hard labour, a system approved by Governor Hahl. The Australians were to insist upon government-appointed *luluais*, often but not always the same men as the Lutheran chiefs, whereas the German colonial administration left the mission undisturbed. The initiative for the strict social code of the Lutheran village seems to have come from converts themselves, eager to embrace the Word of God and forsake the past, whether in true Christian spirit or in the the expectation of material gain.[23]

Christian villagers spread the Word for the Neuendettelsau Mission as they did for other missions. Among the first were four Sattelberg men, Halingke, Mainao, Kupa and Fungmo, who ventured into the mountain valleys of the Hube people in 1908 and set up a mission station at Kulungtufu; by 1912 Mainao was as far west as Ogeramnang and two years later the mission had twenty-two trained evangelists. The evangelists acquired influence by distributing goods, making peace, mediating in village disputes and showing no fear of sorcerers. A letter written by Kupa in

1912 shows how the evangelists, by intervening in local politics, could help to prevent hostilities:

> The man Zililinga died. His relatives and friends gathered at the burial with their weapons in order to avenge his death. When we learnt the people's intention I hurried there with Kawac in order to prevent the evil deed from being done. I succeeded in winning the dead man's clan for peace. But the guests and friends from the neighbourhood wanted nothing of peace. It was only a few men but they shouted so loudly that everyone else was afraid of them. Then I said to them: 'Do you really not want to rest until it comes to a fight and someone lies murdered on the ground? Then when more and more fighting follows you will come to us again and ask us to settle the peace. So I will advise you: don't start the quarrel; bury the dead man in peace!' Then one of the biggest rabble rousers snapped: 'You are a foreigner. What are you doing talking to us?' At these words he drew his bow and took aim at me. But some of the men immediately grabbed his arm and abused him for being so hot-tempered. I demanded the arrow which he had aimed at me. He gave it. I did not want any other token of peace. The Hube are like wild, biting pigs. They reach for their weapons at every opportunity.[24]

Isolation only partly accounts for the Neuendettelsau Lutherans' success. With twenty-six European missionaries in 1913 they were much better staffed than either of the other Protestant missions in German New Guinea. The Rhenish Mission had nine and the Methodists eight. Flierl was a practical man, ensuring from the start that every mission station had land for gardens and cattle, at least 100 hectares, and that the stations were run simply and economically. He encouraged missionaries on coastal stations to plant coconut palms, and near Finschhafen he set up two copra plantations and a sawmill. The 500 hectares of land which he bought near Lae in 1914 were later to become the mission's largest plantation, Malahang.[25]

The Neuendettelsau Mission never achieved financial self-sufficiency, but its investments usefully contributed to income and created a situation in which the mission brought the outside world to New Guinea on its own terms. School pupils were to be paid at the least possible expense, a mission conference noted in 1905, reminding missionaries not to have a bad conscience 'if the mission boys are satisfied with a low wage; our main aim is their instruction and they work at the stations for their own upkeep'. When recruiting youths for mission boarding-schools, missionaries tried to avoid paying the usual advances. They resisted official attempts to make them record such recruits as labourers. Villagers sold taro, yams, bananas, sago, fish and pork to mission stations at uniform prices lower than those paid by the Neu Guinea Compagnie, and the mission was their main source of soap, blankets, bush knives and axes. For many villagers the mission was recruiter, employer, civil and spiritual authority, tradestore and school all in one, and they identified closely with it, speaking of 'our sawmill', 'our plantation' and 'our printery'. The Australians were to find Neuendettelsau mission villages particularly suspicious of the new regime.[26]

The Rhenish Mission

The Rhenish Mission of Barmen was dogged by a series of disasters which left it hardly more influential in 1914 than when Brother Friedrich Eich landed in Kaiser Wilhelmsland in 1887. Brother J. W. Thomas left New Guinea ill and weak in October 1887, the first in a long line of Rhenish missionaries to be driven out of the country by fever. Eich stayed on at Bogadjim, soon to be inconveniently close to the NGC plantations, and within a few years was joined by fellow-missionaries on Siar and Kranket islands in the immediate vicinity of Madang. Attempts to settle at Hatzfeldthafen twice failed, once after a punitive expedition in 1887 when villagers presumed the missionaries to be allies of the white marines and again in 1890, when warriors killed F. W. Scheidt and Friedrich Bösch. After six years the tiny mission had sustained the deaths of a further two missionaries and three wives of missionaries, with nothing to show for the sacrifice.

Karkar Islanders asked to have missionaries but the smallpox epidemic of the 1890s wrought such havoc that the Karkar station was abandoned. Elsewhere the villagers treated the missionaries as traders, useful for their supplies of cloth and knives but for nothing else. One Rhenish missionary, worried about prostitution in villages near the German settlements, saw his task as protecting the women of Bogadjim from white vice. He noted that 'the very beautiful girls and women in their quite scanty clothing arouse lust far too much. I have made the observation that many whites go into the villages only in order to feast their eyes on the beautiful, half-naked women'. Protecting women was a long way from converting them, however, and even the few mission schools in the 1890s failed to arouse interest in the Gospel. A conference of Rhenish missionaries in 1899 concluded that 'not a single native' understood their purpose in being in New Guinea; instead people took the missionaries' pastoral visits to be trading trips and were interested only in tangible gains such as free treatment of wounds. Without exception, the missionary at Bongu complained, every villager lacked a sense of sinfulness.[27]

Frustrated, impatient and self-righteous, the Rhenish missionaries were peculiarly apt to seek the assistance of the colonial authorities and to take a stern view of local custom. They resolved to report infanticide to the government for punishment. Gustav Bergmann on Siar Island thought forced labour imposed by the police in 1900 would have 'a good influence on the natives here' and a few years later, when police again conscripted the Siar, he described the measure as 'good and useful for our people'. Ostermann on Kranket mission station, founded in 1901, insisted on keeping a boy in school against the wishes of his father, and when the father brandished a spear, Ostermann had him punished by the authorities. Another missionary, A. Hoffmann, complained that the magistrate at Madang took no action over his complaints about local murders. More than any other mission, the Rhenish mission identified Christianity with colonial order and turned to the colonial government to enforce it.[28]

At the baptism of the first convert at Bogadjim in December 1903 the Rhenish missionaries' spirits rose in the belief that 'the ice which seemed to encase the hearts of the Papuans had broken, and the complete victory of the Gospel could not be far distant'. The Madang revolt just eight months later, directed as it was at all Europeans whether planters or not, plunged the missionaries once more into gloom. The very peoples whom they thought they knew best, the Yam of Kranket and Siar, had conspired to murder them and the missionaries never fully trusted them again.[29]

On Kranket ill-feeling reached a peak in 1907 as the missionary Heinrich Helmich clashed with the *luluai* Sabu, a relapsed convert who led a campaign of threats and sorcery against the Christians and denounced the missionary as an enemy of his people. In anger, Helmich went to the village and dealt out what he called 'paternal chastisement' to a few of his opponents, who then complained to the Madang District Officer. The trouble lay in the mission's campaign against the island's secret male cult, a custom which Helmich expected the authorities to criticize, but on a visit soon afterwards Governor Hahl upheld the people's right to practise traditional custom and chided Helmich for not attempting to adapt his message accordingly. The Kranket heathens, quick to exploit differences between Europeans, now appealed repeatedly to the District Office to get rid of the missionary, their 'open slanders and lies' (said Helmich) going quite unpunished. On Siar the people had to endure the rantings and beatings of a missionary called Weber, a man obsessed with order and sexual morality, possibly mentally disturbed, who was eventually dismissed by his embarrassed sponsors in Germany.[30]

The Rhenish Mission could look back on a quarter of a century's effort in 1912. In that time it had sent fifty-three men and women into the mission field from Germany, of whom sixteen had died there and eighteen left. Their struggles had produced just eighty-one converts, eight schools and a total financial contribution from New Guineans in 1911 of less than 300 marks or £15 in contemporary sterling. Siar, for twenty years the head mission station, was abandoned in 1910 after what the mission called success 'equal to zero'.[31]

Stagnation came for many reasons. Rapid turnover of staff left the mission without the experience and renown of a Johann Flierl or Louis Couppé. It lacked the sizable landholdings which gave the Neuendettelsau missionaries such a valuable supply of food. Nor did the missionaries advance their cause by advocating a colonial mission, seeing missions and government as partners in the task of civilizing the 'native'. The mission inspector Eduard Kriele, who came to New Guinea in 1909, wanted more 'teamwork between missions and colonial policy'. His colleague W. Diehl welcomed the news that the government would extend the head-tax to mission villages, seeing it as 'cultural progress which will benefit our people and undoubtedly our work as well', part of that systematic official action which would overcome people's unwillingness to work. 'For their own sake' the people would have to learn to work and earn money, said Diehl, and he pointed to the jobs which villagers could do to raise money for the mission if they only possessed the initiative: casual labouring on plantations, gathering wild gutta-percha and working for Europeans as hunters or butterfly collectors. Many villagers believed, in the words of one missionary, 'that our sermons and the government regulations were the same and therefore whenever they failed to follow what we said they could expect difficulties or punishment from the authorities in power'.[32]

Proximity to the plantations and towns of Astrolabe Bay was a disadvantage for the Rhenish missionaries, though not as great as they imagined. The bright lights distracted people from the Gospel. 'The labourers recruited from various districts of New Guinea', Bergmann complained in 1902, 'bring their national dances and suchlike to their new home and the natives like nothing more than to learn from their distant countrymen these new dances, with which a lot of other things are associated . . .'. The preaching of the Gospel could make no headway against these constant novelties, according to Bergmann. On Sunday mornings, instead of going to church, the Siar Islanders crossed to Madang to exchange fruits and vegetables for the tobacco which plantation labourers had been paid the previous evening. The costs of mission were higher than in the remote mission field of the Huon Gulf. At Madang and Stephansort every potential pupil knew the wages and conditions of a NGC labourer and wanted the same for himself. Living close to a district office, the villagers played missionaries off against officials as the occasion suited: missionaries could be useful when the *kiap* wanted to imprison people for stealing from plantations; the *kiap* was a defence against the missionaries' intrusions on traditional custom.

All of these problems, however, were familiar to missionaries in the Gazelle Peninsula, where missions close to settlers nevertheless prospered. What made the crucial difference for the Rhenish Mission was the attitude of the people of Madang and the Rai coast. They did not like Europeans of any kind, refused to believe what the missionaries said and co-operated only for tactical reasons. When the Germans deported many of the Yam people after the conspiracy of 1912 the Rhenish Mission was, in its own words, 'robbed of its object', for few villagers remained in the greater part of the Kranket station district. Typically, the mission's last report before the war thanked the colonial authorities for suppressing polygamy and urged them to do more to make people plant coconuts.[33]

The Holy Spirit Mission of the Society of the Divine Word (SVD)

The Society of the Divine Word, given the responsibility of the new prefecture apostolic of Kaiser Wilhelmsland, settled near Aitape on the northwest coast in 1896. The leader of the first group of six SVD missionaries was a German, Father Eberhard Limbrock, a priest with thirteen years' experience of missionary work in China. Nothing if not a practical man, Limbrock devoted himself to establishing the mission on a sound economic basis. Of the missions in New Guinea, only the Sacred Heart owned more land at the end of World War I and none had developed copra plantations so quickly. For Father Limbrock land, plantations, boats, boathouses, cranes, winches, sawmills and cattle came first and evangelization followed in the fullness of time.[34]

Having been refused entry to Madang because of the opposition of the Rhenish Lutherans, the SVD went instead to Tumleo, one of the four small islands in the Aitape roadstead. The Tumleo people, nearly 300 of them living in four villages, were handsomely built and well fed, makers of large sailing canoes which could carry two tonnes and travel hundreds of kilometres along the coast. Like the Bilbil of Astrolabe Bay, the Tumleo monopolized the manufacture of pots in the region and their island home was therefore a centre of trade. On the mainland coast people speaking a different language welcomed two priests and two brothers who came in July 1898 to found a second station on the grey sand of Vokau village[35] where Father Christian Schleiermacher encountered problems familiar to any missionary in a new field in New Guinea:

> In the first village one finds a group of old kanakas who are about to build a boat. 'Time for school!' we call to them. *Pameum anoe kajem lapil*, that is, 'no, I am making a boat'. 'You can make the boat when school is finished'. This has little effect; finally we take some of them by the arm and pull them away from their work. That helps. They take their tools home, which lasts some minutes. But one must wait and ensure that the will becomes the deed. After they have rolled a cigar and lit it, they finally decide to follow our call. Another group is spread out around the fire, eating tobacco. How many excuses are to be expected here! The whole lot of them stay quietly where they are. Finally one takes some by the hair and drags them away; the crowd begins to move . . . Meanwhile others have noticed what it is all about and at a favourable moment disappeared into the bush. After much talk back and forth we finally reach the school. Here the men are quite well-behaved, at times too quiet, that is, when they are continuing their slumber. They like to hear about religion but do not want to abandon their heathen customs. I spoke to them for three-quarters of an hour about God and His Love, and when I asked them whether they wanted to become Catholics, they exclaimed in unison: 'Yes!' But after they heard that they would have to renounce this, that and the other heathen custom they shouted just as loudly: 'School is over! School is over!'[36]

Of all the missions in German New Guinea, however, the SVD was the least in a hurry to save souls. 'We have to be farmers and planters; we have to import, care for and breed cattle. For sea journeys we must understand sailing and steering', wrote Limbrock, and he pressed the colonial authorities for land, asking Hahl for 10 000 hectares in 1902. Within three years the SVD spread east from Aitape as far as Alexishafen, where the mission built a sawmill to supply its timber and a training centre to teach villagers skills in carpentry and metalwork. To complaints from fellow priests that he was neglecting the spiritual tasks of the mission Limbrock replied that if a house was to be built a foundation was necessary and he continued to assign his colleagues to jobs as plantation managers, road engineers, ship's captains and boat builders. The mission planted coconut palms extensively, experimented successfully with rubber and rice and laid down plantation rail tracks.[37] It spread the Gospel through its plantation labourers, whose children were attracted to the mission schools, and like its counterpart in New Britain, founded orphanages in which the heathen young could be raised in the Faith. 'I explain the Annunciation to them with a picture', Father Franz Vormann wrote of an early SVD school class,

> On the walls there are various panels with coloured pictures; of the creation of the world, the Fall, Cain and Abel, the story of Joseph in Egypt, Moses and the tablets on Sinai. The children have already picked up isolated fragments of the truths which these panels portray but their relationship and spirit remain hidden.[38]

By 1914 the SVD claimed over 3600 converts and had established its first inland station at Marienberg, a small hill about sixty kilometres upstream from the mouth of the Sepik River. Here again the first task of the missionaries was to clear the dense tropical forest for a plantation.

Governor Hahl thought Limbrock was the ideal missionary, a man of action committed to the economic development of the colony and to the spread of German language and culture. School children at Alexishafen spoke to the missionaries in German, not Pidgin, and in 1910 they entertained visiting sailors by singing German songs and displaying their knowledge of the national borders of the Second *Reich*. (More than sixty years later people on Ali Island near Aitape still remembered some German.) Hahl's criterion of a mission's usefulness was patriotic, not religious. A Protestant himself, he disliked the Methodists because so few of them were Germans, and he reacted sharply when Rome decided in 1913 to split the SVD's mission field in two, assigning the coast from Aitape to Dutch New Guinea to a French congregation, the Picpus Fathers. Keeping the Germans in a position of cultural supremacy in New Guinea would depend on training New Guineans to accept German as a lingua franca and on ensuring that the civilization of Europe reached the villager 'in our language and with our thoughts', he complained to the Colonial Office. The education of Germany's colonial subjects, 'our people', ought not to be entrusted to a French missionary society. On this matter as on many others the opinion of Governor Hahl was by no means decisive in Berlin: the pioneer party of Catholic missionaries, due to leave Europe on 7 August 1914, were Germans rather than Frenchmen, but they were members of the Picpus Congregation to which Hahl objected. As it happened, they were prevented from going to New Guinea by the war.[39]

The Society of Mary
The Marist Fathers were old hands in the Pacific, having first come in the 1830s. After brief and disastrous settlements on Woodlark Island (1847) and Umboi Island (1848) they had withdrawn (1855) and did not return to Melanesia until 1898, entrusted by the Sacred Congregation for the

Propagation of the Faith with the evangelization of the Solomon Islands. The Shortland group, where the Marists bought land for a mission station on Poporang Island in 1899, remained German territory only until 1900, when it passed to British control as a consequence of the Anglo-German Treaty over Samoa. Poporang was nevertheless the base from which the ecclesiastical territory of the North Solomons was evangelized. In German times and for long after the Church ignored the international border, treating the North Solomons as a region which encompassed the Shortlands and Choiseul as well as Bougainville and Buka. Until Governor Hahl forbade the practice in 1907, most of the children at Poporang mission school in the British Solomons were taken from Bougainville and Buka in German New Guinea.

Expansion from Poporang northwards was slow, hindered by malaria and local resistance. The Marists, it is true, were asked to come to Kieta by a village leader on Pokpok Island called Sarai, who sold them thirty-five hectares of land for axes, knives, cloth, beads and a whaleboat. He wanted a school, sharing that Melanesian enthusiasm for literacy which often smoothed the way for missionaries in New Guinea. But the missionaries who came to take possession of the land endured many months of hostility from nearby villagers before their presence was accepted.

The advance into Buin, south Bougainville, was equally opposed. At Patupatuai station, established in 1905, Fathers John Rausch and François Alotte made the mistake of taking sides in a local feud by granting asylum to fugitive villagers including a hated sorcerer. In fear of their lives, the Fathers asked for police from Kieta, who engaged in battle with local warriors, killing two and reducing a village to ashes. Hahl was annoyed. His police had been drawn into conflict in Buin unnecessarily, and he told the Marists that they could expect no future protection if hostilities arose from mission interference in villagers' disputes. The Marists stayed on in Buin, made peace and won a small number of converts but the wholesale conversion of the area and the overthrow of the old pagan chiefs did not come until the 1920s. In 1908 when the anthropologist Richard Thurnwald lived for nine months in Buin, mission influence was non-existent: the houses of the greatest warriors were still adorned with numerous skulls and the bodies of the dead cremated on platforms.

Smallest of the three Catholic missions in German New Guinea, the Society of Mary still numbered its converts in hundreds by 1914, whereas its sister missions had thousands of followers. Settlements on Buka in 1910 and the west coast of Bougainville in 1911 extended its influence only slightly. The Bukas in particular, long accustomed to earning Western wealth as plantation labourers and police, saw little novelty in the Mammon being offered by the Marists to lead people to God.[40]

All missions faced the problem of converting people in non-chiefly societies. In Fiji, the Methodist Heath Rickard observed:

a chief said 'I am *lotu*' and hundreds said the same day: 'So are we'. In New Britain, on the contrary, a so-called chief says he is '*lotu*', but even his wife and children say 'we will not': therefore we cannot expect here the great things that were witnessed in Fiji.[41]

Mass conversion arising from the authority of Christianized chiefs was inconceivable in New Guinea, and the missionaries were therefore compelled to find other ways of gathering in the flock. Whether Catholic or Protestant, they employed fundamentally similar tactics of winning the villagers' approval.

The Melanesian villager valued the missionary, at least initially, not for what he preached but for what he possessed, gave away or traded. In all but name the missionary on the frontier in New Guinea was a trader and land purchaser and his goods alone gave him access to pagan village communities. Before the German occupation the Methodists paid for land in New Britain in axes, tomahawks, tobacco, cotton print, beads, boxes of matches, pipes, knives and even flasks of gunpowder. Except for the gunpowder, goods of this kind became the standard currency of land transactions between villagers and all missions.

Once permitted to stay, the missionary made himself indispensable to villagers by his constant supply of such material wealth. To begin with, villagers often stole from the missionaries: the people at Sattelberg greeted Johann Flierl in the 1890s by stealing everything from the sheets on his bed and washing on the line to goats grazing near his house. But a trading relationship developed here, as it did everywhere between missionaries and villagers.

The mission school was an extension of the trading relationship, a form of paid employment. The Marists and Sacred Heart missionaries paid openly for orphans and other children who could be brought to a boarding school, away from the distractions of the village, taught the fundamentals of the Faith and formed into the nucleus of the new Christian community. After a catechumenate of two or three years pupils were paid off with tobacco and cloth and dispatched to their villages with news of the white man's wealth, literacy and beliefs. The Marist Father Joseph Forestier paid £4 each for girls from Buin in 1902, and Marist methods of filling mission schools continued to resemble labour recruiting. Governor Hahl was under no illusions about the schools in Bougainville, and he insisted in 1907 that all children attracted to school by the promise of wages or gifts were to be treated by the Marist mission as indentured labourers subject to the protection of the labour legislation. The Neuendettelsau Lutherans were also recruiters, offering iron tools in return for the months which children spent on the mission station learning bible stories and doing odd jobs for the missionaries. School pupils were cheap labour. 'How much better it has become in the past two years', wrote Flierl in 1892 of the establishment of his first boarding school, 'we no longer need to go begging to Simbang for a messenger or carrier. In a country such as this it is a blessing to have one's own people'.[42]

Material wealth, then, was the first weapon of Christ's followers in their quest for the souls of the New Guinean heathen. The successful missionary put goods before theology. Father Leo Brenninkmeyer, at work in the Baining Mountains of east New Britain in 1913, was asked by people who saw the crucifix on his table what it meant. With all his theological knowledge, he recalled, he was unable to give an answer in 'a few comprehensible words'; they would, he assured his inquirers, learn its significance later. A blanket, clothes and daily rations of pork were the attractions which brought the first village boys to Brenninkmeyer's primitive boarding school.[43]

The missionaries had other ways of appealing to villagers. In a country where virtually every coastal dweller suffered from malaria and ringworm, where common colds frequently developed fatal complications and where any scratch could become a tropical ulcer, the slightest medical skills of the missionary were welcome. On many mission stations missionaries spent a number of hours every day bandaging wounds, distributing medicines and instructing people in hygiene. Every missionary had to learn basic first aid and get used to dealing with medical emergencies. To give one of thousands of examples, the Neuendettelsau missionary Johann Stössel, with one year's medical training at Tübingen, had to amputate the hand of a man who had been mauled by a shark, fix broken bones and perform a cataract operation, as well as assisting at numerous childbirths. Beginning in 1911 the colonial administration began training medical assistants, village men who were capable of disinfecting and bandaging wounds, dispensing simple medicines and diagnosing more serious cases for government doctors. By 1914 *heiltultul*, as they were known, were at work in eighty-five communities in the Namatanai district alone and were being appointed for the first time in the Aitape and Morobe districts. They were Hahl's barefoot doctors, his frontline troops in the battle against depopulation. But for the greater part of German rule the villager, as distinct from the indentured labourer, depended upon missions rather than government for the treatment of illness.[44]

The missionaries' success in making peace and protecting people from their enemies also won converts. The MSC gained a following on the north coast of the Gazelle Peninsula in the 1890s after it intervened to prevent the execution of a man who had been opposing the missionaries in the area. More dramatically, Neuendettelsau Lutheran missionaries enabled the Wampar people of the Markham Valley to cease their hostilities with coastal peoples. The Wampar, called the Laewomba people by the Germans, killed more than 100 people in raids on villages of the Lae people in 1907, and remained undiscouraged by two punitive expeditions, successfully attacking the first in a night raid and avoiding contact with the second. But in April 1909 the Wampar found gifts of boars' tusks, tobacco and dogs' teeth left as tokens of peace by a party of Lutheran missionaries who had ventured up the Markham River into Wampar territory: they responded favourably, presenting the Lae with a sword, participating in a peacemaking feast and welcoming missionaries. The Lutherans made allies on both sides of the conflict. The Lae people, now safe from raids, came in hundreds to greet their new missionary Gottfried Schmutterer in 1911 and the Wampar also accepted their first missionary at Gabmatzung in the same year. The Wampar continued to kill enemies further inland, especially the Atzera. Theirs was a society in which no young man could put on decorations or obtain a wife until he had killed someone. Uninfluenced by the missionaries among them, they left the schools and churches empty and refused to convert until the 1920s. But in a colonial situation which constantly reminded people that the white man, who was a Christian, was also rich and powerful, all missionaries had time on their side. Gaining a foothold was what mattered. The conversion of most peoples was sure to follow in a decade or two.[45]

Conversion meant different things to different missions. The Catholics, believing in the efficacy of the Sacraments, said prayers over the dead, celebrated Mass and baptized babies whether people were converted or not. They laid down plantations, built sawmills, bought land and busied themselves with economic enterprises which would sustain the Church of the future. When villagers eventually asked for baptism the Catholics obliged without excessive inquiry into people's understanding of the Faith. Protestants, with notable exceptions, stressed individual conversion by confession of sin, repentance and willingness to lead a new life, and imposed stricter tests on candidates for entry into the community of believers.

Within individual missions missionaries disagreed sharply about the nature of conversion. To Karl Steck, the Neuendettelsau mission inspector who visited the New Guinea field in 1914, for example, the achievements of Flierl and his colleagues were illusory. Only in the Sattelberg congregation under Christian Keysser did the inspector find a Christian community. Elsewhere, he believed, the Christianity of the Lutherans was a sham: people believed in God, were confident of forgiveness, accepted the Ten Commandments and expected to go to Heaven but had no clear or necessary place for Jesus Christ in their beliefs. The Christ of the Atonement, sacrificed for the sins of the world, was missing. Not surprisingly, Flierl refused to accept these criticisms. He had laboured long and hard to amass the 4000 Christians of the Neuendettelsau mission and believed them to be true converts. As the Lutheran Georg Pilhofer was later to point out, the converts believed that Christ protected them from the dark forces of sorcery, an interpretation of Salvation which belonged to the Christian tradition. The Methodist H. P. Wenzel believed that Methodist converts both understood and followed 'the doctrine of repentance and forgiveness of sins', even though it was 'difficult for the Kanaka to renounce his essential self'.[46]

All missionaries were against those traditional practices which most clearly offended Christian and Western values, such as nakedness, sexual licence, lascivious dancing, polygamy, infanticide and warfare, and all sought to impose on people a missionary version of Western life, in which people wore clothes, men had one wife each, children went to school and everyone went to church on Sunday. Whether or not converts understood the doctrine of the Atonement or the meaning of the mass, then, they all knew that Christians were supposed to forgo certain old customs and adopt certain new ones. Christianity was no mere adoption of belief. It was a revolution in the daily and seasonal life of the village. Writing in 1914 the head of the Rhenish mission saw evidence of 'Christian morality and civilisation' in the fact that the people of southern Astrolabe Bay were making roads and plantations, building bigger huts, burying their dead, devoting less time to heathen festivals and working harder to obtain European goods. That same process, seen from the viewpoint of the village, meant that the authority of old people was undermined, the spirits of the ancestors offended and the political ambitions of heathens thwarted.[47]

Whatever conversion was, it was not simply the achievement of European missionaries. Europeans did not directly control much of the evangelization of New Guinea. They initiated and supervised that process, but in numerous communities considered too small or remote to be worthy of a European missionary, Christianizing was a Polynesian or Melanesian affair. Probably the majority of villagers heard most about Jesus from a Fijian, Tongan, Samoan or Papua New Guinean mission teacher, and some heard it first from young men returning after a stint of plantation work. South Sea Islanders did most of the work of converting the villagers of New Britain and New Ireland to Methodism, bringing with them new fruits such as lemons, oranges and guavas, new varieties of banana, pandanus and yams, together with Fijian and Tongan music and a strict Sabbatarianism. New Guinean catechists carried Catholicism into remote villages in the Gazelle Peninsula, New Ireland, Manus, Bougainville and the north-west coast of the mainland. Lutheranism reached many people in the Huon Peninsula and the Markham Valley on the lips of Kotte and Yabim converts from nearer the coast.

New Guinean mission teachers were no less ethnocentric than their European sponsors. Kupa and his fellow Kotte evangelists were disgusted by the depravity and violence of the Hube, their nearby countrymen in the Huon Peninsula. But the exact version of Christianity which men such as Kupa preached is now beyond recall. Perhaps, like some later evangelists, Kupa thought of Heaven as the place where good people were paid off as they would be on completing a labour contract. To judge from the letters of other Kotte Christians he would have stressed sexual purity, peace and hard work. As the Kotte convert Genzi, aged eighteen, wrote in 1909 of a girl called Madong:

> Wherever she meets me on the track, I always feel the longing to seduce her. But then I think of the fact that Jesus died for me and hold myself back . . . I want to make sure that she is mine and buy her with money, knives and cloth.

For Tilijuc, a Christian labourer in Rabaul, the temptations to betray Jesus were also strong. 'Here', he wrote to his missionary in 1910,

> we are ridiculed when we sing and pray. We do not stop, but answer: Jesus has done so much for us and freed us from the old fear, that is why we will not let go of him. But it really is difficult not to get dirty in the midst of filth. The men laugh at us and sneer. The women

approach us and want to seduce us. I will not disgrace Jesus my Lord
. . . but whether I will stand firm in the long run I do not know.

A Neuendettelsau school pupil called Bilong, home on holidays in 1910,
saw Christians as industrious people:

On the first day at home I helped my people clear the forest for a
field of yams. The men stopped and had a smoke. As they were sitting
there too long I said: today is a work day, we should not do nothing
for so long! One of the men answered: you work on the mission station
only because the overseer is standing nearby! Why act now as if you
were a model of hard work? At these words from the people I thought:
when I am hard working I am thinking not of a person but of God
. . . Only when it grew dark did I stop working. The people said: he
is different from us in our youth, because he thinks of God.[48]

Such fragmentary evidence can do no more than hint at the nature of
conversion in German New Guinea, but a few things can be said with cer-
tainty. One is that, with the exception of the Rhenish missionaries, the
missions won converts in numbers which they regarded as evidence of success. Broadly, the two most successful missions at the end of German rule
were the Sacred Heart missionaries and the Methodists, both in the New
Guinea islands. The Neuendettelsau Lutherans monopolized mission work
in the Huon Gulf, its hinterland and along the coast from Sio to the border
with Australian Papua. The Divine Word Mission had made a promising
beginning on the coast between Alexishafen and Aitape, the Marist Mission
a less promising one on Bougainville and Buka, and the Rhenish Lutherans
on the Madang and Rai coasts had failed.

Second, New Guinean villagers were active participants in the coming
of the new Christian order. The Methodist Heath Rickard thought the
missionaries' influence with the Duke of York Islanders to be 'little short
of omnipotence, since they do almost as directed, and since they and the
history of their land is as wax in our hands to be moulded almost as we
will'.[49] He was wrong, and so were other missionaries who relished the
role of spiritual kings. Villagers were not waiting to be pressed into Christian shape by missionaries. They were attracted to Christianity by advantages for themselves in the foreign Christians' wealth, medicine and power.
They picked and chose from what was on offer, stressing those elements
of the new Faith which made sense, such as protection from sorcery, and
creating Melanesian varieties of Christianity which syncretized new and
old beliefs. The missionaries might have brought Christianity to New
Guinea but the New Guineans made it their own.

8
The Germans as Explorers and Colonizers

New Guinea represented career opportunities not only for missionaries and civil servants, but for explorers and scientists as well. An ascent of the Sepik River, a march across west New Britain, even a trip along familiar coastline was worth publications, recognition and professional advancement to an enterprising ethnographer, geologist, botanist or zoologist. Not all the explorers were Germans. The Hungarian Lajos Biró spent five years collecting plants, animals and artefacts in Kaiser Wilhelmsland and sending them to the National Museum in Budapest. Nor were all explorers experts. Some were wealthy dilettantes who paid for their own exploratory adventures, others were planters and missionaries who made observations in the course of their work. But professional expeditions, staffed by German scientists and sponsored by scientific institutions, the Neu Guinea Compagnie, the Colonial Office and the Navy, undertook the bulk of exploration in the islands in German times and filled the museums of the Fatherland with millions of specimens, from butterflies and stuffed birds to canoes, houses, masks, spears, shields and traditional valuables.

Unlike British and Australian explorers in Papua, the Germans in New Guinea waded through sago swamps or hacked their way through scrub, mainly for the sake of science and in the hope of finding valuable resources. They did not do so in order to bring knowledge of the government to the people, after the manner of British New Guinea's governor Sir William MacGregor, who ascended all the major rivers in his colony, climbed the highest peak in the Owen Stanley Range and twice crossed south-east New Guinea from Port Moresby to the Mambare. The German exploratory enterprise was different from its British counterpart: scientific and economic rather than administrative in purpose, less adventurous but more meticulous and far more significant as a contribution to scholarly knowledge. The Germans walked less but recorded more.

German explorers failed to achieve their economic aims. They discovered traces of gold, oil and coal and modest numbers of gutta-percha trees but not enough of any to justify intensive exploitation. The potential labourers they found in Sepik villages were to be recruited by Australians, not Germans. And by not penetrating to the intermontane valleys of the

Highlands the Germans never saw the most densely populated part of their possession or its good agricultural land.

The NGC took exploration seriously, especially in the early years of the charter when it could afford to mount large expeditions in the hope of finding valuable resources. The first Company governor, Schleinitz, a veteran of the naval expedition which named the Gazelle Peninsula in 1875, sailed along much of the coast of Kaiser Wilhelmsland, hundreds of kilometres up the Sepik River and to west New Britain. Travelling south-east from the Huon Gulf in 1886 he named promontories and capes after the Prussian Minister of Religion, Gustav von Gossler, the former Prussian Minister of War, Bronsart von Schellendorf, and a collection of Prussian generals from August von Göben to Eduard Vogel von Falkenstein. It was easy enough to try to immortalize one's countrymen in the features of a coastline. The more daunting task was to explore the inland, where steep ridges, fast-flowing rivers, dense jungle and men with spears awaited the explorer. The NGC's special scientific expedition, led by the astronomer Carl Schrader, found these obstacles so great that it ignored instructions and confined itself to the coast of Kaiser Wilhelmsland and the Sepik River, collecting plants and rocks for museums but leaving the NGC little the wiser about the practical potential of the colony.[1]

After that the Company left exploration for a number of years to private adventurers, men such as the journalist Hugo Zöller, who was sponsored by the *Kölnische Zeitung* to entertain readers with lurid tales of life in the darkest jungles of New Guinea. He led a party high into the Finisterre Range behind the Rai coast, named a mountain after the owner of his newspaper and wrote a book describing what he called 'the first successful advance into the high mountain ranges of New Guinea'. Zöller had the sense to inflate a minor achievement into a major one.[2]

Otto Ehlers, a professional traveller who reached New Guinea in 1895, was determined to cross the island of New Guinea, a feat never performed in the rugged country where he wanted to go. Warned by the authorities not to attempt the journey, Ehlers nevertheless set out confidently from Bayern Bay near Salamaua, accompanied by another German and forty-three New Guinean carriers, expecting to average six kilometres a day and reach the Gulf of Papua in a month. He had not reckoned with leeches, mites, constant rain and mist, precipitous mountainsides, tropical infections and dysentery. After five weeks the party ran out of food and had to live off grass and leaves, and when twenty survivors stumbled into the village of Motumotu on the Papuan coast, Ehlers was not among them. He and some of the carriers from New Ireland, so the Germans came to believe, had been killed in desperation by two Buka police on the expedition, Ranga and Upia, who then concocted a story that the Germans had drowned. Other explorers were to die in German New Guinea. Bruno Mencke was speared to death by warriors of the St Matthias Islands in 1901 and Wilhelm Dammköhler bled to death in 1909 from arrow wounds inflicted by Babwaf people on the Watut River. But none invited his own end as recklessly as Ehlers.

The Ehlers affair had a violent sequel. Imprisoned for murder, Ranga and Upia escaped and were pursued by an expedition under the Company Governor Curt von Hagen, who was shot dead in an encounter with the prisoners. Once Hagen was buried, the German authorities attempted once more to bring the two Buka to justice, this time with a party of police under the young Albert Hahl, who had no fewer than seven villages in the Madang area burnt down in the search. Hahl did not find the fugitives. Local villagers killed them. Hagen's lasting memorial was a mountain range named after him by two explorers who saw it far away to the south-west from the Bismarck Mountains in 1896, in an area not to be visited by Europeans until Jim Taylor and Mick Leahy walked from Bena Bena to Mount Hagen in 1933.[3]

Gold was the lure which attracted a series of inland expeditions by the Germans between 1896 and 1902. The first, led by the botanist Carl Lauterbach, discovered a second great navigable river in Kaiser Wilhelmsland in addition to the Sepik and, in the optimistic words of the Neu Guinea Compagnie's report, 'emphatically disproved previous assumptions that the interior of Kaiser Wilhelmsland consisted entirely of rugged, inhospitable and impassable mountains'. The second expedition, under Ernst Tappenbeck in 1898, proved that the Ramu River was identical with what Schleinitz had called the Ottilien and established a camp 140 kilometres from the coast to act as a base for further investigation. Lauterbach observed geological formations suggesting the presence of gold in the Bismarck Range in 1896 and collected traces of alluvial gold on the third expedition in 1899 but the NGC's El Dorado in the Ramu Valley never materialized.[4]

The Germans also explored the inland in search of gutta-percha, a kind of wild rubber ideal for use in submarine electric cables. Gutta-percha trees were the goal of an expedition in 1901 by the botanist Rudolf Schlechter, whose expenses were paid by the *Kolonialwirtschaftliches Komitee*, an organization set up by the German Colonial Society to encourage the production of useful raw materials in the colonies. Schlechter succeeded in finding stands of gutta-percha in the Bismarck Range and was awarded a prize of 3000 marks by the *Komitee*, which sent him back to New Guinea in 1905 to spend a further three years investigating the country's potential as a source of wild rubber. Superseded by the invention of wireless telegraphy, gutta-percha was another failed hope of the Germans in New Guinea, total exports from the Old Protectorate in 1913 being worth a mere 7000 marks.[5]

That gateway to the interior, the Sepik, was rediscovered by the Germans after Hahl travelled up the river on the naval vessel *Cormoran* in 1909. The German-Dutch border expedition of 1910 followed the Sepik almost 1000 kilometres upstream until forced back by the coming of the wet season and another large party of explorers entered the mouth of the great river in March 1912. With a geographer, a zoologist, a botanist, an ethnographer, 150 carriers, fifty police, a small powered vessel provided by the German Colonial Society and official backing from the Colonial Office, the Sepik Expedition of 1912-13 was the most ambitious exploratory undertaking in the history of German New Guinea. It produced the first reliable map of the river basin, investigated numerous tributaries and established the presence of sizeable populations even in the most remote mountain ranges. According to the geographer Walter Behrmann, these were populations who could be recruited for work on plantations. 'What is most valuable in the interior of the country', he wrote,

> are the natives themselves. Everyone concerned with colonial questions knows that the labour problem in the plantations is the most difficult of all in tropical colonisation. We observed numerous sturdy tribes of people. They were pacified, the way for recruiting policy was cleared. The natives' desire for European goods was awakened in the most skilful manner possible. A vast recruiting field for the colony was opened up, which is especially favourable because the most developed tribes can be easily reached on river craft within our own colony.[6]

Behrmann was right about the potential of the Sepik for European employers. It became one of the principal sources of labour for the Australians in the 1920s and 1930s.

Other, less professional explorers were in Kaiser Wilhelmsland in the imperial period. Wilhelm Dammköhler, a gold prospector, walked from the Huon Gulf up the Markham Valley to the headwaters of the Ramu and down to the coast at Astrolabe Bay in 1907; attempting to repeat the journey two years later with another prospector called Rudolf Oldörp and without carriers, he was killed by warriors near a tributary of the Watut. Oldörp, suffering from arrow wounds, managed to build himself a raft and spend five days in agony drifting downstream to the coast, where he was rescued and cared for by villagers. The Lutheran missionaries were also explorers, most notably in the journey undertaken in 1913 by Georg Pilhofer and Leonhard Flierl, who walked from the mouth of the Waria River near the Papuan border up to its headwaters and then north-west into the Bulolo valley and down to the Markham.[7]

For the first twenty years of German rule in New Guinea European exploration of the New Guinea Islands was inseparable from the name of Richard Parkinson, originally a teacher from Heligoland, who used his plantation in the Gazelle Peninsula as a base from which to study the geography and peoples of the Bismarck Archipelago and the German Solomons. He published an important first book on the Archipelago as early as 1887 and followed it with a string of articles, collections of excellent photographs which often identified New Guineans by name and finally a magisterial guide to the region, *Dreissig Jahre in der Südsee* (Stuttgart, 1907). Less well known but a similarly acute and sympathetic observer was Emil Stephan, a naval staff-surgeon who recorded the way of life of villagers living along the coast of south-west New Ireland during a voyage on the survey vessel S.M.S. *Möwe* in 1904. Like Parkinson, Stephan came to know the villagers as friends and wrote about them by name and personal history. The frontispiece of his book on New Ireland, a handsome photograph of Palong Pulo, big man of the village of King, is a rarity in German ethnographic literature of the time. Stephan thought of his subjects as people, not as exemplars of supposed 'racial types'. He returned to New Guinea in 1907 to lead the German Naval Expedition to Explore the Bismarck Archipelago but died from blackwater fever at Namatanai, his place taken by the renowned ethnographer of Hawaii and Samoa, Augustin Krämer.[8]

By 1908 official and scientific interest in the New Guinea Islands was at its height. In that year the geographical commission of the Colonial Office, a body set up in 1905 to extend geographical knowledge of the colonies, sent an official exploratory expedition to New Hanover, New Ireland, Buka and Bougainville under Karl Sapper, a former coffee planter turned vulcanologist, and Georg Friederici, an anthropologist. While Sapper peered down the rims of New Britain volcanoes Friederici amassed linguistic and material evidence for his theories of the origins of the Melanesians. It was in 1908, too, that the Hamburg South Seas Expedition, financed at a cost of 600 000 marks by the Hamburg Scientific Foundation, was beginning its tour of the St Matthias and Admiralty Islands, the entire coast of New Britain, part of the coast of the mainland and the lower reaches of the Sepik before turning north for another year's research in German Micronesia. It was led by Friedrich Fülleborn, a doctor and naturalist who had accompanied a major expedition to Lake Nyassa in 1898, and organized by the Director of the Hamburg *Museum für Völkerkunde*, Georg Thilenius, who laboured for the next thirty years editing the first sixteen volumes of detailed results, *Ergebnisse der Südsee-Expedition 1908-1910* (Hamburg, 1914-1938).[9] In Bougainville in 1908 the young anthropologist Richard Thurnwald was observing the people of Buin for the Berlin *Museum für Völkerkunde* and Governor Hahl crossed the island from Arawa Bay over a high pass in the Crown Prince Range, one of the few occasions on which Europeans penetrated the interior of the larger islands before 1914.[10]

While missionaries of the MSC such as Bernhard Bley, August Kleintitschen and Otto Meyer studied the language and customs of the Tolai,[11] the Colonial Office funded practical research in the New Guinea Islands, a forestry expedition in 1913-1914 and, shortly before the war, a demographic research expedition designed to discover the reasons why the New Guinean population was not increasing. Few of the Australians who fought their way against the Germans on the Bitapaka Road in September 1914 and won control of the Protectorate ever understood the scale of the German scientific achievement in New Guinea.

The Germans' economic achievement was something the Australians understood immediately. Colonel William Holmes, commanding the Australian Naval and Military Expeditionary Force, thought Australia should keep the German territories 'as valuable British possessions for colonising purposes'. By 1914 the Old Protectorate of German New Guinea had twice as much cultivated plantation land as Papua, twice as many police, more than twice as many indentured labourers, and copra exports worth eleven times as much. The Australians were impressed. As the traveller Marnie

Masson reported in 1921, 'You can't talk for two minutes to a Papua resident without their apologising for the place; nor, as we have since found, to a Rabaulite without his ridiculing Papua'.[12]

The Germans, comparing New Guinea with other German colonies, were disappointed. The European population of the Old Protectorate numbered 271 in 1900, of whom 200 lived in the Bismarck Archipelago. It doubled by 1907 and again by 1914 but even 1130 Europeans together with 1377 Chinese and a couple of hundred other foreigners were few for such an extensive territory. The Kaiser, members of the *Reichstag*, the Colonial Secretary Solf, the directors of the NGC, settlers and Hahl himself were all dissatisfied with the slow advance of German colonization. After leaving New Guinea Hahl was to complain that German investors had always lacked faith in the colony. He had had to 'go and collect the guests ... before they would believe that a banquet was prepared for them'.[13]

Under the imperial administration as under the NGC the Protectorate did not match the expectations of its administrators. Hansemann, the Berlin banker who made New Guinea his hobby, set his heart on that enthusiasm of the German colonial movement in the 1880s, the colony of settlement, which would people Melanesia with energetic German farmers. When that scheme foundered, he sought to make New Guinea a plantation colony in which a string of companies financed by Berlin capital would produce tobacco, cotton, cacao and coffee for the European market. And when millions of marks and thousands of lives had been lost in that venture Hansemann turned to the German government for the money and concessions to avert insolvency. The government obliged and with an extra four million marks in subsidies, the NGC staggered on to pay its first dividend to shareholders in 1913 after twenty-seven years in business.

Hahl, whose name is virtually synonymous with the imperial administration of German New Guinea, had broader and more humane objectives, though still primarily economic ones. Unlike many German governors in Africa Hahl believed he owed protection to the colonized as well as to the colonizers and endeavoured to reconcile their competing interests. He belonged, like Solf in Samoa, to that minority tradition of German colonial thought which found expression in the views of Bernhard Dernburg and in the *Koloniale Rundschau*, a journal founded by the German Society for the Protection of Aborigines in 1909 to promote a humane approach to colonial policy. Yet at the same time Hahl, like Hansemann, thought New Guineans were too few and too primitive to transform a wilderness into a flourishing colony. He conceived of New Guinea as part of South-East Asia and saw its salvation in the immigration of tens of thousands of industrious Asian peasant farmers. The overwhelmingly Melanesian New Guinea which he left in 1914 fell far short of his hopes for its development.

New Guinea lagged behind the African colonies because the Pacific possessions did not matter to the German government and the *Reichstag*. Copra, the main export of the German Pacific, provided less than 9 per cent of Germany's supplies in 1910 and 1911 compared with 48 per cent imported from British colonies and 40 from the Dutch East Indies. Politically the South Seas had long since served their purpose: Samoa in the domestic propaganda for a bigger navy in 1899, New Guinea in Bismarck's grab for colonies. The German government left New Guinea to the devices of those trading and plantation companies foolhardy enough to seek profit on its malarial coasts. Fourteen years of imperialism without rule under the NGC were succeeded by fifteen years of skeletal colonial administration unevenly extending control over the littoral.

The German imperial administration adopted a colonizing strategy familiar throughout the tropics before World War I. Its aim was a plantation colony, built on the investments of German businessmen who would be attracted to New Guinea by assured title to freehold land, protection from rebellious villagers and abundant, cheap labour.

Shipping presented few difficulties after 1905 when Norddeutscher Lloyd began its inter-island service in return for a monopoly of the carrying trade of the colony. By 1914 its steamers on the run to the Dutch East Indies and Singapore were calling not only at Madang and Rabaul but also at the smaller ports of Aitape, Potsdamhafen, Finschhafen, Morobe and the Witu Islands so that settlers at these outstations could export direct to Europe via Singapore and import their copra bags without using the main entrepots.

The Germans alienated about 280 000 hectares of land in the Old Protectorate, perhaps 40 per cent of which passed into foreign control in the last few years of German rule, when high copra prices caused a rush for estates along the coasts of Kaiser Wilhelmsland and the German Solomons. German land policy was so attractive to the Australian firm Burns Philp that in 1913 it moved its subsidiary, the Choiseul Plantation Company, from the British Solomons to Bougainville, where the company's islands manager bought 5000 hectares of freehold land. Wages in German New Guinea, about 40 per cent lower than in the Solomons, were an added lure. Only a small proportion of New Guinea's land passed into foreign possession under the Germans but it was in the richest coastal localities and represented considerable loss for particular communities in the Gazelle Peninsula, around Madang and in the Witu Islands.[14]

The Germans' most remarkable success was in mobilizing the villagers of coastal New Guinea as a plantation labour force. About 20 000 villagers worked for the foreigners by 1914, most of them under indenture, compared with fewer than 3000 in 1899. They signed on because the *luluai* told them to or because they wanted to see the world and impress their friends, or as a way of raising the money which their relatives needed to pay head-tax, or more rarely as a result of being held at gunpoint by a desperate labour recruiter on some remote bush track. Other people wielded picks and shovels on the roads, required to do so because they could not find the one-mark pieces to pay head-tax. It was a labour system designed to encourage investors. As Joseph Meek, the Sydney manager of Lever Brothers, said in 1916, German colonial policy in New Guinea had

always been carried out with the idea of encouraging as many planters
as possible to settle under their administration . . . they did what they
could to get labour, facilitating the planter in every way; and they even
went to the extent of advising planters just starting not to pay above
a given wage for labour, or else they would come in and spoil the labour
market.[15]

The Germans believed firmly in flogging disobedient labourers. Under
German colonial law, 'natives' were a separate legal category defined as
'members of the native tribes of the Protectorate' and 'members of other
coloured tribes'. All New Guinean villagers in the German possession
became 'natives', subject to penalties which did not apply to Europeans,
and the most significant such penalty was corporal punishment, administered by authorized planters on their plantations as well as by government
officials at district offices. Often themselves beaten as schoolchildren or
military cadets, the Germans made a practice of flogging 'natives' throughout their colonial empire. Of 18 868 sentences handed down in German
East African courts in 1912, for example, 8057 directed that offenders be
flogged; the equivalent figure for sentences in British East African courts
was 380 out of 9113.[16]

For Hahl, the labour system became too much of a success, bringing
villagers on to the plantations in numbers which he thought threatened
the survival of the population. The planters, consumed by the desire for
immediate profit, wanted unrestricted recruiting whatever its demographic
consequences. Hahl counselled patience and caution lest the labour supply
dry up from over-use, and spent the latter half of his governorship strug-
gling against planters for more humane labour legislation, a ban on the
recruiting of women and the closure of districts to the recruiters. His most
ambitious schemes were never realized. The development plan of 1913,
if enacted, would have brought agricultural extension officers to Rabaul,
Namatanai, Madang and the Sepik, an agricultural laboratory to Rabaul,
a scheme to encourage cattle raising and a further expansion of government
control, but the proposal foundered for lack of funds from Berlin.

As German colonial governor Hahl was checked in the exercise of his
powers by settlers in the colony and by politicians, bureaucrats and businessmen in Berlin. The Government Council in the colony could do no
more than offer advice to the governor, and in theory Hahl could have
ignored the unofficial members of the Council whenever he liked, even
though they formed a majority. When he did this in introducing the copra
export duty in 1908, however, the unofficial councillors resigned in protest,
in order to embarrass him. A series of such resignations, widely publicized
in Germany, would have tarnished New Guinea's reputation for welcoming
new planters and might conceivably have lost Hahl his job. He was in any
case dealing with friends and associates at meetings of the Government
Council and had no desire to oppose them at every turn, especially as he
depended increasingly upon them for government revenue. On most issues
Hahl therefore chose to co-operate with the Council, making concessions
to the settlers rather than confronting them and delaying reforms if necess-

ary in order to win broader settler support. As his wrangles with the Council over the labour and population issues show, Hahl was by no means free to act as he thought fit.

Berlin constrained him even more. It was here that the expert officials of the Colonial Department of the Foreign Office and its successor the Colonial Office determined the fate of colonial policy initiated by governors in Buea, Lomé, Dar-es-Salaam, Windhuk, Apia and Rabaul. With a mere eleven officials in 1899 the Colonial Department could hardly oversee every detail of colonial administration, yet even in the early years of imperial rule in German New Guinea the veto of the Berlin bureaucracy was decisive in land and labour policy. Behind the bureaucrats, telling them what to do, stood the men of the NGC. By 1913, when the Colonial Office had expanded to thirty-seven officials, reforms had permitted governors greater say in preparing budgets but the centralization of policy-making was otherwise undiminished, and no governor decided any major issue of policy without Colonial Office approval. It was to the Colonial Office that the plantation companies came when they wanted a labour ordinance revised, a land claim reconsidered, a concession granted or an official removed. In the case of New Guinea, where government by chartered company lasted longer than anywhere in the colonial empire, Berlin officials had become accustomed to deferring to the knowledgeable businessmen of the metropolis. 'Hahl's hands were tied by the acts of his predecessors', as the historian of the Australian military occupation Seaforth Mackenzie remarked, 'and, later, were forced by the large companies with influence at Berlin'.[17]

Berlin, too, was the seat of the *Reichstag*, whose Budget Commission annually scrutinized all income and expenditure by the governments of the colonies. Weak in the constitutional structure of the *Reich*, the *Reichstag* sought to augment its importance by demonstrating its financial control over colonial administration, one of the few areas where it possessed such authority. The outcome was by no means favourable to New Guinea. Most of the time New Guinea was the forgotten colony. In 1905 and 1906, for example, when the Catholic Centre Party was leading a parliamentary attack on corruption and maladministration in the colonies, *Reichstag* deputies concentrated on the rebellions against the Germans in Africa, and if they noticed the Pacific at all their interest was in Samoa.

Then came Dernburg's 'era of reform'. For the African colonies it meant a boom in railway construction, financed by private loans and underwritten by the imperial government; for New Guinea it meant a drastic decline in revenues. Reaching Berlin from his colony of German Samoa in March 1908 Wilhelm Solf went straight to the Colonial Office, where he found officials inundated with the annual task of ensuring the passage of colonial budgets through the *Reichstag*. 'In the forefront of interest are the African railways', he wrote. 'Then come the African colonies, South-West Africa in particular. By comparison with the great territories the South Seas colonies are in the background and are therefore treated not inconsiderately but rather as being of no consequence . . .'. Hahl in New Guinea found only neglect in his treatment by the *Reichstag* and the Colonial Office at this time. The Dernburg régime, he said later, was the one which had nothing left for the South Seas. And when the *Reichstag* eventually decided to fund New Guinea more generously it was too late.[18]

Berlin ignored New Guinea for other reasons. Hahl was a prosaic man, easily overlooked in the metropolis, and he was a commoner in a colonial service in which three out of every four governors were noblemen. He lacked the social contacts and political influence of an Albrecht, Freiherr von Rechenberg, governor of East Africa from 1906 to 1912, or a Count Julius von Zech auf Neuenhofen, governor of Togo from 1903 to 1910, and he had little of the charm, wit, learning and ambition which enabled another commoner, Wilhelm Solf, to go from the governorship of a Pacific colony to the colonial secretaryship.

As the neglected colony of the empire, New Guinea was the least affected by German colonial rule, its contacted population of fewer than 200 000 representing a mere fraction of its inhabitants. For a colonial power in possession of a territory for thirty years Germany did not get very far in asserting its sovereignty over Melanesians. Yet those villagers who came under German influence or control experienced significant changes in technology, mobility, knowledge of the outside world, health and political fortune, changes which prefigured the impact of Australian colonizers on the rest of the population in the succeeding decades.

Iron, familiar to many coastal dwellers in the islands in 1884 but not to the people on the mainland, brought a revolution to New Guinean village life. It vastly reduced the work of clearing bush for gardens, making paths, building houses and carving ceremonial objects. Millions of axes, knives, adzes, nails and hoops of iron passed from the hands of the foreigners into those of New Guinean villagers between 1884 and 1914, and villagers themselves traded those tools far beyond territory known to the Germans. Villagers needed no persuading to embrace the new technology. People naturally preferred iron fish-hooks to traditional shell ones, and they liked hoop iron because pieces of it could be fitted immediately to axes in place of polished stone. Other European goods also saved labour. Leather belts, worn by many Tolai men even in the 1880s, lasted longer than bark; glass rings were more durable than those made of clay; empty beer bottles, favourites of the St Matthias Islanders in the early years of the century, held liquids better than clay pots; and in the 1890s the Madangs liked the Germans' used rice-sacks as blankets in place of the customary strips of bark.[19]

German rule made possible an unprecedented movement of people within New Guinea and between Melanesia and Western Samoa. A few coastal communities had been mobile in precolonial times: the voyaging traders of the mainland coast such as the Tami, the Bilbil and the Tumleo, for example, and the villagers from New Ireland, New Britain and Buka who had gone on labour traders' vessels to Queensland, Fiji and Samoa in the early 1880s. But the great majority of New Guineans had lived their lives close to home, fearing annihilation by enemies if they ventured too far afield. The coming of the Germans meant that, for the first time, scores of thousands of coastal people travelled long distances and lived for years in plantation barracks, where they met people of other language-groups with different spirits, love magic, sorcery, dances and plants. These unsung journeys, recorded only as labour recruiting statistics, were exploration, contributing more to change in the villages than the exploration undertaken by the Europeans. Melanesian exploration of the territory which the Germans called *Neuguinea* gave villagers a new perspective on their place in the world, undermined old assumptions about their power, importance and centrality and spread a common language of communication, Pidgin.

Rudimentary Western education came to thousands of New Guineans during the German era, principally from the missions. The government contributed in a minor way to education by setting up a 'school for natives' in 1907, first situated on the hills behind Rabaul at Namanula and later moved down to the bay. By September 1908 the school had sixty boys, thirty from the Gazelle Peninsula, twenty-two from the German Solomons, five from New Hanover and one from New Ireland, together with two of 'Malay-Chinese descent'. In the early years teachers taught in Kuanua, the language of the Tolai, introducing German as the medium of instruction in 1911. Some at least of the twenty-three young men who graduated with six years' schooling in 1913 were fluent in German and became clerks and teachers in the government service. By that time 120 boys were attending the school, including fifteen from the Admiralty Islands, and were learning practical skills in carpentry, bookbinding and metalwork. State education in German New Guinea did not extend to girls and was in part a form of cheap labour performed by the boys who set the type each fortnight for the government gazette, but it was more than the Australians were doing in Papua, where no government school existed.[20]

The Germans both facilitated the spread of disease and combated it with Western medicine. Repeated outbreaks of influenza, pneumonia and dysentery, possibly encouraged by the new mobility of the population, afflicted people in villages and on plantations. To take one example: 1200 people were estimated to have died in a dysentery epidemic on Manus in 1912 and in the following year the Manus suffered an 'acute coughing and influenza epidemic'. Malaria killed thousands of New Guineans unaccustomed to it, from hill peoples of Bougainville to islanders of Wuvulu. Smallpox cut a swathe through the coastal population of the mainland and part of New Britain in the mid-1890s, and venereal diseases were rife in many parts of coastal New Guinea by the time the Germans left, especially in New Ireland. Beriberi was affecting so many labourers in northern New Ireland by 1909 that the government established a special beriberi hospital. Of all the New Guineans' afflictions, this was the most attributable to colonial rule, since it was the direct result of poor diet, a disease of the labourer rather than the villager.[21]

By the standards of colonies in the Pacific the Germans exacted a high price in deaths for their colonization of New Guinea. Among the 26 000 or so indentured labourers employed in German territories in Melanesia between 1887 and 1903 the average annual death rate was estimated by Hahl to be over 28 per cent, whereas a British Colonial Office official could describe as 'ghastly' a figure of less than 5.5 per cent recorded for Indians in Fiji in 1895. (London warned the governor of Fiji that the emigration of Indians might have to be stopped.) The highest annual mortality rate among Pacific Islanders indentured in Queensland was 14.8 per cent in 1884 and from 1886 to 1904 it never exceeded 6.2 per cent. Even the severe outbreak of dysentery on the Lakekamu goldfield of Papua in 1910 was minor compared with the epidemics which raged on the NGC plantations in the 1890s.[22]

On the other hand the Germans saved the Tolai from decimation by smallpox in 1896 and continued to protect New Guineans from the disease by large-scale inoculation. They cleaned and dressed countless infected wounds, sores and tropical ulcers, the most prevalent of all Melanesian afflictions, and in their last years they had begun training a corps of New Guinean *heiltultul* to patrol the villages with bandages and disinfectants. Life for many villagers with suppurating infections, yaws, hookworm, tuberculosis, gonorrhoea and other common diseases was made bearable, prolonged or saved. And the Germans in New Guinea were the first to adopt regular doses of quinine as a prophylactic for malaria after the renowned pathologist Robert Koch visited Stephansort in 1899 and proved the value of the new treatment. Quinine was an advance, not a revolution in the treatment of malaria. Some people could not sleep after taking it and others could not bear it at all. The more fundamental discovery had been that of the Englishman Ronald Ross, who showed that anopheles mosquitoes were the bearers of the malaria parasite.[23]

The Germans changed the distribution of power between village communities, strengthening some at the expense of others. Inland peoples everywhere from the Huon Gulf and the Rai coast to Manus attacked coastal communities whose strong, young men had gone away to plantations. German 'control' often took the form of military intervention in local conflicts, intended to bring a measure of justice to the colonial frontier but based on poor intelligence. When the Germans intervened in local wars they relied on villagers to tell them what was happening. The village of Galavit in the inland Baining Mountains of the Gazelle Peninsula was attacked and destroyed in February 1913 and a German punitive expedition sent to punish the guilty warriors. The sequence of events was typical of German rule in New Guinea: news of the attack was volunteered by a man called To Magaga, who said that he was afraid to return home and who provided a plausible account of the identity of the wrongdoers, their evil deeds and their threats to kill his people; he asked the government to punish his enemies severely and the government obliged. His tale may have been true or false. The truth of this affair and a hundred others like it will never be known but it is obvious that the Germans' ignorance of local languages, customs and politics left them open to manipulation by ambitious villagers. Except in the longest-settled districts of the colony, where the government had an opportunity of hearing two sides of a dispute, German officials and their police could never be arbiters; they could only be allies, placing their force at the disposal of an apparently wronged New Guinean community. The interpreters were in a key position to determine the outcome of German interventions, for they were the filters through which knowledge of the situation on the non-Pidgin-speaking frontier of control had to pass before it reached the government. In the Galavit case the German officer in charge of the police thought his interpreters were using their position 'for their own advantage'.[24] By their choice of *luluais, tultuls* and catechists the foreigners promoted the influence of particular individuals and by denouncing recalcitrant big men, sorcerers and pagans they undermined the influence of others.

The Germans themselves often had only a vague idea of their impact on village politics. Their greatest lack was information about villagers' motives, beliefs and intentions. The district officer greeted by dancing and feasting was likely to think the celebrations were in his honour and would show his pleasure with a few token gifts. But villagers often expected to be feasted in return, on a scale which repaid the debt they had created, and meant to challenge the Germans to a reciprocal show of generosity or even to shame them. Peace-making between warring groups, attributed by the Germans to the government's stern resolve and use of force, could also arise from decisions made by people who welcomed the message of peace brought by the missionaries or were following pre-Christian custom. At the time of the *balum* circumcision festival held every ten years or so by the Kawa people and their neighbours along the northern coast of the Huon Gulf, for example, invitations went to all trading partners and a truce was called for the entire period of preparation, building the initiates' house and feasting.[25]

Melanesia was hard country for any colonial power. Its very geography was anti-colonial, placing natural barriers in the way of the Germans at every turn: the high mountains, steep ridges, landslides and volcanic peaks of much of New Britain, New Ireland, Manus and Bougainville, the coastal mountain ranges of the mainland rising to the rugged heights of the Finisterres and Saruwageds in the Huon Peninsula, the mosquito-infested mangrove and sago-palm swamps of the river deltas, and almost everywhere the gorges swollen with flooded creeks after heavy rain, the tangle of exposed roots on the floor of lowland tropical forests and the huge trees blotting out sight of the sky. No wonder the Germans liked the atolls, the smaller islands, the coasts and the Gazelle Peninsula.

The Germans had to contend as well with a population speaking hundreds of different languages, living as hundreds of distinct peoples and according to experience and predilection treating Europeans as enemies, temporary allies, masters or friends. However the Germans were received by villagers in one place, they could be sure of one thing: their reception a few kilometres away might be quite different and no New Guinean was in a position to take responsibility for that difference. The result was that the Germans and their New Guinean allies of the moment inched forward on a colonial frontier at a time when German troops in Africa were winning decisive wars against unified populations within a couple of years. New Guineans yielded their independence slowly, village by village rather than region by region. Thirty years proved too brief for Germany to overcome New Guinea's natural defences against intruders except on the coasts.

In the limited area where they held sway the Germans achieved more of what colonizers wanted to achieve than the British or Australians in the neighbouring colonies of Papua and the Solomons before 1914. They laid down more plantations, built more roads and bridges, provided better shipping, lived in more imposing official residences and at Rabaul constructed a capital with amenities far superior to those offered by Port Moresby. 'Life in the Bismarck Archipelago under the German regime', wrote an admirer in 1923, 'was a delightful thing. The planters had beautiful homes, cheap black labour, every encouragement from the Government, good roads, telephones, a sanitorium in the hills . . . ice, fresh milk and meat, amusements and all kinds of social festivities'.[26] The Germans also left behind a more impressive legacy of scholarly knowledge about Melanesia and did more to educate villagers and improve their health.

Such development came at a price. The Germans were more callous than the British and Australians, permitting mass mortality on the plantations of Kaiser Wilhelmsland in the 1890s, for example. They were stricter disciplinarians, wielding the whip and stick more often. They tolerated greater loss of life in hostilities between police and villagers on the frontier of control, and treated rebels more harshly, executing them with firing squads, confiscating land and deporting whole communities. They recruited more labourers, paying them less and interpreting labour legislation more frequently to the advantage of the planter. By various methods they alienated more land from villagers' control.

Yet in the end no single picture of the German impact on New Guinea emerges. In a country where people's common identity was historically defined by clan or language-group, history itself becomes particularized, each community which encountered the Germans having its own history of German rule. Beneficent towards some New Guineans, the Germans were brutal in their dealings with others and their impact must be seen as a mosaic composed of numerous, unique interactions between colonizer and colonized.

Appendixes

Tables II and III are based on a count of labourers recruited through Kokopo from 1887 to 1903 which Hahl commissioned in 1903 to help him in the growing dispute over recruiting areas.[1] Of the 18617 labourers listed, 62.6 per cent had worked in the Gazelle Peninsula and the Duke of York group, 18.5 per cent in Kaiser Wilhelmsland, and 17.4 per cent in Samoa. Over half (50.7 per cent) came from New Ireland and the islands east of it, 23.4 per cent from Buka and Bougainville, 14.9 per cent from the Gazelle Peninsula, and 7.9 per cent from New Hanover. Taken together, New Ireland and New Hanover supplied 58.6 per cent of all labourers, 70 per cent of those taken to Samoa, and 57.5 per cent of those employed in the Gazelle Peninsula. The number who had died while under contract was so high that the Colonial Department decided not to publish the figures lest they give a false impression of the situation in 1904.[2] In the Gazelle Peninsula 12.8 per cent had died under contract, in Finschhafen 14.6 per cent, in Samoa 23.3 per cent, and in the Astrolabe Bay and western Kaiser Wilhelmsland 40.3 per cent. In all, 18.7 per cent of labourers recruited through Kokopo had died on the plantations, and 22 per cent of the largest group, the New Irelanders.[3] The figures exclude recruiting of labourers for employment in northern New Ireland, because in the original these are the same in every particular as those given for labourers employed in the Astrolabe Bay, Potsdamhafen, and Berlinhafen, owing to an error in transcription. The number of labourers missed is probably 203, because the DHPG refers to the 1904 statistics in a letter to the Colonial Office,[4] giving the total recruited as 18 820 and the total number of deaths as 3508 or 18.65 per cent. The general argument remains unaffected by this omission of 1.1 per cent of recruits. The mortality rate of those recruited through Madang in these years, who possibly numbered 7000, was undoubtedly higher. For the whole Protectorate from 1887 to 1903 Hahl put the number of labourers' deaths on the plantations at about 7500 out of 26 000 or 28.8 per cent.[5]

[1] Hahl to KA, 3 Jun 1904, RKA 2309. [2] Minute by Rose, 1 Nov 1904, RKA 2309.
[3] Hahl to KA, 4 Sep 1904, RKA 2309. [4] DHPG to RKA, 16 Jun 1913, RKA 2313.
[5] *Amtsblatt*, 15 Jan 1910.

I

Indentured Labourers in the Old Protectorate, 1899-1914

Year	Bismarck Archipelago & German Solomons	Kaiser Wilhelmsland	Total
1899	c. 1600	c. 1100	c. 2700
1900	c. 2000	c. 940	c. 2940
1901	c. 2500	c. 900	c. 3400
1902	(3323)	1109	?
1903	3435	1217	4652
1904	3954	1052	5006
1905	3504	1755	5259
1906	?	?	6025
1907	5224	1776	7000
1908	5962	2313	8275
1909	5993	2318	8311
1910	6291	3178	9469
1911	8112	2872	10984
1912	9306	4316	13622
1913	11035	3955	14990
1914	13600	3929	17529

II

Contract Labourers Registered at Kokopo, New Britain, 1887-1903, showing place of origin and place of work

PLACE OF RECRUITMENT	PLACE OF EMPLOYMENT							
	Finschhafen	Samoa	Berlinhafen Potsdamhafen Astrolabe Bay	Western Islands	Duke of York Group, Gazelle Peninsula	Huon Gulf Expedition 1901?	Various	Total
Gazelle Peninsula	484	600	543		1084	52	17	2780
Elsewhere in New Britain					80		2	82
Witu Islands			22		43			65
Southern New Ireland	36	757	352		1380		30	2555
Northern New Ireland and Nusa Straits	71	1009	947		3089	39	22	5177
New Hanover	1	368	48		1054			1471
St Matthias and Kerue					16			16
Western Islands				28	5			33
Admiralties					32			32
Islands East of New Ireland		127	436		1135	11	7	1716
Nissan, Pinipel and Carraret Is.			13		67		1	81
Buka	37	63	338		1952		20	2410
Bougainville		295	100		1503		57	1955
British (to 1899 German) Solomons		12			82		7	101
Kaiser Wilhelmsland			3		124	16		143
Total	629	3231	2802	28	11646	118	163	18617

III

Deaths of Contract Labourers Registered at Kokopo,
New Britain, 1887-1903, showing place of origin and place of work

PLACE OF RECRUITMENT	PLACE OF EMPLOYMENT							Total
	Finschhafen	Samoa	Berlinhafen Potsdamhafen Astrolabe Bay	Western Islands	Duke of York Group, Gazelle Peninsula	Huon Gulf Expedition 1901?	Various	
Gazelle Peninsula	76	91	197		78		1	443
Elsewhere in New Britain					1	1		2
Witu Islands			6		5			11
Southern New Ireland	3	218	150		221		4	596
Northern New Ireland and Nusa Straits	13	256	399		350	1	3	1022
New Hanover		85	9		158			252
St Matthias and Kerue								
Western Islands				14	2			16
Admiralties					4			4
Islands East of New Ireland		46	194		161	1		402
Nissan, Pinipel and Cartaret Is.			2		7			9
Buka		2	130		246			378
Bougainville		54	42		239			335
British (to 1899 German) Solomons		1			14		1	16
Kaiser Wilhelmsland					1			1
Total	92	753	1129	14	1487	3	9	3487

IV

Indentured Labourers Recruited in the Bismarck Archipelago and the German Solomons for the Samoa plantations of the DHPG showing the number who died under contract, 1887-1912

	Recruitments	Deaths
1887	269	108
1888	87	31
1889		
1890	343	121
1891	52	18
1892		
1893	158	50
1894	297	67
1895	179	25
1896	164	63
1897	220	39
1898	206	19
1899	240	62
1900	247	54
1901	98	14
1902	384	79
1903	103	29
1904	332	58
1905	201	40
1906	179	31
1907	159	11
1908	204	53
1909	291	44
1910	350	58
1911	348	56
1912	174	7
	5285	1137
		(21.5 per cent)

Source: Enclosure in Hahl to RKA, 16 Nov. 1913, RKA 2313

V

Cultivated Area of Non-Indigenous Plantations in the Old Protectorate of German New Guinea, 1899-1914, in hectares

Year	Bismarck Archipelago & German Solomons	Kaiser Wilhelmsland	Total
1899	*c.* 2 500	?	?
1900	*c.* 3 500	?	?
1901	*c.* 3 300	1 200	*c.* 4 500
1902	4 626	1 441	6 067
1903	6 999	1 690	8 689
1904	8 198	1 313	9 511
1905	8 522	3 557	12 079
1906	9 965	3 565	13 530
1907	11 102	4 727	15 829
1908	11 988	4 781	16 769
1909	13 465	4 771	18 236
1910	?	?	20 520
1911	18 247	5 564	23 811
1912	19 199	6 641	25 840
1913	22 337	6 991	29 328
1914	26 109	8 081	34 190

VI

Copra Exported from the Old Protectorate, 1899-1913

Year	Bismarck Archipelago & German Solomons (tonnes)	Kaiser Wilhelmsland (tonnes)	Total Value (Marks)	Total value as proportion of value of all exports (per cent)
1899-1900 (1 Apr.-31 Mar.)	?	?	716 141	64
1900-1901 (1 Apr.-31 Mar.)	?	200	?	?
1901-1902 (1 Apr.-31 Mar.)	?	94	?	?
1902-1903 (1 Apr.-31 Mar.)	2 867	395	816 216	73
1903 (calendar year)	3 294	271	749 205	62
1904 (calendar year)	4 225	222	937 194	79
1905 (calendar year)	4 465	451	1 234 208	93
1906 (calendar year)	4 194	197	1 418 921	91
1907 (calendar year)	4 877	817	1 807 957	91
1908 (calendar year)	5 587	699	1 549 460	91
1909 (calendar year)	7 910	743	2 172 251	88
1910 (calendar year)	8 778	466	3 039 122	84
1911 (calendar year)	8 571	981	3 331 930	79
1912 (calendar year)	10 234	1 063	4 052 052	81
1913 (calendar year)	(14 526)		6 173 680	77

Notes

Introduction

[1] Unless otherwise specified, the term 'German New Guinea' in this book refers to the German colonial possessions in Melanesia.

[2] Pethebridge to Minister for Defence, 10 Mar. and 27 May 1915, Pethebridge Reports 1914-1916; Lieut. Basil Holmes, 'Diary in Connection with Expedition to Kawieng', entry for 31 Oct. 1914, Australian War Memorial Library, Canberra.

Chapter 1

[1] Johnston to Secretary, Dept. of Defence, 27 Jan. 1920, Ex German New Guinea Miscellaneous Reports Jan.-Feb. 1920, Australian War Memorial Library, Canberra.

[2] Oertzen to Bismarck, 4 Dec. 1884, Reichskolonialamt records, Vol. 2797, Zentrales Staatsarchiv, Potsdam [hereinafter RKA].

[3] Quoted in R. P. Gilson, *Samoa 1830-1900. The Politics of a Multi-Cultural Community* (O.U.P., Melbourne, 1970), pp. 179-80.

[4] *The Cyclopaedia of Samoa, Tonga, Tahiti, and the Cook Islands* (Sydney, 1907), p. 79.

[5] Theodor August Ludwig Weber was born in Hamburg in 1844. He left Hamburg for Samoa in April 1862 and took control of J. C. Godeffroy und Sohn when he was 20. As Hamburg and German Consul, 1865-79, and local manager of Godeffroy, he was the most powerful man in Samoa until his death in 1889.

[6] Consul to Bismarck, Apia, 24 Jan. 1874, RKA 2808.

[7] F. Hernsheim, *Südsee-Erinnerungen (1875-1880)* (Berlin, 1883), p. 102.

[8] Gilson, *Samoa*, p. 309.

[9] H. U. Wehler, *Bismarck und der Imperialismus* (Cologne & Berlin, 1970), p. 211; P. M. Kennedy, *The Samoan Tangle. A Study in Anglo-German-American Relations 1878-1900* (Dublin, 1974), p. 16.

[10] Gilson, *Samoa*, p. 353.

[11] Staatsarchiv Hamburg, Familienarchiv Hernsheim No. 1: 'Lebenserinnerungen von Eduard Hernsheim' (n.d.), passim; Max von Koschitzky, *Deutsche Colonialgeschichte* pt 2 (Leipzig, 1888), p. 234; B. von Werner, *Ein deutsches Kriegsschiff in der Südsee* (Leipzig, 1889), pp. 379-451.

[12] Fritz Stern, *Gold and Iron. Bismarck, Bleichröder and the Building of the German Empire* (London, 1977), p. 397; Philipsborn to Bismarck, 3 Dec. 1889, Auswärtiges Amt records, vol. 13107, Zentrales Staatsarchiv, Potsdam [hereinafter AA].

[13] Gustav Godeffroy to Bleichröder, 10 Dec. 1879, quoted in Stern, *Gold and Iron*, p. 398.

[14] Bismarck to Stolberg, 21 Dec. 1879, AA 13109; Wehler, *Bismarck und der Imperialismus*, p. 220.

[15] Zembsch to AA, 9 Sept. 1880, AA 13112.

[16] DHPG and Seehandels-Gesellschaft in Liquidation to AA, 31 May 1881, AA 13113.

[17] AA to Zembsch, 23 Apr. 1881; minute, 11 Mar. 1881, AA 13112.

[18] Wehler, *Bismarck und der Imperialismus*, pp. 223-5.

[19] Stuebel to Bismarck, 18 Dec. 1883, RKA 2791.

[20] Report by Oertzen, Feb. 1883, encl. in Stuebel to Bismarck, 6 Aug. 1883, RKA 2787.

[21] D. C. Gordon, *The Australian Frontier in New Guinea, 1870-1885* (New York, 1951), pp. 124-6; P. W. van der Veur, *Search for New Guinea's Boundaries, From Torres Strait to the Pacific* (Canberra and the Hague, 1966), p. 15.

[22] Weber to Consul, 11 May 1883, encl. in Stuebel to Bismarck, 14 May 1883; DHPG to AA, 27 June 1883, RKA 2928.

[23] W. O. Aydelotte, *Bismarck and British Colonial Policy. The Problem of South West Africa 1883-1885* 2nd ed. (Philadelphia, 1970), p. 12.

[24] DHPG Papers: 'Bilanz pro 1882', Staatsarchiv Hamburg; R. Parkinson, *Im Bismarck-Archipel. Erlebnisse und Beobachtungen auf der Insel Neu-Pommern (Neu-Britannien)* (Leipzig, 1887), pp. 28-9; evidence of J. C. Hoyer, mate on Niuafoou, 1 Mar. 1884, encl. in Stuebel to Bismarck, 25 Apr. 1884, RKA 2788; AA memo., 23 Nov. 1885, RKA 2316.

[25] Karcher to Admiralty, 6 July 1883, [British] Foreign office Confidential Print 5128.

[26] Hernsheim to Bismarck, 29 May 1883; Stuebel to Bismarck (and enclosures), 6, 8 and 31 Aug. 1883, RKA 2787; Plessen to Granville, 4 Sept. 1883, F.O. Conf. Print 5112.

[27] Stuebel to Bismarck, 1 Oct. 1883, RKA 2830.

[28] Gordon, *Australian Frontier*, pp. 191-2; Loftus to Derby, 31 Dec. 1883, C3839, *Further Correspondence Respecting New Guinea and Other Islands, and the Convention at Sydney of Representatives of the Australasian Colonies* (London, 1884), p. 8; Derby to Gladstone, 7 Dec. 1883, quoted in Aydelotte, *Bismarck and British Colonial Policy*, p. 14.

[29] Aydelotte, *Bismarck and British Colonial Policy*, p. 49; H. A. Turner, 'Bismarck's Imperialist Venture: Anti-British in Origin?' in Prosser Gifford and Wm R. Louis (eds), *Britain and Germany in Africa. Imperial Rivalry and Colonial Rule* (New Haven, 1967), pp. 68-9.

[30] Hansemann to Oppenheim, 30 May 1884, vol. 112, Hausarchiv Sal. Oppenheim jr. & Cie., Cologne; Kusserow to Bismarck, 20 Aug. 1884, RKA 2790.

[31] Marjorie Jacobs, 'Bismarck and the Annexation of New Guinea', *Historical Studies*, Vol. V (Nov 1951), pp. 23-5; Gordon, *Australian Frontier*, p. 260.

[32] DHPG to AA, 6 Aug. 1884, RKA 2791; DHPG to Bismarck, 9 Jan. 1885, RKA 2831; Robertson & Hernsheim to Bismarck, 23 Jan. 1885, RKA 3071; P. M. Kennedy, 'Bismarck's Imperialism: the Case of Samoa, 1880-1890', *Historical Journal*, Vol. XV (June 1972), pp. 268-75.

[33] Aydelotte, *Bismarck and British Colonial Policy*, p. 192.

34 Wehler, *Bismarck und der Imperialismus*, passim.

35 Stuebel to Bismarck, 20 Apr. 1884, RKA 2791.

36 Extract of Report on the Condition of the Samoan Islands, by Mr. J. B. Thurston, C.M.G. (British Commissioner), F.O. Conf. Print 5417.

37 DHPG Papers: 'Bilanzen', 1884–87, Staatsarchiv Hamburg.

Chapter 2

1 *Nachrichten über Kaiser Wilhelms-Land und den Bismarck-Archipel* 1886, pp. 64–5; *Deutsche Kolonialzeitung* 1887, p. 416; P. G. Sack, *Land Between Two Laws. Early European Land Acquisitions in New Guinea* (Canberra, 1973), p. 138.

2 *Nachrichten*, 1887, pp. 192–3.

3 C. L. Sentinella, transl. and ed., *Mikloucho-Maclay: New Guinea Diaries 1871-1883* (Madang, 1975), p. 313; *Nachrichten*, 1886, p. 117.

4 Sentinella *Mikloucho-Maclay*, pp. 18–19; Knappe to Bismarck, 4 Sept. 1886, RKA 2977.

5 H. Münch, *Adolph von Hansemann* (Munich and Berlin, 1932), p. 243; Comité der Neu Guinea Compagnie [NGC] to Sal. Oppenheim jr. & Cie., 25 July 1885, Hausarchiv Sal. Oppenheim jr. & Cie., Cologne; *Nachrichten* 1885, p. 34.

6 Koschitzky, *Deutsche Colonialgeschichte*, pt 2, pp. 228–9.

7 *Nachrichten*, 1886, p. 31.

8 *Nachrichten* 1886, pp. 9, 114; Knappe to Bismarck, 3 Sept. 1886, RKA 2977.

9 Knappe to Bismarck, 4 Sept. 1886, RKA 2977.

10 Oertzen to Bismarck, 29 Jan. 1887, RKA 2977.

11 Oertzen to Bismarck, 23 Dec. 1886, RKA 2977; NGC to Bismarck, 18 Nov. 1887, RKA 2978.

12 Heusner to Admiralty, 19 Dec. 1887 and AA to Rose, 2 May 1890, RKA 2978; NGC to Schellendorf, 19 Oct. 1887, RKA 2670.

13 Sack, *Land Between Two Laws*, pp. 138–9.

14 Proclamation at Finschhafen 18 Sept. 1888, RKA 2997; NGC to AA, 21 June 1888, RKA 2408; Hansemann to Bismarck, 22 Nov. 1888 and NGC to Hohenlohe, 5 Jan. 1895, RKA 2939.

15 *Nord-Australische Zeitung* (Brisbane), 20 Oct. 1888.

16 Rose to AA, 1 July 1890, RKA 2997.

17 *Nachrichten*, 1888, pp. 233–4; ibid., 1890, p. 70.

18 *Nachrichten*, 1889, p. 34.

19 O. Schellong, *Alte Dokumente aus der Südsee. Zur Geschichte der Gründung einer Kolonie. Erlebtes und Eingeborenenstudien* (Königsberg, 1934), pp. 170-3; *Nachrichten*, 1894, pp. 24–5.

20 Ordinances, 15 and 16 Aug. 1888, *Verordnungsblatt für das Schutzgebiet der Neu Guinea Compagnie*, 18 Sept. 1888.

21 Hansemann to Bismarck, 18 Mar. 1889; ambassador to Bismarck, the Hague, 25 May and 29 June 1889; AA to NGC, 3 July 1889, RKA 2299; Rose to Caprivi, 21 Dec. 1890, RKA 2301.

22 P. Sack and D. Clark, ed. and transl., *German New Guinea. The Annual Reports* (Canberra, 1979), p. 35.

23 Rose to Bismarck, 13 Feb. 1890, RKA 2960; Rose to Caprivi, 21 Oct. 1890, RKA 2301; Rose to Caprivi, 19 Nov. 1891, RKA 2302.

24 Rose to Caprivi, 2 Sept. and 5 Oct. 1890, RKA 2409; Kolonialabteilung des

Auswärtigen Amtes [Colonial Department of the Foreign Office, hereinafter KA] to Rose, 13 Jan. 1891, RKA 2939; NGC to KA, 10 Feb. 1891, RKA 2409; Rose to KA, 27 Feb. 1891, RKA 2980.

25 'Neuguinea Compagnie Akten Detzner, 1886-1923'; G. Pfalzer and E. Daub, 'Neu Guinea Friedhofsache', Hauptarchiv Neuendettelsau, Bavaria; *Nachrichten*, 1891, pp. 5, 7, 17, 26.

26 *Nachrichten*, 1891, p. 9; AA to Rose, 2 May 1890, RKA 2978.

27 Rose to KA, 27 July 1891, RKA 2980.

28 Rose to KA, 1 Sept. 1891, RKA 2980.

29 Rose to KA, 27 Nov. 1891, RKA 2980.

30 Rose to KA, 27 July 1891, RKA 2980.

31 Rose to KA, 9 Nov. 1892; Rose to KA, 27 Jan. 1891, and Kaiser Wilhelms-Land-Plantagen-Gesellschaft to KA, 30 Apr. 1891, RKA 2425.

32 Rose to KA, 1 Sept. 1891, RKA 2980.

33 KA to NGC, 9 Nov. 1891 and reply, 22 Dec. 1891, RKA 2980.

34 KA memo., 23 Sept. 1891 and Rose to KA, 27 Feb. 1891, RKA 2980; Rose to KA, 9 Nov. 1892, RKA 2982.

35 *Die Nation*, 30 Nov. and 7 Dec. 1895; Rose to KA, 24 Dec. 1891, RKA 2980.

36 Astrolabe Compagnie. Voranschlag der Ausgaben und Einnahmen pro 1892/93, RKA 2427.

37 *Deutsches Kolonialblatt*, 1892, p. 472.

38 B. Hagen, *Unter den Papua's. Beobachtungen und Studien über Land und Leute, Thier- und Pflanzenwelt in Kaiser Wilhelmsland* (Wiesbaden, 1899), p. 15.

39 *Free Press* (Singapore), 3 Dec. 1892; NGC to KA, 11 Apr. 1893, RKA 2303.

40 AA to Hatzfeldt, 10 Sept. 1893, RKA 2304.

41 Rosebery to Hatzfeldt, 23 Oct. 1893, F.O. Conf. Print 6442, no. 65.

42 *Soerabaya-Courant*, 24 Sept., 1 Oct., 22 Oct. 1892, 8 Mar. 1893.

43 Consul to AA, Batavia, 15 Oct. 1894, RKA 2305.

44 Hagen, *Unter den Papua's*, p. 36.

45 NGC to KA, 18 June 1895, RKA 2940; Janke to Oberkommando der Marine [hereinafter Navy], 6 May 1896, encl. in Navy to KA, 14 Aug. 1896, RKA 2985; H. Blum, *Neu-Guinea und der Bismarckarchipel. Eine wirtschaftliche Studie* (Berlin, 1900), p. 135.

46 NGC to KA, 29 May 1896, RKA 2985; KA memo., 22 Dec. 1897, RKA 2404.

47 NGC to Mission Society, 3 Mar. 1898; Müller to NGC in Stephansort, 12 Dec. 1898, 'Neuguinea Company Akten Detzner, 1886-1923', Hauptarchiv Neuendettelsau, Bavaria.

48 Hoh to mission inspector, 20 Apr. 1898, Letters of A. Hoh, Hauptarchiv Neuendettelsau, Bavaria.

49 Bamler to mission inspector, 20 June 1898, letters of G. Bamler, Hauptarchiv Neuendettelsau, Bavaria; NGC to Skopnik, 16 Oct. 1898, encl. in NGC to KA, 23 Oct. 1898, RKA 2414.

50 *Stenographische Berichte über die Verhandlungen des Reichstages: Anlagebände*, 1895-6, no. 378; KA to Kolonialrat, 25 Sept. 1896, RKA 2941.

51 *Die Neu-Guinea-Compagnie in Kaiser-Wilhelmsland* (Hamburg, 1888).

52 'Das deutsche Schutzgebiet der Neu Guinea Compagnie in der Südsee', 24 Nov. 1892, RKA 2980; Sack and Clark, *Annual Reports*, p. 82.

53 Hahl to KA, 4 Sept. 1904, RKA 2309.

54 *Der Vertrag zwischen dem Reich und der Neu Guinea Compagnie wegen Uebernahme der Landeshoheit* (Berlin, 1899), p. 11.

Chapter 3

[1] *Deutsche Kolonialzeitung*, 1887, pp. 524-6.

[2] Parkinson, *Im Bismarckarchipel*, p. 77.

[3] Ibid., pp. 137-9.

[4] Ibid, p. 104.

[5] R. Parkinson, *Dreissig Jahre in der Südsee. Land und Leute, Sitten und Gebräuche im Bismarckarchipel und auf den deutschen Salomo-Inseln* (Stuttgart, 1907), pp. 254-5, 270, 298-9, 641-7; E. Walden and H. Nevermann, 'Totenfeiern und Malagane von Nord Neumecklenburg', *Zeitschrift für Ethnologie* Vol. LXXII (1940), pp. 11-38; A. Kraemer, *Die Malaggane von Tombara* (Munich, 1925), passim.

[6] Oertzen to Bismarck, 25 Mar. 1886, and enclosures, RKA 2976.

[7] Danks to Kelynack, 16 June 1886, Methodist Church Overseas Mission Records, 53, Mitchell Library, Sydney; Oertzen to Knorr, 15 June 1886, encl. in Oertzen to Bismarck, 21 June 1886; Knorr to Admiralty, 21 June 1886, RKA 2976.

[8] Oertzen to Bismarck, 23 Dec. 1886, RKA 2977.

[9] Oertzen to Bismarck, 29 Jan. 1887, RKA 2997.

[10] Rooney to Brown, 5 July 1887, papers of Rev. Isaac Rooney, microfilm, Mitchell Library, Sydney.

[11] Robertson & Hernsheim to AA, 8 Aug. 1885; Oertzen to Bismarck, 12 Jan. 1887; AA to NGC, 8 Sept. 1887, RKA 2298.

[12] Schmid of DHPG to Rottenburg, 8 Apr. 1885, RKA 2800; AA to Bismarck, 18 Apr. 1885, RKA 2801; Oertzen to Bismarck, 20 Mar. 1886, RKA 2298; Hahl to RKA, 16 Nov. 1913, RKA 2313.

[13] Biermann to Caprivi, 8 Mar. 1894, RKA 2317; Directorate's Reports, 1890, 1891, 1892, DHPG papers, Staatsarchiv Hamburg.

[14] Krüger to DHPG, 9 Mar. 1893, RKA 2926.

[15] Investigation into murder of Bradley, 15 Oct. 1889, Miscellaneous Records of the Territory of New Guinea, AA 63/83, B.39, Australian Archives, Canberra; Inquest into death of Hoppe, 25 Dec. 1888, AA 1963/83, B. 43; Prittwitz to Admiralty, 18 Sept. 1889, RKA 2978.

[16] Rose to Bismarck, 29 May and 23 Oct. 1890, RKA 2979.

[17] Quoted in Rose to Bismarck, 29 May 1890, RKA 2979.

[18] Rose to Bismarck, 9 May 1890, RKA 2979; Rose to Caprivi, 7 Sept. 1891, RKA 2980; Rose to Gertz, 30 Apr. 1892, RKA 2981.

[19] NGC to KA, 4 July 1894 and 31 July 1895, RKA 2984; Hahl to Wallmann, 27 July 1897, RKA 2986; Bennigsen to KA, 8 Aug. 1899, RKA 2987.

[20] Evidence of Maranon, Herbertshöhe, 7 Apr. 1897, B. 45, AA 63/83 Aust. Archives; Hahl to Wallmann, 27 July 1897, RKA 2986.

[21] Rose to Caprivi, 27 June 1890; NGC to KA, 23 Aug. 1890, RKA 2979.

[22] 'Neu-Guinea nach den Berichten der dortigen kaiserlichen Beamten', KA memo, 1892, RKA 2981; report by Rose on trip on *Bussard*, 1892, RKA 2982.

[23] Schmiele to NGC, 5 Nov. 1892, RKA 2982.

[24] E. Sarfert and H. Damm, *Luangiua und Nukumanu* (Hamburg, 1929-31), pp. 34, 284, 310-11.

[25] Kirkpatrick to Hixon, 19 June 1893, encl. in Pelldram to AA, 13 July 1893, RKA 2982.

[26] Report by Rose on trip on *Bussard*, 1892, RKA 2982.

[27] Rose to Caprivi, 30 Oct. 1892, RKA 2982; *Rabaul Record*, 1 July 1917.

[28] Geissler to Caprivi, 14 Aug. 1893 and Fischer to Navy, 8 Feb. 1893, RKA 2983.

[29] Testimony of Jonas Forsayth at Ralum and Rickard to Schmiele, 29 Mar. 1890, B. 39, AA 63/83, Aust. Archives.

[30] Parkinson to Schmiele, 1 Apr. 1890, B. 39, AA 63/83, Aust. Archives.

[31] Schmiele to Rose, 8 and 21 Apr. 1890, encl. in Rose to Bismarck, 26 May 1890, RKA 2979; description of hanging, 2 Sept. 1891, B. 39, AA 63/83, Aust. Archives.

[32] Schmiele to Rose, 2 Apr. 1890, encl. in Rose to Bismarck, 26 May 1890, RKA 2979.

[33] Rose to Caprivi, 7 Nov. 1890, RKA 2979.

[34] Kolbe to Schmiele, 18 Sept. 1893, RKA 2983.

[35] Letter from Ralum, 21 Nov. 1893, encl. in Rose to KA, 8 Jan. 1894, RKA 2983.

[36] *Nachrichten*, 1894, p. 18; *The New Guinea Memoirs of Jean Baptiste Octave Mouton*, ed. P. Biskup (Canberra, 1974), p. 115.

[37] R. F. Salisbury, *Vunamami. Economic Transformation in a Traditional Society* (Berkeley and Los Angeles, 1970), p. 80; NGC to KA, 11 Jan. 1894, RKA 2983.

[38] Schmiele to NGC, 26 Dec. 1893, encl. in NGC to KA, 21 Mar. 1894, RKA 2983.

[39] Fischer to Navy, 8 Feb. 1893, RKA 2982.

[40] Sack and Clark, *Annual Reports*, pp. 104-8.

[41] See my 'Albert Hahl: Governor of German New Guinea' in James Griffin, ed., *Papua New Guinea Portraits: the Expatriate Experience* (Canberra, 1978), pp. 28-47.

[42] Hahl to KA, 5 Mar. and 25 Aug. 1896, RKA 2985.

[43] Hahl to KA, 25 Aug. 1896, RKA 2985.

[44] P. J. Hempenstall, *Pacific Islanders Under German Rule. A Study in the Meaning of Colonial Resistance* (Canberra, 1978), p. 133.

[45] Hahl to KA, 25 Aug. 1896, RKA 2985.

[46] *Nachrichten*, 1897, pp. 55-6.

[47] Herbertshöhe Station report, 22 Oct. 1895; trial proceedings 5 June 1896; Hahl to Rüdiger, 10 June 1896; Hahl to Hagen, 22 Aug. 1896; Hahl to Geissler, 4 Sept. 1897, B. 40 AA 63/83, Aust. Archives.

[48] Merten to Navy, 20 May 1897, RKA 2986.

[49] Hahl to Skopnik, 26 Sept. and 25 Oct. 1898; NGC to KA, 5 Mar. 1899, RKA 2987.

Chapter 4

[1] Hahl to KA, 23 July 1901, RKA 2419.

[2] Sack and Clark, *Annual Reports*, p. 211.

[3] Bennigsen to KA, 8 Aug. and 24 Sept. 1899, RKA 2987.

[4] Schnee to KA, 9 Apr. 1899, RKA 2987.

[5] *Deutsches Kolonialblatt*, 1904, pp. 127-36.

[6] Bennigsen to KA, 5 June 1900, RKA 2988 and Bennigsen to KA, 8 Aug. 1899, RKA 2987.

[7] Bennigsen to KA, 26 Feb. 1900, RKA 2987; Bennigsen to KA, 25 and 27 Apr., 24 Aug. 1900; Grapow to the Kaiser, 28 Feb. 1901, RKA 2988.

[8] Sack and Clark, *Annual Reports*, pp. 217, 220.

[9] Sack, *Land Between Two Laws*, p. 170.

[10] Boether to Bennigsen, 21 Aug. 1900, encl. in Bennigsen to KA, 8 Oct. 1900

and minute by Rose, 20 Jan. 1901, RKA 2988; Sack, *Land Between Two Laws*, p. 170.

11 Rose to Schnee, 7 Aug. 1902, Heinrich Schnee Papers, vol. 31, Geheimes Staatsarchiv Preussischer Kulturbesitz, Berlin-Dahlem; H. Schnee, *Als letzter Gouverneur in Deutsch-Ostafrika. Erinnerungen* (Heidelberg, 1964), p. 48.

12 Bennigsen to KA, 2 and 20 June 1900, RKA 2307.

13 Ordinance, 31 July 1901, RKA 2308.

14 NGC directors' report, 2 Dec. 1901, RKA 2419.

15 Disconto-Gesellschaft and others to Reichskanzler, 10 May 1901; Disconto-Gesellschaft to KA, 8 May 1906, RKA 2433.

16 Schmidt-Dargitz to Schnee, 27 May 1899, Schnee Papers, vol. 52, Geheimes Staatsarchiv, Berlin-Dahlem.

17 Ibid.

18 Knake to KA, 11 Aug. 1902, RKA 2989; see Hempenstall, *Pacific Islanders under German Rule*, pp. 147-50.

19 Hahl· to KA, 10 Aug. 1903, RKA 2946.

20 Proclamations, 18 July 1903 and 5 Feb. 1904, B. 213, AA 63/83, Aust. Archives; C. D. Rowley, *The Australians in German New Guinea 1914-1921* (Melbourne, 1958), pp. 216-17.

21 Hahl to Friedrich Wilhelmshafen District Office, 2 Nov. 1903; Friedrich Wilhelmshafen District Office to Hahl, 2 June 1909, B. 213, AA 63/83, Aust. Archives.

22 Rowley, *Australians in German New Guinea*, p. 221.

23 E. Stephan and F. Graebner (eds), *Neu-Mecklenburg (Bismarck Archipel) Die Küste von Umuddu bis Kap St. Georg. Forschungsergebnisse bei den Vermessungsfahrten von S.M.S. Möwe im Jahre 1904* (Berlin, 1907), pp. 22-3, 114, 152-6, 217.

24 Kornmajer to Hahl, 20 Feb. 1905, B. 58, AA 63/83, Aust. Archives.

25 RKA to Hahl, 3 Mar. 1901; Friedrich Wilhelmshafen District Office to Hahl, 2 June 1909, B. 213, AA 63/83, Aust. Archives.

26 B. Frommund, *Deutsch Neuguinea eine Perle der Südsee. Erlebnisse und Eindrücke eines Deutschen auf Deutsch-Neuguinea 1905-1908* (Hamburg, 1926), pp. 54-5.

27 'Bericht betreffend die Unruhen am Varzin im April, Mai und Juni 1902', 5 Aug. 1902, encl. in Knake to KA, 11 Aug. 1902, RKA 2989.

28 P. A. Kleintitschen, *Die Küstenbewohner der Gazellehalbinsel (Neupommern— deutsche Südsee) ihre Sitten und Gebräuche* (Hiltrup, 1906), pp. 306-7.

29 Wolff to KA, 20 May 1902, RKA 2669; Knake to KA, 23 Oct. 1902, RKA 2989.

30 *Ostasiatischer Lloyd*, 15 Aug. 1902.

31 *Kölnische Volkszeitung*, 13 Jan. 1903; *Vorwärts*, 17 Jan. 1903.

32 Minute by Rose, 19 Jan. 1903; Hahl to KA, 22 Jan. 1903, RKA 2989.

33 Grapow to the Kaiser, 28 Feb. 1901, RKA 2988; Stuckhardt to Hahl, 18 May 1904, encl. in Hahl to RKA, 8 June 1904, RKA 2990.

34 Bennigsen to KA, 2 Apr. 1901, RKA 2988.

35 Hahl to KA, 23 Dec. 1903, RKA 2990; Hahl to KA, 1 Mar. 1905, RKA 2991; *Neu Guinea Compagnie. Geschäftsbericht der Direction 1905/1906*, p. 12.

36 Hahl to KA, 8 June 1904, RKA 2990.

37 KA memo., 27 Jan. 1906, RKA 2992.

38 Hahl to KA, 3 Sept. 1904, RKA 2991.

39 Stuckhardt to governor, 23 Oct. 1906, encl. in Krauss to KA, 28 Nov. 1906, RKA 2992.

40 Hahl to KA, 21 Oct. 1904, RKA 2991.

41 'Bericht des Polizeimeisters Beyer über die Bestrafung der Bili Bilis', 25 Nov. 1904, RKA 2991.
42 Hahl to KA, 9 Oct. 1905, RKA 2991.
43 Hahl to commander, S.M.S. *Condor*, 11 Oct. 1908, RKA 2993; W. Diehl, 'Wie ziehen'wir unsere jungen Christen zu finanziellen Leistungen heraus?', 14 Sept. 1909, Rhenish Mission Archives, Wuppertal-Barmen.
44 Hempenstall *Pacific Islanders Under German Rule*, pp. 180-90.
45 Bennigsen to KA, 1 June 1900, RKA 2988; *Deutsches Kolonialblatt* 1904, p. 130; Hahl to KA, 16 Nov. 1901, RKA 2989; R. Neuhauss, *Deutsch-Neu-Guinea* (Berlin, 1911), Vol. III, p. 314. Hahl to KA, 14 July 1905, RKA 2991; Hahl to RKA, 14 July 1909, RKA 2993.
46 Hahl to KA, 29 Nov. 1903, RKA 2990; Hahl to KA, 8 Aug. 1904, RKA 3113; Krauss to KA, 3 May 1906, RKA 2992.
47 Krauss to KA, 16 June and 29 Nov. 1906, RKA 2992.
48 *Etat für das Schutzgebiet Neu-Guinea auf das Rechnungsjahr 1905*, Vol. 1117, *Reichstag* records (RT), Zentrales Staatsarchiv Potsdam; Hahl to KA, 8 Feb. 1907, encl. in Hahl to Wiegand, 16 Apr. 1908, Norddeutscher Lloyd records, 7,2010, Staatsarchiv Bremen; Hahl to KA, 6 Aug. 1904, RKA 2990; memo. by Rose, 10 Jan. 1905, RKA 2991.
49 Ernst Frizzi, 'Ein Beitrag zur Ethnologie von Bougainville and Buka mit spezieller Berücksichtigung der Nasioi', *Baessler-Archiv*, vi (1914), 2-3, 36-42.
50 Lieverenz to governor, encl. in Krauss to KA, 19 May 1906, RKA 2992.
51 Döllinger to governor, encl. in Krauss to KA, 18 Oct. 1906, RKA 2992; Hahl to RKA, 29 July 1908, RKA 2993.
52 Hahl to RKA, 8 May 1908, RKA 2310.
53 *Samoanische Zeitung*, 9 Sept. 1905; Sack and Clark, *Annual Reports*, pp. 255, 263.
54 Hahl to KA, 8 Feb. 1907, encl. in Hahl to Wiegand, 16 Apr. 1908, Norddeutscher Lloyd records 7,2010, Staatsarchiv Bremen.
55 *Reichstag*, 75. Sitzung, 26 Mar. 1906, RT 1118.

Chapter 5

1 Sack and Clark, *Annual Reports*, p. 313.
2 Hahl to RKA, 27 Oct. 1911, RKA 2994; *Etat für das Schutzgebiet Neuguinea ... 1913*, RT 1119.
3 Hahl to RKA, 21 Oct. 1912, RKA 2995.
4 Pethebridge to Minister for Defence, 27 May 1915, Pethebridge Reports, Australian War Memorial Library, Canberra.
5 Sack and Clark, *Annual Reports*, p. 277.
6 Rodatz to governor, 13 July 1908, encl. in Hahl to RKA, 12 Oct. 1908, RKA 2993.
7 Hahl to RKA, 15 Dec. 1908, RKA 2993.
8 Schober to Hahl, 20 Dec. 1910, RKA 2312; Hahl to Mommsen, 5 Aug. 1913, RKA 2655.
9 Van der Veur, *Search for New Guinea's Boundaries*, p. 44; Paul Ebert, *Südsee-Erinnerungen* (Leipzig, 1924), pp. 61-2; D. G. Pilhofer, *Die Geschichte der Neuendettelsauer Mission in Neuguinea* (Neuendettelsau, 1961), Vol. I, p. 165.
10 Klink to Hahl, 10 Nov. 1910 and 8 Mar. 1911; Berghausen to RKA, 9 Oct. 1911, RKA 2994.

[11] Hahl to Government Council, 4 Oct. 1913, RKA 2313; Carlile to Pethebridge, 20 Jan. 1916, Ex German N. G. Miscellaneous Reports, and Davies to Nelson, 4 Mar. 1915, encl. in Pethebridge to Minister for Defence, 29 May 1915, Pethebridge Reports, Australian War Memorial Library, Canberra.

[12] *Cormoran* commander to the Kaiser, 19 Dec. 1901, RKA 2653; Full to Hahl, 7 Jan. 1909, RKA 2993.

[13] Diary of Richard Thurnwald, entry for 20 Dec. 1913, New Guinea Collection, Library of the University of Papua New Guinea.

[14] Osswald to RKA, 31 May 1910, RKA 2994.

[15] *Amtsblatt für das Schutzegebiet Neu-Guinea*, 1 and 15 July 1911.

[16] A. Hahl, 'Achtzehn Jahre in Deutsch-Neuguinea', *Zeitschrift der Gesellschaft für Erdkunde zu Berlin* (1920), No. 1/2, p. 21.

[17] Berghausen to Osswald, 8 Feb. 1911, RKA 2994; Ian Willis, *Lae. Village and City* (Melbourne, 1974), p. 41.

[18] Scholz to Hahl, 4 July 1912; Hahl to RKA, 24 July 1912; Scholz to RKA, 2 Oct. 1912, RKA 2995.

[19] Hahl to RKA, 14 May 1913, RKA 2995.

[20] Prey to Hahl, 9 May 1913, RKA 2995.

[21] Hahl to KA, 10 May 1903, RKA 2989.

[22] Kirchhoff to the Kaiser, 12 Apr. 1904, RKA 2990.

[23] Hahl to KA (received 23 July 1904), RKA 2990; Hahl to RKA, 3 Jan. 1908, RKA 2992.

[24] Hahl to RKA, 11 June and 14 July 1909, RKA 2993.

[25] *Etat für das Schutzgebiet Neu-Guinea . . . 1911*, RT 1119.

[26] Hahl to *Cormoran* commander, 5 Feb. 1914, RKA 2656; Navy to RKA, 4 Mar. 1914, RKA 2996.

[27] *Amtsblatt*, 15 Mar. 1911.

[28] Hahl to RKA, 14 May 1913, RKA 2342.

[29] Scholz to RKA, 3 and 8 Sept. 1912, RKA 2995; for detailed accounts, see P. Lawrence, *Road Belong Cargo. A Study of the Cargo Movement in the Southern Madang District New Guinea* (Melbourne and Manchester, 1964), pp. 71-2, and Hempenstall, *Pacific Islanders Under German Rule*, pp. 188-9.

[30] Sack and Clark, *Annual Reports*, p. 355; Hahl to RKA, 26 Dec. 1913 and 19 Jan. 1914, RKA 2996.

[31] Hahl to RKA, 24 May 1913, and reply, 8 Sept. 1913, RKA 3108.

[32] KA to Hahl, 25 Jan. 1907, RKA 2763; *Amtsblatt* 1 May 1910.

[33] *Planet* commander to the Kaiser, 9 Dec. 1907, 5121 *Friedensakten betreffend Deutschland, Kolonien in Australien*, Bundesarchiv-Militärarchiv Freiburg; Hahl to RKA, 27 Oct. 1911, RKA 2994.

[34] Salisbury, *Vunamami*, pp. 122-3; *Amtsblatt*, 15 Feb. and 1 Apr. 1910.

[35] Hahl to RKA, 4 Aug. 1908, RKA 2438.

[36] *Amtsblatt*, 1 Apr. 1910; Carlile to his mother, 12 Sept. 1915, Letters of E. K. Carlile, File 181.11, Australian War Memorial Library; Klug to Hahl, 20 Oct. 1913, RKA 2996.

[37] C. Keysser, 'Die Seele der Papuachristen in der ersten Generation, Teil IV Briefe und Lieder', Hauptarchiv Neuendettelsau, Bavaria.

[38] Stuckhardt to Hahl, 29 June 1905, RKA 2991; Hahl to RKA, 12 Oct. 1908, RKA 2993; C. Leidecker, *Im Lande des Paradiesvogels. Ernste und Heitere Erzählungen aus Deutsch-Neuguinea* (Leipzig, 1916) pp. 127-9.

[39] Neuhauss, *Deutsch-Neu-Guinea*, Vol. I, p. 459; Hahl to RKA, 16 Oct. and 7 Dec. 1913, RKA 2313.

[40] Keysser, 'Seele der Papuachristen', Hauptarchiv Neuendettelsau, Bavaria.
[41] 'Strafliste des Gouvernementspferdestalles', B. 73, AA 63/83, Aust. Archives.
[42] Hamburgische Südsee A.G., New Guinea Company, Heinrich Rudolph Wahlen G.m.b.H. and D.H.P.G. to Administrator, 4 Sept. 1915, Hamburgisches Welt-Wirtschafts-Archiv.
[43] *Amtsblatt*, 1 May 1909, 1 Nov. 1910.
[44] Hahl to RKA, 9 Mar. 1913, RKA 2313; RKA to NGC, 21 Mar. 1908, RKA 5770; Hahl to RKA, 25 Oct. 1908, RKA 2311.
[45] Hahl to RKA, 27 Oct. 1911, RKA 2994.
[46] H. Zöller, *Deutsch-Neuguinea und meine Ersteigung des Finisterre-Gebirges* (Stuttgart, 1891), p. 281.

Chapter 6

[1] Hahl to RKA, 8 Feb. 1907, encl. in Hahl to Wiegand, 16 Apr. 1908, Norddeutscher Lloyd records 7,2010, Staatsarchiv Bremen.
[2] Hahl to RKA, 27 Oct. 1911, RKA 2994.
[3] *Government Gazette. British Administration German New Guinea*, 15 Nov. 1914.
[4] Hahl to RKA, 8 Feb. 1907, encl. in Hahl to Wiegand, 16 Apr. 1908, Norddeutscher Lloyd records 7,2010, Staatsarchiv Bremen.
[5] *Etat für das Schutzgebiet Neu-Guinea . . . 1911*, RT 1119.
[6] Paul Hambruch, 'Wuvulu und Aua (Maty- und Durour-Inseln) auf Grund der Sammlung F. E. Hellwig aus den Jahren 1902 und 1904', *Mitteilungen aus dem Museum für Völkerkunde in Hamburg* 4 Beiheft zum Jahrbuch der Hamburgischen Wissenschaftlichen Anstalten, XXV 1907, pp. 8, 23, 128, 142.
[7] Hahl to KA, 13 July 1904, RKA 2990; Hambruch, 'Wuvulu und Aua', pp. 11-22.
[8] Krauss to KA, 29 Nov. 1906, RKA 2992.
[9] Ebert, *Südsee-Erinnerungen*, p. 144.
[10] T. B. Bayliss-Smith, 'The Central Polynesian Outlier Populations since European Contact', in V. Carroll (ed.), *Pacific Atoll Populations* (Hawaii, 1975), pp. 286-343; Hahl to RKA, 17 Aug. 1909, RKA 2993.
[11] Hahl to RKA, 27 Oct. 1911, RKA 2994.
[12] Consul to AA, 11 Mar. 1903; consul to Colonial Secretary of the Straits Settlements, 21 Dec. 1903 (copy), encl. in consul to AA, 29 Dec. 1903, RKA 2308; Hahl to KA, 3 June 1904, RKA 2309.
[13] P. Biskup, 'Foreign Coloured Labour in German New Guinea. A Study in Economic Development', *Journal of Pacific History*, Vol. V (1970), pp. 85-107; Rowley, *Australians in German New Guinea*, p. 75.
[14] Hahl to RKA, 17 Jan. 1913, RKA 2313.
[15] Hahl to RKA, 14 May 1913; AA to RKA, 30 Apr. 1914, RKA 2342; A. Hahl, *Gouverneursjahre in Neuguinea* (Berlin, 1937), p. 248.
[16] Hahl to RKA, 16 Feb. 1912, RKA 2995; Sack, *Land Between Two Laws*, pp. 166-8, 182-4.
[17] Forsyth to Pethebridge, 26 Nov. 1915, Ex German N. G. Miscellaneous Reports, Australian War Memorial Library, Canberra.
[18] Johnston to Secretary, Defence Dept., 7 Feb. 1919, Ex German N.G. Miscellaneous Reports, Australian War Memorial Library, Canberra.
[19] Hahl to KA, 13 Nov. 1903, RKA 2308; Hahl to KA, 10 Aug. 1903, RKA 2946.

20 *Samoanische Zeitung*, 3 Sept. 1904.

21 Minutes of Govt. Council meetings of 2 Mar. and 2 Nov. 1906, RKA 3103; memo., 5 July 1907, RKA 2310.

22 Colonial Society to Hahl, 3 Dec. 1907; RKA to Hahl, 24 Feb. 1908, RKA 2310.

23 *Reichstag* debates, 17 Mar. 1908, RT 1035.

24 H. Schnee, ed., *Deutsches Kolonial-Lexikon* Vol. I, p. 617, Vol. III, p. 152, 313; (Leipzig, 1920) K. Hausen, *Deutsche Kolonialherrschaft in Afrika. Wirtschafts-interessen und Kolonialverwaltung in Kamerun vor 1914* (Zürich and Freiburg, 1970), pp. 53-8; meeting of Budget Commission, 26 Mar. 1912, RT 1119.

25 Budget Commission meetings, 10 and 11 Feb. 1909; *Reichstag* debates, 15 Feb. 1909, RT 1118; *Reichstag* debates, 31 Jan. 1910, RT 1119.

26 Wendland to Hahl, 3 Dec. 1908, RKA 2312.

27 Kolbe to Hahl, 20 Jan. and 16 Feb. 1909, RKA 2312; RKA to Hahl, 14 July 1909; Hahl to RKA, 28 Oct. 1909, RKA 2311; A. A. Graves Pacific Island Labour in the Queensland Sugar Industry, 1862-1906, Oxford D. Phil. thesis 1979, p. 96.

28 *Amtsblatt*, 15 Jan. 1910.

29 Hahl to RKA, 21 Nov. 1907, RKA 2310; Hahl to RKA, 25 Oct. 1908 and 5 July 1909, RKA 2311.

30 Memo., 13 Mar. 1909; Hahl to RKA, 30 Apr. and 5 July 1909, RKA 2311.

31 *Amtsblatt*, 15 Jan. 1910.

32 Haber to Rabaul District Office, 5 June 1914, B.65, AA 63/83, Aust. Archives.

33 *Amtsblatt*, 1 May, 1 June, 15 Oct. and 15 Nov. 1911; 1 Nov. 1912.

34 *Amtsblatt*, 15 Sept. 1912; Osswald to RKA, 28 Sept. 1912, RKA 2313.

35 *Amtsblatt*, 1 Nov. 1912; Osswald to RKA, 28 Sept. 1912, and Hahl to RKA, 10 Feb. 1913, RKA 2313. Since the creation of the *Gesellschaft mit beschränkter Haftung* (G.m.b.H.) or limited liability company in 1892, the older *Aktiengesellschaft*, with its stricter rules for founding and organization, has been the typical form of larger companies.

36 Forsayth G.m.b.H. to governor, 23 Sept. 1913 and to RKA, 21 Nov. 1912, RKA 2313.

37 Firms to Solf, 4 Feb. 1913; minutes of meeting, 17 Apr. 1913, RKA 2313.

38 Solf to von Koenig, 30 Apr. 1904, Wilhelm Solf Papers, vol. 25, Bundesarchiv Koblenz.

39 Hahl to RKA, 10 Apr. and 20 Oct. 1913, RKA 2313.

40 Hahl to RKA, 16 Oct. 1913, RKA 2313.

41 Hahl to RKA, 10 Mar. 1914, RKA 2313.

42 *Amtsblatt*, 1 Dec. 1913.

43 Meeting of Budget Commission, 26 Mar. 1912; *Etat für das Schutzgebiet Neuguinea . . . 1913*, RT 1119.

44 RKA and Treasury to Chancellor, 1 Nov. 1912 and reply, 4 Nov. 1912, records of *Reichskanzlei*, vol. 940, Zentrales Staatsarchiv Potsdam.

45 *Amtsblatt*, 15 April 1914.

46 Hahl to RKA, 5 Mar. 1914, RKA 2313.

47 Metzner and Enders et. al. to RKA, 1 Mar. 1914, RKA 2313; NGC, Hernsheim & Co. and H.A.S.A.G. to Australian Royal Commission, 24 Sept. 1919, Hamburgisches Welt-Wirtschafts-Archiv.

48 *Australian Parl. Papers 1917-1919* Vol. V, p. 691; Hahl to RKA, 7 Aug. 1909, RKA 2763.

49 *Amtsblatt*, 1 Dec. 1911; Hahl to RKA, 10 Feb. 1913, RKA 2313.

Chapter 7

[1] Oertzen to Bismarck, 6 Aug. 1885, RKA 2566.

[2] New Guinea Company to Bismarck, 23 Aug. 1886, RKA 2566; Sack and Clark, *Annual Reports*, p. 12; K.-J. Bade, 'Colonial Missions and Imperialism: The Background to the Fiasco of the Rhenish Mission in New Guinea', in J. A. Moses and Paul M. Kennedy (eds.), *Germany in the Pacific and Far East, 1870-1914* (University of Queensland Press, St Lucia, 1977), pp. 313-46.

[3] Horst Gründer, 'Deutsche Missionsgesellschaften auf dem Wege zur Kolonial-mission', in K.-J. Bade (ed.), 'Imperialismus und Kolonialmission', unpub. MS (Erlangen 1979); note by Bismarck, 29 Sept. 1889, RKA 2570.

[4] Journal of Rev. G. Brown, entry for 15 Aug. 1875, quoted in J. L. Whittaker, N. G. Gash, J. F. Hookey and R. J. Lacey (eds.), *Documents and Readings in New Guinea History. Prehistory to 1889* (Jacaranda Press, Qld, 1975), p. 367; Oertzen to Bismarck, 6 Aug. 1885, RKA 2566.

[5] Letter by Danks, 20 Aug. 1881, quoted in Whittaker et al. (eds.), *Documents and Readings*, pp. 412-13; Rickard to editor of *Border Post*, 3 July 1883, Methodist Church Overseas Mission Records 328, Mitchell Library; Rooney to Emberson, 20 Dec. 1881, Isaac Rooney Papers (microfilm), Mitchell Library.

[6] W. Deane (ed.), *In Wild New Britain. The Story of Benjamin Danks Pioneer Missionary* (Sydney, 1933), p. 184; Danks to Kelynack, 16 Feb. 1886, quoted in Whittaker et al. (eds.), *Documents and Readings*, p. 417.

[7] Consul to AA, Sydney, 8 June 1906, RKA 2567; N. Threlfall, *One Hundred Years in the Islands. The Methodist/United Church in the New Guinea Islands Region 1875-1975* (Rabaul, 1975), p. 92.

[8] Brandeis to KA, 13 May 1894; Rose to Brown, 25 Sept. 1890 and reply, 11 Feb. 1891; marginal note by Rose on Schmiele to New Guinea Company, 14 June 1894, RKA 2566.

[9] Hahl to KA, 10 Aug. 1903, RKA 3133; Hahl to KA, 5 Oct. 1904, RKA 2567.

[10] Hahl to KA, 27 Oct. 1905, RKA 2567.

[11] Fellmann and Cox to Danks, 3 May 1910, Methodist Church Overseas Mission Records 111, Mitchell Library; Weber Diary, vol. 3, pp. 658-71, Herz Jesu Mission, Münster. I am indebted to Dr Peter Hempenstall for this information.

[12] Mary Venard, *The History of the Daughters of Our Lady of the Sacred Heart in Papua New Guinea* (Port Moresby, 1978), pp. 75-99.

[13] Rose to KA, 24 Jan. 1895, RKA 2566.

[14] Hempenstall, *Pacific Islanders*, p. 137; Hahl to KA, 25 Aug. 1896, RKA 2985.

[15] Rascher to Dicks, 4 Oct. 1899, Rascher File, Herz Jesu Mission, Münster. I am indebted to Dr Peter Hempenstall for this information.

[16] Hempenstall, *Pacific Islanders*, pp. 147-50.

[17] Leo Brenninkmeyer, *15 Jahre beim Bergvolke der Baininger. Tagebuchblätter* (Hiltrup, 1928), pp. 28-9.

[18] J. Hüskes (ed.), *Pioniere der Südsee. Werden und Wachsen der Herz-Jesu-Mission von Rabaul. Zum goldenen Jubiläum 1882-1932* (Hiltrup, 1932), pp. 58-66.

[19] Ibid., pp. 165-71.

[20] Pilhofer, *Geschichte der Neuendettelsauer Mission*, Vol. I, p. 110.

[21] Ibid., p. 113.

[22] Ibid., p. 138.

[23] C. Keysser, *Eine Papuagemeinde* 2nd ed. (Neuendettelsau, 1950), pp. 69-71, 235-7; Pilhofer, *Geschichte der Neuendettelsauer Mission*, Vol. I, p. 256.

[24] C. Keysser, 'Seele der Papuachristen', Hauptarchiv Neuendettelsau, Bavaria.

²⁵ Pilhofer, *Geschichte der Neuendettelsauer Mission*, Vol. II, p. 84.
²⁶ Minutes of mission conferences at Simbang, 30 Jan. 1905. Deinzerhöhe, 21-26 Nov. 1908, Sattelberg, 27 Nov.-3 Dec. 1909; Steck to mission board, 2 Mar. 1914, Konferenz-Protokolle I and II, Hauptarchiv Neuendettelsau.
²⁷ 'Welche Gefahren drohen durch Ausdehnung von Plantagen unserm Volke...?' c. 1893, Arff Papers; conference report, Jan. 1899; Bongu station annual report, 1899, Rhenish Mission Archives, Wuppertal-Barmen.
²⁸ Siar station annual reports, 1900 and 1903; conference reports, 10 Apr. 1902 and 29 Jan. 1903, Rhenish Mission Archives.
²⁹ 'Bericht über die Entwicklung der Rheinischen Mission in Neuguinea', 8 Nov. 1912, Rhenish Mission Archives.
³⁰ Ragetta (i.e. Kranket) station annual report 1907, Rhenish Mission Archives; Hahl to RKA, 8 July 1909, RKA 2569.
³¹ 'Bericht über die Entwicklung...', 8 Nov. 1912, Rhenish Mission Archives.
³² Report by W. Diehl, 14 Sept. 1909, Rhenish Mission Archives; Bade, 'Colonial Missions and Imperialism...', pp. 339-40.
³³ Siar station annual report, 1901, Rhenish Mission Archives; Bade, 'Colonial Missions and Imperialism...', p. 338; P. Sack and D. Clark (eds), *German New Guinea. The Draft Annual Report for 1913-14* (Canberra, 1979), p. 142.
³⁴ R. M. Wiltgen, 'Catholic Mission Plantations in Mainland New Guinea: their origin and purpose', in K. S. Inglis (ed.), *The History of Melanesia* (Canberra and Port Moresby, 1969), pp. 329-62.
³⁵ M. J. Erdweg, 'Die Bewohner der Insel Tumleo, Berlinhafen, Deutsch-Neu-Guinea', *Mitteilungen der Anthropologischen Gesellschaft in Wien*, xxxii (1902), pp. 274, 370.
³⁶ H. auf der Heide, *Die Missionsgenossenschaft von Steyl* (Steyl, 1900), pp. 489-90.
³⁷ Wiltgen, 'Catholic Mission Plantations', passim.
³⁸ Auf der Heide, *Die Missionsgenossenschaft*, p. 489.
³⁹ Gühler, military-political report, 15 Sept. 1910 and Hahl to RKA, 31 July 1913, RKA 2580.
⁴⁰ This account is based on H. Laracy, *Marists and Melanesians. A History of Catholic Missions in the Solomon Islands* (Canberra, 1976), passim; R. Thurnwald, 'Im Bismarckarchipel und auf den Salomoinseln 1906-1909', *Zeitschrift für Ethnologie*, Vol. XLII (1910), pp. 98-147; Hahl to RKA, 29 July 1907, RKA 2580.
⁴¹ Rickard to Kelynack, 13 Jan. 1886, Methodist Church Overseas Mission Records 328, Mitchell Library.
⁴² Laracy, *Marists*, p. 75; Hahl to RKA, 29 July 1907, RKA 2580; Pilhofer, *Geschichte der Neuendettelsauer Mission*, Vol. I, p. 105.
⁴³ Brenninkmeyer, *15 Jahre beim Bergvolke der Baininger*, pp. 28-30.
⁴⁴ Pilhofer, *Geschichte der Neuendettelsauer Mission*, Vol. II, pp. 76-7; Sack and Clark, *Report for 1913-14*, pp. 59, 95, 101.
⁴⁵ I. Willis, *Lae. Village and City* (Melbourne, 1974), pp. 33-9; Pilhofer, *Geschichte der Neuendettelsauer Mission*, pp. 171-5; Hempenstall, *Pacific Islanders*, pp. 191-2.
⁴⁶ Pilhofer, *Geschichte der Neuendettelsauer Mission*, Vol. II, pp. 30-42; Sack and Clark, *Report for 1913-14*, p. 117.
⁴⁷ Sack and Clark, *Report for 1913-14*, p. 141.
⁴⁸ Keysser, 'Seele der Papuachristen', Hauptarchiv Neuendettelsau.
⁴⁹ Richard to Kelynack, 22 Nov. 1882, Methodist Church Overseas Mission Records 328, Mitchell Library.

Chapter 8

[1] A. Wichmann, *Nova Guinea. Uitkomsten der Nederlandsche Nieuw-Guinea-Expeditie*, vol. II, pt. 2, *Entdeckungsgeschichte von Neu-Guinea (1885 bis 1902)* (Leiden, 1912), p. 418; *Nachrichten*, 1886, p. 5; 1888, pp. 183-241.

[2] H Zöller, *Deutsch-Neuguinea und meine Ersteigung des Finisterre-Gebirges* (Stuttgart, 1891).

[3] Wichmann, *Entdeckungsgeschichte*, pp. 617-19; Hahl, *Gouverneursjahre*, pp. 64-6; Bennigsen to KA, 11 Apr 1901, RKA 2988.

[4] Sack and Clark, *Annual Reports*, pp. 123, 135-6, 167-8.

[5] Wichmann, *Entdeckungsgeschichte*, p. 787.

[6] W. Behrmann, *Im Stromgebiet des Sepik. Eine deutsche Forschungsreise in Neuguinea* (Berlin, 1922), pp. 346-7.

[7] Willis, *Lae*, pp. 25-6.

[8] E. Stephan and F. Graebner (eds), *Neu-Mecklenburg (Bismarck-Archipel). Die Küste von Umuddu bis Kap St. Georg* (Berlin, 1907).

[9] H. Beck, *Germania in Pacifico. Der deutsche Anteil an der Erschliessung des Pazifischen Beckens* (Mainz, 1970), pp. 277-88; H. Vogel, *Eine Forschungsreise im Bismarck-Archipel* (Hamburg, 1911), passim.

[10] R. Thurnwald, 'Im Bismarckarchipel und auf den Salomoinseln 1909-1909', *Zeitschrift für Ethnologie*, XLII (1910), pp. 98-147.

[11] Examples of the work of the MSC missionaries are Kleintitschen's *Küstenbewohner der Gazellehalbinsel*, Bley's linguistic contributions to Parkinson, *Dreissig Jahre in der Südsee*, and Meyer's articles on the Watom Islanders published in *Anthropos*, 1908-1910 and 1913.

[12] Holmes to Dept of Defence, 26 Dec 1914, Holmes Diary of Events 1914-1915, Australian War Memorial Library, Canberra. The exact comparison between German and Australian territories is as follows:

	New Guinea 1 Jan 1914	Papua 31 Mar 1914
Cult. Plantation Land (acres)	84 483	42 921
Police	*c.* 650	293
Indentured Labourers	17 529	7681
Copra Exports (value)	*c.* £308 000	£ 26 063
	(1913)	(1913-14)

The quotation from Marnie Masson is from M. Bassett, *Letters from New Guinea 1921* (Melbourne, 1969), p. 11.

[13] *Amtsblatt*, 1 May 1914; P. Biskup, 'Foreign Coloured Labour in German New Guinea', *Journal of Pacific History*, V (1970), pp. 85-107; Hahl to Solf, 28 Nov 1914, Wilhelm Solf Papers, Bundesarchiv Koblenz.

[14] Rowley, *Australians in German New Guinea*, pp. 56, 89-90; information about Burns Philp & Co. kindly supplied by Dr C. W. Newbury.

[15] 'British and Australian Trade in the South Pacific. Evidence', p. 17, *Commonwealth of Australia Parliamentary Papers 1917-1919*, vol. 5.

[16] *Nachrichten*, 1886, p. 104; L. H. Gann and P. Duignan, *The Rulers of German Africa 1884-1914* (Stanford, 1977), p. 184.

[17] Gann and Duigan, *Rulers of German Africa*, pp. 53-4; 255-6; S. S. Mackenzie, *The Australians at Rabaul. The Capture and Administration of the German Possessions in the Southern Pacific* (*Official History of Australia in the War of 1914-18*, vol. X) (Sydney, 1927), p. 224.

18 Solf to Schultz, 26 Mar. 1908; Hahl to Solf, 28 Nov. 1914, Wilhelm Solf Papers, vols 132 and 109, Bundesarchiv Koblenz.
19 Kornmajer to Hahl, 9 Jun. 1904, RKA 2990; O. Dempwolff, 'Die Erziehung der Papuas zu Arbeiten', *Koloniales Jahrbuch*, XI (1898), p. 11.
20 Sack and Clark, *Annual Reports*, pp. 281, 298, 326, 342, 361, and *Report for 1913-14*, pp. 146-52.
21 Sack and Clark, *Annual Reports*, p. 311, 360; and *Report for 1913-14*, p. 64.
22 *Amtsblatt*, 15 Jan. 1910; K. L. Gillion, *Fiji's Indian Migrants. A History to the End of Indenture in 1920* (Melbourne, 1962), p. 92; O. W. Parnaby, *Britain and the Labor Trade in the Southwest Pacific* (Durham, N. C., 1964), p. 205; H. Nelson, *Black, White and Gold, Goldmining in Papua New Guinea 1878-1930* (Canberra, 1976), pp. 199-206.
23 Sack and Clark, *Annual Reports*, p. 185.
24 Prey to Hahl, 8 May 1913, RKA 2995.
25 S. Lehner, 'Bukaua', in Neuhauss, *Deutsch Neu-Guinea*, vol. 3, p. 403.
26 L. Overell, *A Woman's Impressions of German New Guinea* (London, 1923).

Bibliography

A. MANUSCRIPT SOURCES

Zentrales Staatsarchiv, Potsdam, German Democratic Republic

(i) Reichskolonialamt series

2298-2313	Arbeitersachen Neuguinea, 1884-1914
2316-2317	Arbeiterfrage in Samoa, 1885-1899
2342	Anwerbung javanischer Arbeiter für Neuguinea und Samoa, 1913-1915
2402-2406	Plenarversammlungen der Direktion der Neuguinea Kompagnie, 1886-1909
2408, 2409 & 2414	Beamte der Neuguinea Kompagnie im Schutzgebiet derselben, 1885-1891, 1897-1899
2418-2420	Die Geschäftsberichte der Neuguinea Kompagnie, 1887-1911
2425	Die Kaiser Wilhelmsland Plantagen Gesellschaft, 1890-1895
2427-2429	Die Astrolabe Kompagnie, 1891-1897
2432-2434	Das Huon Golf Syndikat, 1900-1907
2438	Bismarck-Archipel-Gesellschaft m.b.H. 1907-1910
2566-2567	Die evangelische Mission in Deutsch-Neu-Guinea, 1885-1906
2570-2580	Die katholische Mission in Deutsch-Neu-Guinea, 1885-1911
2649-2656	Entsendung deutscher Kriegsschiffe nach der Australischen und Südsee-Station, 1895-1914
2670	Organisierung einer Polizeitruppe für das Schutzgebiet der Neuguinea Kompagnie, 1884-1899
2763	Steuerwesen in Neuguinea, 1900-1912
2787-2797	Die diesseitigen Beziehungen zu den Marschall-Inseln, Karolinen, Duke of York Inseln, Neu-Irland und Neu-Britannien, sowie den Ralick- und Ellice-Inseln usw., 1883-1885

2800-2801   Niederlassung in Kaiser Wilhelmsland (Neuguinea) sowie auf dem Bismarck-Archipel, 1884-1885
2808   Handels- und Schiffahrtsverhältnisse mit den Samoa- und Tonga-Inseln, insbesondere Abschluss von Freundschaftsverträgen mit diesen Inseln, 1874-1876
2830-2831   Ibid., 1883-1885
2926   Diebstähle auf den Pflanzungen auf Samoa, 1886-1896
2928   Geheim. Deutsche Kolonial-Bestrebungen in der Südsee, 1883
2939-2944   Uebernahme der Verwaltung des Schutzgebiets der Neu-Guinea Kompagnie auf das Reich, 1888-1908
2946   Verhandlungen des Gouvernements mit den Ansiedlern über Verwaltungsangelegenheiten, 1903-1914
2959-2961   Verordnungen für das Schutzgebiet der Neuguinea Kompagnie, 1886-1907
2976-2996   Allgemeine Verhältnisse—Neuguinea, 1886-1914
2997   Wirtschaftliche Entwicklung des Schutzgebiets der Neuguinea Kompagnie, 1888-1896
3071   Allgemeine Verhältnisse auf den Marschall-Inseln, 1885
3103-3104   Bildung eines Gouvernementsrats bei dem Gouvernement in Neuguinea, 1900-1913
3113   Regierungsstationen in Deutsch-Neuguinea, 1904-1906
5769-5772   Gesundheitsverhältnisse in Deutsch-Neuguinea, 1896-1914

(ii) Auswärtiges Amt series (records of the Politische and Handelspolitische Abteilungen)
Volumes 13107, 13109, 13112 and 13113

(iii) Reichstag series
Volumes 1035, 1117, 1118 and 1119

(iv) Reichskanzlei series
Volumes 920, 930 and 940

Staatsarchiv Hamburg
Archiv der Deutschen Handels- und Plantagengesellschaft der Südsee-Inseln zu Hamburg, 1878-1917
Familienarchiv Hernsheim

Hamburgisches Welt-Wirtschafts-Archiv
Individual documents held as part of the book collection:
(i) 'Denkschrift über die Arbeiterverhältnisse im Schutzgebiet Deutsch Neu-Guinea', typescript dated Sept. 1913

(ii) 'Entwurf einer Verordnung des Gouverneurs von Deutsch Neuguinea, betreffend die Auswanderung und Ausführung von Eingeborenen, die Anwerbung und Beschäftigung von Eingeborenen als Arbeiter, sowie die Erhaltung der Disciplin unter den eingeborenen Arbeitern (Arbeiter-Verordnung)', Rabaul, 1914

(iii) Letter from the New Guinea Company, Hamburgische Südsee A.G., H.R. Wahlen Ges., and the D.H.P.G. to the Administrator, 4 Sept. 1915, with reference to the amendment of Native Labour Regulations 45 and 46.

(iv) Letter from the New Guinea Company, Hernsheim & Co. A.G. and Hamburgische Südsee A.G. to the Secretary of the Australian Royal Commission, Rabaul, 24 Sept. 1919.

Geheimes Staatsarchiv Preussischer Kulturbesitz, Berlin-Dahlem
Heinrich Schnee Papers

Staatsarchiv Bremen
Norddeutscher Lloyd Collection, 7,2010

Hausarchiv Sal. Oppenheim jr. & Cie., Cologne
Vol 112: Die kolonialen Unternehmungen I, Samoa und Neu-Guinea, 1879-1914

Bundesarchiv-Militärarchiv, Freiburg
Records of Admiralstab der Marine, bundles 5079 and 5121. Oskar von Truppel Papers

Bundesarchiv Koblenz
Wilhelm Solf Papers

Hauptarchiv Evang.-Luth. Missionsanstalt, Neuendettelsau, Bavaria
Konferenz-Protokolle I, 1891-1919
Neuguinea Company Akten Detzner, 1886-1923
Letters of Adam Hoh, 1891-1917
Letters of Georg Bamler, 1887-1928
Christian Keysser Papers: 'Die Seele der Papuachristen in der ersten Generation. Teil IV, Briefe und Lieder' (These are letters and songs of Papua New Guineans in the Huon Peninsula region translated by Keysser into German)

Archiv der Rheinischen Mission, Wuppertal-Barmen
G/a2 Bogadjim Neu-Guinea 1900-1909
G/a9 Siar Neu-Guinea 1900-1911
G/a10-18 Pflanzungen (Statistik) Neu-Guinea, 1908-1932
G/b1 Neu-Guinea Conferenzprotokolle u. Varia, 1890-1898
G/b2 Referate Neu-Guinea
G/b7 Arff Papers

Library of the Australian War Memorial, Canberra
Diary of Events in connection with the Australian Naval and Military Expedition under the command of Colonel W. Holmes 10 Aug. 1914-22 February 1915

Lieut. Basil Holmes, Diary in Connection with Expedition to Kawieng, 1914
Reports by Brigadier-General S. A. Pethebridge, 1914-1915
Letters of Lieut. E. K. Carlile

Australian Archives, Canberra
Miscellaneous Records of the Territory of New Guinea, series AA 63/83: bundles B39, B40, B43, B45, B58, B65, B73, B213

Mitchell Library, Sydney
Microfilm FM 4/2346: papers of Rev. Isaac Rooney, principally letters from the Duke of York Islands, 1881-1888
Methodist Church Overseas Mission Records:
53: Letter Book of Rev. Benjamin Danks, 1884-1910
111-13: New Britain, 1909-1913
328: Letter Book of Rev. R. Heath Rickard, 1882-1893

Library of the University of Papua New Guinea, Port Moresby
Diary of Richard Thurnwald, 1913-1915

PRINTED SOURCES

I OFFICIAL

(i) Government Publications
Amtsblatt für das Schutzgebiet Deutsch-Neuguinea Simpsonhafen/Rabaul, vols 1-6, 1909-1914
Auszugsweise Zusammenstellung der wichtigsten in Deutsch-Neu-Guinea (Bismarck-Archipel, Deutsche Salomons-Inseln und Kaiser Wilhelms-land) geltenden Verordnungen, Berlin, 1903
Deutsches Kolonialblatt, Amtsblatt für die Schutzgebiete des Deutschen Reichs, Berlin, vols 1-25, 1890-1914
Government Gazette. British Administration German New Guinea, vol. 1, 1914-1915
Jahresberichte über die Entwicklung der deutschen Schutzgebiete in Afrika und der Südsee, 1898-1899 to 1908-1909, published in Berlin in the following year in each case as supplements to the *Deutsches Kolonialblatt*
Die deutschen Schutzgebiete in Afrika und der Südsee. Amtliche Jahresberichte, 1909-1910 to 1912-1913, Berlin, 1911-1914
Nachrichten über Kaiser Wilhelms-Land und den Bismarck-Archipel Neu Guinea Compagnie, Berlin, vols. 1-14, 1885-1898
Reichs-Marine-Amt Südsee-Handbuch–part II *Der Bismarck-Archipel* Berlin, 1912–part III *Kaiser-Wilhelms-Land* Berlin, 1913
British Administration (Late) German New Guinea, *Statistics Relating to Commerce, Native Tax, Population, Live Stock and Agriculture, Etc., In Connexion With The Late German New Guinea Possessions Compiled from German Official Publications, Etc.* 2nd edn, Melbourne, 1916

(ii) British Foreign Office Confidential Prints, held in the Library of Rhodes House, Oxford

5112 *Correspondence Respecting the Islands of the Pacific 1875-1883*, May 1885
5128 *Précis of German White Book. German Interests in the South Sea Part II*, Feb. 1885.
5417 *Extract of Report on the Condition of the Samoan Islands by Mr J. B. Thurston, C.M.G. (British Commissioner)*, 1886
6442 *Further Correspondence Respecting the Pacific Islands July to December 1893*, 1894

(iii) Parliamentary Papers

a. Germany

Denkschrift, betreffend den Uebergang der Landeshoheit über das Schutzgebiet der Neu-Guinea-Kompagnie auf das Reich in *Anlagen zu den Verhandlungen des Reichstags*, 1895-96 session, no. 378

b. Great Britain

Reports Concerning the State of Affairs in the Western Pacific, *Parl. Papers 1884* Vol. LV (c. 4126)
Report on the German Colonies in Africa and the South Pacific, *Parl. Papers 1895*, Vol. CII
Report for the Year 1893-94 on the German Colonies in Africa and the South Pacific, *Parl. Papers 1896*, Vol. LXXXIV
Report for the Year 1909 on the Trade and Agriculture of German New Guinea, *Parl. Papers 1910*, Vol. XCVIII

c. Australia

Inter-State Commission of Australia, report on British and Australian Trade in the South Pacific, *Parl. Papers Session 1917-19*, Vol. V
Parliament of the Commonwealth of Australia, Melbourne, *Interim and Final Reports of the Royal Commission on Late German New Guinea*, 1920
Parliament of the Commonwealth of Australia, Melbourne, *Report to the League of Nations on the Administration of the Territory of New Guinea, from September 1914 to 30th June, 1921*, 1922
Official Handbook of the Territory of New Guinea administered by the Commonwealth of Australia under Mandate from the Council of the League of Nations, Canberra, 1937

II UNOFFICIAL

(i) Periodicals, Newspapers, Pamphlets, Handbooks

Adressbuch für Deutsch-Neuguinea, Samoa, Kiautschou, 11th edn, Berlin, 1911
Deutsche Kolonialzeitung. Organ des deutschen Kolonialvereins Frankfurt a.M., vols. 1-31, 1884-1914, select issues
Koloniale Rundschau. Monatsschrift für die Interessen unserer Schutzgebiete und ihrer Bewohner, vols. 1-5, Berlin, 1909-1914, select issues

Der Ostasiatische Lloyd. Organ für die deutschen Interessen im Fernen Osten, Shanghai, 1886-1914, select issues
Rabaul Record, 1 July 1917
Samoanische Zeitung, Apia, 1901-1914
Der Tropenpflanzer. Zeitschrift für tropische Landwirtschaft Organ des Kolonial-Wirtschaftlichen Komitees, Berlin, 1897-1912
Vereinigung der Südseefirmen, *Denkschrift. Betr.: Den hohen Wert der deutschen Südsee für unsere Volkswirtschaft an den hohen Reichstag*, Hamburg, Bremen, Berlin, 1917

(ii) Books, articles and dissertations
Aydelotte, W.O. *Bismarck and British Colonial Policy. The Problem of South West Africa 1883-1885*. 2nd edn, Philadelphia, 1970.
Backhaus, E. *Die Arbeiterfrage in der deutschen Südsee. Eine wirtschaftlich-juristische Kolonialstudie*. Berlin, n.d.
Bade, K. J. 'Colonial Missions and Imperialism: the Background to the Fiasco of the Rhenish Mission in New Guinea', in J. A. Moses and P. M. Kennedy (eds), *Germany in the Pacific and Far East 1870-1914*, St Lucia, Qld, 1977, pp. 313-16.
—— *Friedrich Fabri und der Imperialismus in der Bismarckzeit. Revolution—Depression—Expansion*. Freiburg i.B., 1975.
Bassett, M. *Letters from New Guinea 1921*. Melbourne, 1969.
Baumgart, W. 'Die deutsche Kolonialherrschaft in Afrika. Neue Wege der Forschung'. *Vierteljahrschrift für Sozial- und Wirtschafts-geschichte* Vol. LVIII (1971), pp. 468-81.
Bayliss-Smith, T. P. 'The Central Polynesian Outlier Populations since European Contact' and 'Ontong Java: Depopulation and Repopulation' in V. Carroll ed., *Pacific Atoll Populations*, Hawaii, 1975, pp. 266-343 and 417-84.
Beck, H. *Germania in Pacifico. Der deutsche Anteil an der Erschliessung des Pazifischen Beckens*. Mainz, 1970.
Behrmann, W. *Im Stromgebiet des Sepik. Eine deutsche Forschungsreise in Neuguinea*. Berlin, 1922.
Biskup, P. 'Albert Hahl—Sketch of a German Colonial Official', *Australian Journal of Politic sand History* Vol. XIV (Dec. 1968), pp. 342-57.
—— 'Foreign Coloured Labour in German New Guinea. A Study in Economic Development', *Journal of Pacific History* Vol. V (1970), pp. 85-107.
—— (ed.). *The New Guinea Memoirs of Jean Baptiste Octave Mouton*. Canberra, 1974.
Bley, H. *South-West Africa under German Rule 1894-1914*. London, 1971.
Blum, H. *Neu-Guinea und der Bismarckarchipel. Eine wirtschaftliche Studie*. Berlin, 1900.
—— 'Das Wirthschaftsleben der deutschen Südseeinseler', *Preussischer Jahrbücher* XCVIII (Nov. 1899), pp. 294-319.
Brenninkmeyer, L. *15 Jahre beim Bergvolke der Baininger. Tagebuchblätter*. Hiltrup, 1928.

Brücke, O. *Die Entwicklung und weltwirtschaftliche Bedeutung der Kopra-und Kokosölproduktion und Konsumtion.* Nuremberg, 1930.

Burger, F. *Aus Neupommerns dunklen Wäldern. Erlebnisse auf eine Forschungsreise durch Neu-Guinea.* 2nd edn, Minden, 1925.

Cayley-Webster, H. *Through New Guinea and the Cannibal Countries.* London, 1898.

Class, P. *Die Rechtsverhältnisse der freien farbigen Arbeiter in den deutschen Schutzgebieten Afrikas und der Südsee.* Ulm, 1913.

Coppius, A. *Hamburgs Bedeutung auf dem Gebiete der deutschen Kolonialpolitik.* Berlin, 1905.

Corris, P. '"Blackbirding" in New Guinea Waters, 1883-84', *Journal of Pacific History,* Vol. III (1968), pp. 85-105.

——— *Passage, Port and Plantation. A History of Solomon Islands Labour Migration 1870-1914.* Melbourne, 1973.

The Cyclopedia of Samoa, Tonga, Tahiti and the Cook Islands. Sydney, 1907.

Davidson, J. W. *Samoa mo Samoa. The Emergence of the Independent State of Western Samoa.* Melbourne, 1967.

Deane, W. (ed.). *In Wild New Britain. The Story of Benjamin Danks Pioneer Missionary.* Sydney, 1933.

Dempwolff, O. 'Die Erziehung der Papuas zu Arbeitern', *Koloniales Jahrbuch* Vol. XI (1898), pp. 1-14.

Ebert, P. *Südsee-Erinnerungen.* Leipzig, 1924.

Erdweg, M. J. 'Die Bewohner der Insel Tumleo, Berlinhafen, Deutsch-Neu-Guinea', *Mitteilungen der Anthropologischen Gesellschaft in Wien,* Vol. XXXII (1902), pp. 274-310, 317-99.

Finsch, O. *Neu-Guinea und seine Bewohner* Bremen, 1865.

——— *Samoafahrten. Reisen in Kaiser Wilhelmsland und Englisch-Neu-Guinea in den Jahren 1884 u. 1885 an Bord des deutschen Dampfers 'Samoa'.* Leipzig, 1888.

——— 'Ueber Naturprodukte der westlichen Südsee, besonders der deutschen Schutzgebiete', *Deutsche Kolonialzeitung* 1887, pp. 519-30, 543-51 and 593-6.

Firth, S. G. 'Albert Hahl: Governor of German New Guinea', in J. Griffin (ed.), *Papua New Guinea Portraits. The Expatriate Experience.* Canberra, 1978, pp. 28-47.

——— 'German Firms in the Western Pacific Islands, 1857-1914', *Journal of Pacific History,* Vol. VIII (1973), pp. 10-28.

——— 'The New Guinea Company, 1885-1899: a case of unprofitable imperialism', *Historical Studies,* Vol. XV (Oct. 1972), pp. 361-77.

——— 'The Transformation of the Labour Trade in German New Guinea, 1899-1914', *Journal of Pacific History,* Vol. XI (1-2) (1976), pp. 51-65.

Flierl, J. *Forty Years in New Guinea.* Chicago, 1927.

——— *Gottes Wort in den Urwäldern von Neuguinea.* Neuendettelsau, 1929.

——— *Gedenkblatt der Neuendettelsauer Heidenmission in Queensland und Neu-Guinea.* Tanunda, South Aust., 1909.

Frizzi, E. 'Ein Beitrag zur Ethnologie von Bougainville und Buka mit spezieller Berücksichtigung der Nasioi', *Baessler Archiv* Beiheft, Vol. VI (1914), pp. 1-52.

Frommund, B. *Deutsch-Neuguinea eine Perle der Südsee. Erlebnisse und Eindrücke eines Deutschen auf Deutsch-Neuguinea 1905-1908*. Hamburg, 1926.

Gann, L. H. and Duignan, P. *African Proconsuls. European Governors in Africa*. New York, 1978.

—— *The Rulers of German Africa 1884-1914*. Stanford, 1977.

Giesebrecht, F. *Die Behandlung der Eingeborenen in den deutschen Kolonien*. Berlin, 1898.

Gifford, P. and Louis, W. R. (eds). *Britain and Germany in Africa. Imperial Rivalry and Colonial Rule*, New Haven, 1967.

Gillion, K. L. *Fiji's Indian Migrants. A History to the End of Indenture in 1920*. Melbourne, 1962.

Gilson, R. P. *Samoa 1830-1900. The Politics of a Multi-Cultural Community*. Melbourne, 1970.

Giordani, P. *The German Colonial Empire*. London, 1916.

Gordon, D. C. *The Australian Frontier in New Guinea 1870-1885*. New York, 1951.

Graves, A. A. Pacific Island Labour in the Queensland Sugar Industry, Oxford D. Phil. thesis, 1979.

Griffin, J., Nelson, H. and Firth, S. *Papua New Guinea. A Political History*. Melbourne, 1979.

Gründer, H. 'Deutsche Missionsgesellschaften auf dem Wege zur Kolonialmission', in K. J. Bade (ed.), 'Imperialismus und Kolonialmission. Deutschland in Uebersee', MS due for publication by Atlantis Verlag, Freiburg i.B., 1982.

Hagen, B. *Unter den Papua's. Beobachtungen und Studien über Land und Leute, Thier- und Pflanzenwelt in Kaiser Wilhelmsland*. Wiesbaden, 1899.

Hager, C. *Kaiser Wilhelms-Land und der Bismarck-Archipel*. Leipzig, 1886.

Hahl, A. 'Achtzehn Jahre in Deutsch-Neuguinea', *Zeitschrift der Gesellschaft für Erdkunde zu Berlin* (1920), no. 1/2, pp. 12-24.

—— *Deutsche Kolonien in der Südsee*. Hamburg, 1938.

—— *Deutsch-Neuguinea*. Berlin, 1936.

—— *Gouverneursjahre in Neuguinea*. Berlin, 1937. This reminiscence of Hahl's period as governor is now published in an English version as *Governor in New Guinea*, edited and translated by P. G. Sack and D. Clark, Canberra, 1980.

—— 'Ueber die Entwicklung von Neuguinea', *Jahrbuch über die deutschen Kolonien* V (1912), pp. 160-80.

—— 'Wirtschaftliche und technische Fragen in Neu-Guinea', *Kolonialwirtschaftliches Komitee, Verhandlungen des Vorstandes*, 1910, pp. 6-17.

Hambruch, P. 'Wuvulu und Aua (Maty- und Durour-Inseln) auf Grund der Sammlung F. E. Hellwig aus den Jahren 1902 und 1904', *Mitteilun-*

gen aus dem Museum für Völkerkunde in Hamburg, no. 4, *Beiheft zum Jahrbuch der Hamburgischen Wissenschaftlichen Anstalten*, Vol. XXV (1907), pp. 1-156.

Harding, T. G. *Voyagers of the Vitiaz Strait. A Study of a New Guinea Trade System*. Seattle, 1967.

Hassert, K. *Deutschlands Kolonien. Erwerbungs- und Entwicklungs-geschichte, Landes- und Volkskunde und wirtschaftliche Bedeutung unserer Schutzgebiete*. 2nd edn, Leipzig, 1910.

Hausen, K. *Deutsche Kolonialherrschaft in Afrika. Wirtschaftsinteressen und Kolonialverwaltung in Kamerun vor 1914*. Freiburg i.B., 1970.

Heide, H. auf der. *Die Missionsgenossenschaft von Steyl. Ein Bild der ersten 25 Jahre ihres Bestehens*. Steyl, 1900.

Hempenstall, P. J. *Pacific Islanders under German Rule: a study in the meaning of colonial resistance*. Canberra, 1978.

—— 'The Reception of European Missions in the German Pacific Empire: the New Guinea Experience', *Journal of Pacific History* Vol. X (1-2) (1975), pp. 46-64.

—— 'Resistance in the German Pacific Empire: Towards a Theory of Early Colonial Response', *Journal of the Polynesian Society*, Vol. LXXXIV (Mar. 1975), pp. 5-24.

Hernsheim, F. *Südsee-Erinnerungen 1875-1880*. Berlin, 1883.

Hesse-Wartegg, E. von. *Samoa, Bismarckarchipel und Neuguinea. Drei deutsche Kolonien in der Südsee*. Leipzig, 1902.

Hüskes, J. (ed.). *Pioniere der Südsee. Werden und Wachsen der HerzJesu-Mission von Rabaul. Zum goldenen Jubiläum*. Hiltrup, 1932.

Hutter, F. et al. *Das Ueberseeische Deutschland. Die deutschen Kolonien in Wort und Bild*, Vol. II, Leipzig, 1911.

Iliffe, J. *A Modern History of Tanganyika*. Cambridge, 1979.

—— *Tanganyika under German Rule 1905-1912*. Cambridge, 1969.

Inglis, K. S. (ed.). *The History of Melanesia*. Canberra and Port Moresby, 1969.

—— *The Study of History in Papua and New Guinea*. Port Moresby, 1967.

Jacobs, M. 'Bismarck and the Annexation of New Guinea', *Historical Studies Australia and New Zealand* Vol. V (Nov. 1951), pp. 14-26.

—— 'The Colonial Office and New Guinea, 1874-84', *Historical Studies Australia and New Zealand*, Vol. V (May 1952), pp. 106-18.

—— 'German New Guinea', in P. Ryan (ed.), *Encyclopedia of Papua and New Guinea*, Melbourne, 1972, Vol. I., pp. 485-98.

Kennedy, P. M. 'Bismarck's Imperialism: the Case of Samoa, 1880-1890', *Historical Journal*, Vol. XV (June 1972), pp. 261-83.

—— *The Samoan Tangle. A Study in Anglo-German-American Relations 1878-1900*. Dublin, 1974.

Keysser, C. *Anutu im Papualande*. Nuremberg, 1926.

—— '*Das Bin Bloss Ich*'. *Lebenserinnerungen*. Neuendettelsau, 1966.

—— *Eine Papuagemeinde*. 1st edn, Kassel, 1929; 2nd edn, Neuendettel-sau, 1950.

Kleintitschen, A. *Die Küstenbewohner der Gazellehalbinsel (Neupommern— deutsche Südsee) ihre Sitten und Gebräuche.* Hiltrup, 1906.

Kolisch, O. *Die Kolonialgesetzgebung des Deutschen Reichs mit dem Gesetze über die Konsulargerichtsbarkeit.* Hanover, 1896.

Koschitzky, M. von. *Deutsche Colonialgeschichte,* Vol. II, Leipzig, 1888.

Kotze, S. von. *Aus Papuas Kulturmorgen. Südsee-Erinnerungen.* Berlin, 1905.

Kraemer, A. *Die Malaggane von Tombara.* Munich, 1925.

Krämer-Bannow, E. *Bei kunstsinnigen Kannibalen der Südsee. Wanderungen auf Neu Mecklenburg 1908-9.* Berlin, 1916.

Kunze, G. *Im Dienst des Kreuzes auf ungebahnten Pfaden.* 2nd edn, Barmen, 1901.

Laracy, H. *Marists and Melanesians. A History of Catholic Missions in the Solomon Islands.* Canberra, 1976.

Lawrence, P. *Road Belong Cargo. A Study of the Cargo Movement in the Southern Madang District New Guinea.* Manchester, 1964.

Leidecker, C. *Im Lande des Paradiesvogels. Ernste und Heitere Erzählungen aus Deutsch Neu-Guinea.* Leipzig, 1916.

Lyng, J. *Island Films.* Sydney, 1925.

———— *Our New Possession (late German New Guinea).* Melbourne, 1920.

Mackellar, C. D. *Scented Isles and Coral Gardens. Torres Straits, German New Guinea and the Dutch East Indies.* London, 1912.

Mackenzie, S. S. *The Australians at Rabaul. The Capture and Administration of the German Possessions in the Southern Pacific (Official History of Australia in the War of 1914-18,* Vol. X) 4th edn, Sydney, 1937.

Manganau, O. 'My Grandfather's Experience with the Germans', *Oral History* (Port Moresby), no. 6 (1973).

Meinecke, G. (ed.). *Deutschland und seine Kolonien im Jahre 1896.* Berlin, 1897.

Meyer, H. *Das deutsche Kolonialreich. Eine Länderkunde der deutschen Schutzgebiete.* Vol. II, Leipzig and Vienna, 1910.

Mikloucho-Maclay: New Guinea Diaries 1871-1883, transl. by C. L. Sentinella. Madang, 1975.

Moses, J. A. 'The German Empire in Melanesia 1884-1914. A German Self-Analysis', in K. S. Inglis (ed.), *The History of Melanesia.* Port Moresby and Canberra, 1969, pp. 45-76.

Moses, J. A. and Kennedy, P. M. (eds), *Germany in the Pacific and Far East 1870-1914.* St Lucia, Qld, 1977.

Münch, H. *Adolph von Hansemann.* Munich and Berlin, 1932.

Nelson, H. *Black, White and Gold. Goldmining in Papua New Guinea 1878-1930.* Canberra, 1976.

Neuhauss, R. *Deutsch-Neu-Guinea.* 3 vols, Berlin, 1911.

Oliver, D. *Bougainville. A Personal History.* Melbourne, 1973.

Overell, L. *A Woman's Impressions of German New Guinea.* London, 1923.

Overlack, P. 'German New Guinea: a diplomatic, economic and political survey', *Journal of the Royal Historical Society of Queensland,* Vol. IX (1972-73), pp. 128-51.

Panoff, M. 'Travailleurs, recruteurs et planteurs dans l'Archipel Bismarck de 1885 à 1914', *Journal de la Société des Océanistes*, Vol. XXXV (Sept. 1979), pp. 159-73.

Parkinson, R. *Dreissig Jahre in der Südsee. Land und Leute, Sitten und Gebräuche im Bismarckarchipel und auf den deutschen Salomoinseln.* Stuttgart, 1907.

—— *Im Bismarckarchipel. Erlebnisse und Beobachtungen auf der Insel Neu-Pommern (Neu-Britannien).* Leipzig, 1887.

Parnaby, O. W. *Britain and the Labor Trade in the Southwest Pacific.* Durham, N.C., 1964.

Pfeil, J. Graf von. *Studien und Beobachtungen aus der Südsee.* Braunschweig, 1899.

Pilhofer, D. G. *Die Geschichte der Neuendettelsauer Mission in Neuguinea.* 3 vols, Neuendettelsau, 1961-63.

Pullen-Burry, B. *In a German Colony, or Four Weeks in New Britain.* London, 1909.

Rechinger, L. and K. *Streifzüge in Deutsch-Neu-Guinea und auf den Salomons-Inseln.* Berlin, 1908.

Reed, S. W. *The Making of Modern New Guinea.* Philadelphia, 1943.

Romilly, H. H. *Letters from the Western Pacific and Mashonaland 1878-1891.* London, 1893.

—— *The Western Pacific and New Guinea: Notes on the Natives, Christian and Cannibal, with some account of the Old Labour Trade.* London, 1886.

Rowley, C. D. *The Australians in German New Guinea 1914-1921.* Melbourne, 1958.

Rudin, H. R. *Germans in the Cameroons 1884-1914. A Case Study in Modern Imperialism.* London, 1938.

Sack, P. G. *Land Between Two Laws. Early European Land Acquisitions in New Guinea.* Canberra, 1973.

Sack, P. and B. *The Land Law of German New Guinea. A Collection of Documents.* Canberra, 1975.

Sack, P. and Clark, D. (ed. and transl.). *German New Guinea. The Annual Reports.* Canberra, 1979.

—— *German New Guinea. The Draft Annual Report for 1913-14.* Canberra, 1980.

Salisbury, R. F. 'Early Stages of Economic Development in New Guinea', *Journal of the Polynesian Society*, Vol. LXXI (Sept. 1962), pp. 328-39.

—— *Vunamami. Economic Transformation in a Traditional Society.* Berkeley and Los Angeles, 1970.

Sarfert, E. and Damm, H. *Luangiua und Nukumanu.* Hamburg, 1929-31.

Scarr, D. *Fragments of Empire. A History of the Western Pacific High Commission 1877-1914.* Canberra, 1967.

Schafroth, M. M. *Südsee-Welten vor dem grossen Krieg.* Bern, 1916.

Schellong, O. *Alte Dokumente aus der Südsee. Zur Geschichte der Gründung einer Kolonie. Erlebtes und Eingeborenenstudien.* Königsberg in Preussen, 1934.

Schmack, K. *J. C. Godeffroy & Sohn. Kaufleute zu Hamburg. Leistung und Schicksal eines Welthandelshauses.* Hamburg, 1938.

Schnee, H. *Als letzter Gouverneur in Deutsch-Ostafrika. Erinnerungen.* Heidelberg, 1964.

—— *Bilder aus der Südsee. Unter den kannibalischen Stämmen des Bismarck-Archipels.* Berlin, 1904.

—— (ed.). *Deutsches Kolonial-Lexikon.* 3 vols, Leipzig, 1920.

Scragg, R. F. R. *Depopulation in New Ireland. A Study of Demography and Fertility.* Port Moresby, 1957.

Souter, G. *New Guinea: The Last Unknown.* Sydney, 1963.

Stephan, E. and Graebner, F. (eds). *Neu-Mecklenburg (Bismarck Archipel). Die Küste von Umuddu bis Kap St Georg. Forschungsergebnisse bei den Vermessungsfahrten von S.M.S. Möwe im Jahre 1904.* Berlin, 1907.

Stern, F. *Gold and Iron. Bismarck, Bleichröder and the Building of the German Empire.* London, 1977.

Stoecker, S. (ed.). *Kamerun unter deutscher Kolonialherrschaft.* 2 vols, Berlin, 1960 and 1968.

Strandmann, H. Pogge von. 'Domestic Origins of Germany's Colonial Expansion under Bismarck', *Past and Present*, no. 42 (Feb. 1969), pp. 140-59.

—— The Kolonialrat, its Significance and Influence on German Politics from 1890 to 1906, Oxford D. Phil. thesis, 1970.

Suchan-Galow, E. von. *Die deutsche Wirtschaftstätigkeit in der Südsee vor der ersten Besitzergreifung 1884.* Hamburg, 1940.

Tappenbeck, E. *Deutsch-Neuguinea.* Berlin, 1901.

Taylor, A. J. P. *Germany's First Bid for Colonies 1884-1885. A Move in Bismarck's European Policy.* London, 1938.

Threlfall, N. *One Hundred Years in the Islands. The Methodist/United Church in the New Guinea Islands Region 1875-1975.* Rabaul, 1975.

Thurnwald, R. 'Die eingeborenen Arbeitskräfte im Südseeschutzgebiet', *Koloniale Rundschau*, Vol. II (Oct. 1910), pp. 607-32.

—— 'Im Bismarckarchipel und auf den Salomoinseln 1906-1909', *Zeitschrift für Ethnologie*, Vol. XLII (1910), pp. 98-147.

Townsend, G. W. L. *District Officer. From untamed New Guinea to Lake Success, 1921-46.* Sydney, 1968.

Townsend, M. E. *The Rise and Fall of Germany's Colonial Empire 1884-1918.* New York, 1930.

Van der Veur, P. W. *Search for New Guinea's Boundaries. From Torres Strait to the Pacific.* Canberra and the Hague, 1966.

Venard, M. *The History of the Daughters of Our Lady of the Sacred Heart in Papua New Guinea.* Port Moresby, 1978.

Vogel, H. *Eine Forschungsreise im Bismarckarchipel.* Hamburg, 1911.

Walden, E. and Nevermann, H. 'Totenfeiern und Malagane von Nord Neumecklenburg', *Zeitschrift für Ethnologie*, Vol. LXXII (1940), pp. 11-38.

Washausen, H. *Hamburg und die Kolonialpolitik des deutschen Reiches.* Hamburg, 1968.

Wegener, G. *Deutschland im Stillen Ozean, Samoa, Karolinen, Marshall-Inseln, Marianen, Kaiser-Wilhelmsland, Bismarck-Archipel und Salomo-Inseln.* Bielefeld and Leipzig, 1903.

Wehler, H.-U. *Bismarck und der Imperialismus.* Cologne and Berlin, 1969.

Wendland, W. *Im Wunderland der Papuas. Ein deutscher Kolonialarzt erlebt die Südsee.* Berlin, 1939.

Werner, B. von. *Ein deutsches Kriegsschiff in der Südsee.* Leipzig, 1889.

Werner, E. *Kaiser-Wilhelms-Land. Beobachtungen und Erlebnisse in den Urwäldern Neuguineas.* Freiburg i.B., 1911.

Whittaker, J. L., Gash, N. G., Hookey, J. F. and Lacey, R. J. (eds). *Documents and Readings in New Guinea History. Prehistory to 1889.* Milton, Qld, 1975.

Wichmann, A. *Nova Guinea. Uitkomsten der Nederlandsche Nieuw-Guinea-Expeditie*, Vol. II, Part 2, *Entdeckungsgeschichte von Neu-Guinea (1885 bis 1902).* Leiden, 1912.

Wilda, J. *Reise auf S.M.S. 'Möwe'. Streifzüge in Südseekolonien und Ostasien.* Berlin, 1903.

Willis, I. *Lae. Village and City.* Melbourne, 1974.

Wiltgen, R. M. 'Catholic Mission Plantations in Mainland New Guinea: their origin and purpose', in K. S. Inglis (ed.). *The History of Melanesia.* Canberra and Port Moresby, 1969, pp. 329-62.

Wolfers, E. P. *Race Relations and Colonial Rule in Papua New Guinea.* Sydney, 1975.

Zöller, H. *Deutsch-Neuguinea und meine Ersteigung des Finisterre-Gebirges.* Stuttgart, 1891.

Index